CASE STUDIES IN SUICIDE

EXPERIENCES OF MENTAL HEALTH PROFESSIONALS

Paul F. Granello

The Ohio State University

Gerald A. Juhnke

The University of Texas at San Antonio

Merrill
Upper Saddle River, New Jersey
Columbus, Ohio

Library of Congress Cataloging in Publication Data

Granello, Paul F.
  Case studies in suicide: experiences of mental health professionals / Paul Granello, Gerald A. Juhnke. — 1st ed.
    p. ;   cm.
  Includes bibliographical references and index.
  ISBN-13: 978-0-13-225516-5
  ISBN-10: 0-13-225516-2
  1. Suicide—Case studies.   I. Juhnke, Gerald A.   II. Title.
  [DNLM: 1. Suicide—psychology—Case Reports.   2. Psychotherapy—methods—Case Reports.   3. Self-Injurious
    Behavior—therapy—Case Reports.   4. Suicide—prevention & control—Case Reports. WM 165 G756c 2010]
  RC569.G73 2010
  616.85'8445—dc22   2008047735

Vice President and Executive Publisher: Jeffery W. Johnston
Acquisitions Editor: Meredith D. Fossel
Editorial Assistant: Nancy J. Holstein
Senior Managing Editor: Pamela D. Bennett
Art Director: Jayne Conte
Cover Design: Diane C. Lorenzo
Cover Image: ©Ferrell McCollough/SuperStock
Operations Specialist: Renata Butera
Director of Marketing: Quinn Perkson
Marketing Manager: Amanda L. Stedke
Marketing Coordinator: Brian Mounts

This book was set in Garamond by GGS Higher Education Resources, A Divison of Premedia Global, Inc. It was printed and bound by Bind Rite Graphics. The cover was printed by Bind Rite Graphics.

Pearson® is a registered trademark of Pearson plc
Merrill® is a registered trademark of Pearson Education, Inc.

Pearson Education Ltd.   Pearson Education Australia Pty. Limited
Pearson Education Singapore Pte. Ltd.   Pearson Education North Asia Ltd.
Pearson Education Canada, Ltd.   Pearson Educación de Mexico, S.A. de C.V.
Pearson Education—Japan   Pearson Education Malaysia Pte. Ltd.

10 9 8 7 6 5 4 3 2 1

ISBN 13: 978-0-13-225516-5
ISBN 10: 0-13-225516-2

Merrill
is an imprint of

www.pearsonhighered.com

*This book is dedicated in living memory to Mr. Leon J. Granello;
the countless individuals who struggle with mental illness and suicide;
and the mental health professionals who faithfully serve those
contemplating suicide.*

CONTENTS

PREFACE

About 34,000 Americans commit suicide annually. This equates to approximately 93 suicides each day or 1 suicide every 16 minutes. Suicide is the 11th leading cause of all American deaths and the second leading cause of deaths for persons aged 15 to 24. Daily 12 American youth end their lives via suicide. However, it is not only America's youth who commit suicide. At the other end of the age continuum, persons 65 years of age and older account for nearly 15% of all American suicides. Yet these numbers provide only an infinitesimal glimpse into the enormity of suicide in America. Estimates suggest that for each completed suicide, approximately 25 nonfatal suicide attempts occur. The resulting number is greater than the city population of either San Francisco or Atlanta.

Given suicide's prevalence, one would anticipate that counseling and mental health professionals would receive intensive training related to suicide assessment and intervention. Regretfully, this is not the case. On average, most mental health professionals receive no more than a half day of training specific to suicide assessment or intervention. Additionally, counselors and other mental health professionals often do not openly discuss their professional experiences with suicidal clients.

Hence, the editors have created this suicide case studies book to describe the clinical and personal experiences of counselors and mental health professionals who have served suicidal clients. We want them to tell their stories and experiences because we believe these will provide real-life learning opportunities for our readers. The case vignettes contained within the book are true, with only minor changes made to ensure client anonymity. Each one provides practical, realistic, and useful "how to" guidance and is authored by a highly skilled and experienced counseling professional.

While we could have chosen to include only successful case studies with fairy tale endings, we did not. Instead, we believe it is important to learn from the experiences of the seasoned professionals who lost clients. As you read, it will become strikingly apparent that treating suicidal clients and their families extracts a toll on counseling professionals. Clearly, compassion fatigue and emotional exhaustion result when counseling professionals fail to "make time" for themselves.

We welcome you to this book. For those of you who are entering the counseling profession or are graduate students, savor the stories and learn from this diverse collection of skilled practitioners. If you already are a seasoned counselor or mental health professional, we anticipate that you will "connect" with the counselors in the case vignettes and see similarities between your work and that of the authors. In either case, this book will provide learning opportunities that will help you more effectively assess and intervene with suicidal clients and better respond to your personal and professional needs as you serve those intent on ending their lives.

Most of all, we hope that this book will remind each of us that clients are more than the sum of their diagnoses or behaviors. Behind each suicidal behavior is a person seeking hope, love, and validation. May we as counselors and helping professionals always remain respectful of and compassionate toward those seeking to find meaning and control—even through the very acts designed to end their lives.

ACKNOWLEDGMENTS

We would like to acknowledge the many wonderful colleagues and family members that support us in our work. Particularly, we would like to recognize the following persons: Mr. Leon J. Granello, Mr. Leon V. Granello, Dr. Darcy Haag Granello, Ms. Deborah Juhnke, Mr. Bryce Juhnke, Ms. Brenna Juhnke, Dr. Debra Wasserman, Dr. Mark Young, Dr. Richard McKeon, Dr. Alan Hovestadt, Dr. Brian Glaser, Dr. David Lundberg, Dr. Kenneth Coll, Dr. Albert Valadez, Dr. Thelma Duffey, Ms. Debra Copeland, Ms. Cheryl Holton, Ms. Meredith Sarver Fossel, and Mr. Kevin Davis.

We would also like to thank the reviewers of our manuscript for their comments and insights: Peter Manzi, Buffalo State College; Al Carlozi, Oklahoma State University; Nicholas Mazza, Florida State University; and Valerie G. Balog, University of North Carolina–Charlotte.

ABOUT THE AUTHORS

Dr. Paul F. Granello Ph.D., LPCC, is a Licensed Professional Clinical Counselor and an Associate Professor of Counselor Education at The Ohio State University. Paul is a founder and Chief Science Officer of the Ohio Suicide Prevention Foundation. In addition, he has over $2.2 million in grants to provide suicide prevention in Ohio. He has coauthored a book on suicide assessment and treatment, *Suicide: An Essential Guide for Helping Professionals and Educators*, with Dr. Darcy Haag Granello. He has published 20 scientific articles in peer-reviewed national journals and has authored 10 book chapters on suicide, anxiety, and computers in counseling as well as wellness. Paul has presented peer-reviewed papers at state, national, and international conferences on topics related to suicide, psychotherapy outcomes, and wellness.

Gerald A. Juhnke, Ed.D., LPC, NCC, MAC, ACS, CCAS, is a Professor and the Doctoral Program Director for The University of Texas at San Antonio's Counselor Education and Supervision Program. Jerry has authored, coauthored, or coedited five books and over 35 refereed scholarly journal articles. He has specialized in the areas of suicide, life-threatening behaviors, and family addictions since 1986. Jerry is a former President of two counseling associations, the International Association of Addictions and Offender Counselors and the Association for Assessment in Counseling. He is a former Editor of *The Journal of Addictions and Offender Counseling* and is a former Cochair of the American Counseling Association's Council of Journal Editors. Jerry has received numerous professional counseling awards, including the American Counseling Association's Ralph E. Berdie Research Award, the International Association of Addictions and Offender Counselors' *Journal of Addictions and Offender Counseling* Research Award, and most recently, the International Association of Addictions and Offender Counselors' Addictions Educator Excellence Award. He has provided counseling services and supervised counselors in diverse settings, including independent practice, community mental health, corrections, and universities. Jerry has served as a lecturer–consultant to the U.S. Army's Soldier and Family Support Branch, as well as to The University of Texas Health Science Center Division of Community Pediatrics, school districts, psychiatric hospitals, courts, and municipalities.

CASE REFERENCE CHART

Name	Age	Race/ Culture	Therapy Setting	Presenting Problems/ Diagnosis	Suicidality	Page
Jenny	17 Adolescent	Caucasian	Hospital Inpatient	Mood & Interpersonal Relationship Issues	Suicide Attempt Resulting in Physical Injury	23
Mandy	13 (Adolescent)	Hispanic	Middle School Outpatient	Family Reunification Issues & School Bullying	Suicide Ideation	30
Stephanie	14 (Adolescent)	Caucasian	High School Outpatient Agency	Depression & Self-Abusive Behavior	Suicide Attempt	39
Nancy	14 (Adolescent)	Native American	Therapeutic Community	Depression & Substance Abuse	Suicide Attempt	50
Mike	16 (Adolescent)	Caucasian	Outpatient Private Practice	Depression	Suicide Attempt	58
Tori	19 (Adolescent)	African American	Outpatient Agency	Depression & Sexual Abuse Survivor	Suicide Plan	65
Megan	19 (Young Adult)	Caucasian	College Counseling Center	Depression & Eating Disorder	Suicide Attempt	74
Amanda	28 (Adult)	Hispanic	Outpatient Agency	Depression & Relationship Issues	Suicide Attempt	84
John	42 (Adult)	Caucasian	Outpatient Addictions Program	Addictions & Sexual Behavior	Completed Suicide	94
Frieda	43 (Adult)	Caucasian	Intensive Care Unit	Bipolar Disorder & Personality Disorder	Multiple Suicide Attempts	103
Sergio	47 (Adult)	Hispanic	Outpatient Private Practice	Depression & Sexual Addiction	Completed Suicide	115
Mark	27 (Adult)	Caucasian	Outpatient Agency	Depression & HIV Positive	Suicide Attempt	125

Name	Age	Race/ Culture	Counseling Setting	Presenting Problem/ Diagnosis	Suicidality	Page
Terri	38 (Adult)	Caucasian	Outpatient Agency	Bipolar Disorder, OCD, & Borderline Personality Disorder	Completed Suicide	135
John & Marlene	44 & 41 (Adults)	Caucasian	Outpatient Private Practice	Depression & Religious Issues	Suicide Ideation	145
Earl	74 (Older Adult)	Caucasian	Partial Hospital Program	Depression	Completed Suicide	155

The Importance of Suicide Training

- Suicide is a significant public health problem in the United States. In 2005, there were over 32,637 completed suicides in the United States.
- Each day 89 people die by completing suicide.
- Suicide is the third leading cause of death for adolescents and young adults (ages 15–24).
- Mental health professionals are generally not adequately trained in graduate school to properly assess, intervene with, and treat suicidal clients.
- Many clinicians will have a client complete suicide at some time during their practice. (American Association of Suicidology, 2008)

THE PURPOSE OF THIS BOOK

Case Studies in Suicide is written with a single, overriding purpose—to help front-line clinicians and counseling graduate students understand the practical suicide assessment, intervention, case management, and referral strategies that are necessary for working with suicidal clients. Each of the cases in this book represents a true clinical case experience and is written by a skilled counseling professional. You will find that these professionals have selflessly worked to deliver quality care to one of the most challenging populations for which to provide therapy: the suicidal client.

THE CASE-BASED APPROACH

One of the best ways to learn is through example and modeling. Perhaps this is why all professional training programs in health care place such emphasis on practicum, internship, and other supervisory experiences. The study of real cases is used as an instructional method across many fields, including education, medicine, and business (Greenhalgh, 2007).

Each professional who contributed a case to this book is hoping that both graduate students and professionals will benefit from reading about actual treatment experiences with suicidal clients. We believe that by increasing their knowledge of the various ways mental

health professionals work with suicidal individuals in real, day-to-day clinical settings, students and professionals will feel more prepared for their work and, most important, provide more competent care to at-risk clients.

THE NEED FOR IMPROVED GRADUATE TRAINING CONCERNING SUICIDE

In spite of the number of completed suicides each year and the governmental calls for action in suicide prevention, there appears to be very little preparation and training in suicide risk assessment for many mental health professionals. Only 40% to 50% of psychology programs offer formal training in risk assessment (Bongar & Harmatz, 1991; Mazza, Elizabeth, & Freeman, 2003). Coder, Nelson, and Aylward (1991) found that 63% of school counselors in their study stated they had received training in adolescent suicide, although it was unclear whether this training occurred during graduate school or as professional development. Nevertheless, *only 38% of high school counselors believe they could recognize a student at risk for suicide* (King, Price, Talljohann, & Wahl, 1999).

There is, in fact, almost no information available regarding the attention that is given to client suicide in counselor education programs (Foster & McAdams, 1999). Given this lack of published research, at the time of writing this book we collected anecdotal information via CESNET. Our web-based survey was completed by representatives from 54 separate counselor education programs that were geographically distributed around the country. Table 1.1 summarizes these survey results.

Unfortunately, it appears that the amount of training currently provided on suicide varies widely, with a few programs providing good training and most programs providing little or poor training—and shockingly, 11% of programs responding to our survey provide *no* training on suicide to their counseling students at this time.

One explanation for this lack of training could be the continued presence of a traditional attitude toward suicide assessment: They will learn that on the job. The current state of training on suicide for most counseling graduate students is wholy inadequate, especially given that research has shown that many students will have a suicidal client during their internships. The attitude that students will learn about suicide intervention and prevention on the job is not only inaccurate but also, if followed, ethically irresponsible.

Whatever the causes that have contributed to the current situation, the simple fact appears to be that *most graduate students will begin their practica and internships with little or no training in the clinical skills needed to properly assess and manage suicidal clients*. By reading and using this book as part of your classroom preparation for working with suicidal clients, you will be better able to cope with the realities of the current practice environment in which you must begin work.

THE BENEFITS OF SUICIDE CASE STUDY FOR THE PROFESSIONAL

The cases presented in this book will have value not only for graduate students but also for counselors who are currently in practice. First, as illustrated above, most of us did not receive sufficient training in assessing and managing suicidal clients during our graduate programs. We may have encountered our first suicidal client during our internships or practica. At that time, many of us had the benefit of a ready network of agency and faculty supervisors to help us in managing our anxiety in relation to suicide. However, many mental health

TABLE 1.1   Survey of Counselor Educators on Suicide Training

Question	Response	
Q1: Do you *currently provide training on suicide crisis intervention* in your master's program?	**Yes:** 88.9%	**No:** 11.1%

Examples of reasons given if the response was "No":

- "No one has suggested it and it is a taboo"
- "Not in the curriculum, but would be a good elective to add"
- "Not as a formalized component, but usually some exposure is offered in a voluntary workshop format"
- "A crisis intervention course which will contain suicide intervention is slated to be offered but has not been developed"

Question	Response	
Q2: If you answered "Yes" to question 1, *what types of informational content do you include in your suicide training*? (Check all that apply.)	Suicide statistics	64.8%
	Suicide risk factors	88.9%
	Suicide protective factors	64.8%
	Suicide assessment	92.6%
	Suicide intervention	75.9%
	Suicide and special populations	27.8%
	Suicide referral procedures	85.2%
	Suicide prevention	63.0%
	Suicide postvention	35.2%
	Suicide resources	63.0%
Q3: *In what format is your training* on suicide usually presented? (Choose as many as apply.)	Class lecture within specific course	66.7%
	Infusion across several courses	61.1%
	Program workshop outside of specific Course	16.7%

Q4: In what *courses do you currently provide information* on suicide?

- Crisis intervention strategies in all practica and internships
- Practicum, internship
- Special Problems: Life-Threatening Behaviors
- A yearly topic in master's seminar
- Crisis Intervention (an elective)
- Counseling Process (pre-practicum)
- Assessment in Counseling (risk assessment piece)
- Ethical, Professional, and Legal Issues
- Not in a course; is a separate workshop that takes up four hours of one afternoon in the first semester

Question	Response	
Q5: Students in your program *are first exposed to information about suicide* . . .	Before their practicum	66.0%
	During their practicum	16.0%
	After their practicum but before their internship	4.0%
	During their internship	6.0%
	Other	8.0%
Q6: What *types of teaching methodology* do you use in presenting suicide information to your students? (Check all that apply.)	Lecture	87.0%
	Discussion	87.0%
	Case study	55.6%
	Video/movie	22.2%
	Role play	37.0%
	Assigned reading	53.7%

professionals practice in relative isolation in private practices or even within agencies, leaving them without the benefit of readily available supervisory or consultative input.

Through the cases in this book, therapists can have some professional contact with colleagues that have all had a similar clinical challenge. As clinicians, we may have, out of necessity, trained ourselves on the job, through reading and attending workshops. Although almost all of our colleagues agree that it is a very valuable learning experience to share cases with each other and discuss ways we could improve our care, this rarely happens; it is difficult to set aside the time for this opportunity with our busy work schedules. This book represents a great way to hear the voices of colleagues as they discuss suicidal client cases.

A last reason for utilizing this text is found in a harsh clinical fact: Many clinicians in practice will have a client commit suicide at some time during their careers. Yet there are very few articles in the literature on how to cope with the fallout of a client suicide. Often professionals may not have the supervisory supports they had when in training, or they may be reluctant to discuss the case with a colleague due to feelings of embarrassment or failure. The cases in this book are all presented by regular counselors—not "super-therapists."

Reading these cases will help you normalize your clinical experiences with suicidal clients and increase your clinical vision regarding suicidal clients. Perhaps you can use this book as a starting point to engage professional colleagues in discussions about suicidal clients. Finally, while reading these cases, you may learn new counseling methods, be reminded of previous learning that you had forgotten, or simply learn that you are part of a larger family of helpers, all of whom struggle with treating suicidal clients.

HOW TO MAKE THE BEST USE OF THIS BOOK

The purpose as stated above makes it clear that this book is intended to be a practical, realistic, and useful learning resource for both graduate students in training and clinicians in the field. In order to make the most of each of the cases contained herein, you may wish to approach them from a *self-reflection* frame of reference. By adopting this self-reflective orientation, you will be able to learn from what others have done and possibly consider incorporating some their strategies into your own clinical work.

One way to maximize your self-reflection is to pause from time to time as you are reading each case and literally take a minute to reflect. To assist you with reflecting on each case, there are two types of questions at the end of each case. "Suicide Issue Questions" are intended for discussion with others, in addition to stimulating your own thinking, and relate to a wider suicide treatment issue that has been part of a specific case. We have also included some standardized "Skill Builder Questions" across all the cases. You can jot down some notes on these and then share them with a classmate, supervisor, or colleague.

We believe that one of the best ways to learn how to assess and effectively intervene with suicidal clients is by reading what other experienced clinicians have done when faced with difficult cases. While the cases have undergone some editing and structuring so that there is some uniformity among them, a significant effort has been made to preserve the unique perspective, writing style, and personality of the clinician who has written each case. As noted earlier, the cases in this book are real; they are not "perfect" or contrived vignettes. Each one is intended to communicate real-life counseling with a diverse representation of clients. The cases involve people of different genders, of different cultural backgrounds, and with various psychological disturbances, and they take place in different treatment settings.

Each contributor has made efforts to preserve the confidentiality of his or her client by changing names, locations, and sometimes potentially identifying details in the case.

Further, each case illustrates how these counselors grappled with providing care for the suicidal client. We all know that when working with difficult clients, hindsight is frequently 20/20, and we may, as we read these cases, now see that other approaches would have been more desirable or more in line with our approach to therapy. You are invited to think about the cases from your own orientation and unique agency or practice situation.

References

American Association of Suicidology. (2008). *U.S.A. suicide: 2005 official final data* (Fact sheet). Retrieved September 17, 2008, from http://www.suicidology.org

Bongar, B., & Harmatz, M. (1991). Clinical psychology graduate education in the study of suicide: Availability, resources, and importance. *Suicide & Life-Threatening Behaviors, 21*(3), 231–244.

Coder, T. L., Nelson, R. E., & Aylward, L. K. (1991). Suicide among secondary students. *School Counselor, 38*(5), 358–361.

Foster, V. A., & McAdams, C. R., III. (1999). The impact of client suicide in counselor training: Implications for counselor education and supervision. *Counselor Education & Supervision 39*(1), 22–33.

Greenhalgh, A. M. (2007). Case method teaching as science and art: A metaphoric approach and curricular application. *Journal of Management Education, 31*, 181–194.

King, K. A., Price, J. H., Talljohann, S. K., & Wahl, J. (1999). How confident do high school counselors feel in recognizing students at risk for suicide? *American Journal of Health Behavior, 23*(6), 457–467.

Mazza, D., Elizabeth, T., & Freeman, K. A. (2003). Graduate training and the treatment of suicidal clients: The students' perspective. *Suicide & Life-Threatening Behavior, 33*, 211–218.

Suicide Foundations

In this chapter, we will provide basic suicide background information. Given the complexity of suicide as a psychosocial phenomenon, our intent is to provide a foundational knowledge rather than an exhaustive explanation. Entire books have been written on some of the sections you are about to read. Once you have completed this basic suicide orientation and the case studies presented in this book, we encourage you to consult additional resources—for example, *Suicide: An Essential Guide for Helping Professionals and Educators* (Granello & Granello, 2007)—for a complete and in-depth review of the suicide literature. Table 2.1 lists some very good Internet resources.

TABLE 2.1 **Internet Resources on Suicide**

Site	URL
American Association of Suicidology	http://www.suicidology.org
Suicide Prevention Resource Center	http://www.sprc.org
Suicide Prevention Action Network	http://www.spanusa.org
Ohio Suicide Prevention Foundation	http://www.ohiospf.org
Center For Disease Control	http://www.cdc.gov

BASIC SUICIDE TERMINOLOGY

When you need to become familiar with a new topic, learning its professional vocabulary is often a good place to start. Following are some of the fundamental terms used by sociologists and others who study suicide:

Suicide: "Self kill"; the act of taking one's own life intentionally.

Suicidology: The study of suicide.

Complete suicide: To die by suicide.

Attempt suicide: To undertake behaviorally to commit suicide.

Suicide ideation: The act of thinking about attempting suicide.

Para-suicide: A self-threatening act against the self, such as cutting; may or may not result in injury or completed suicide.

Survivor: Any family member, friend, or individual who has been affected by the suicide of another.

Suicidal risk factor: Any variable or factor the presence or absence of which leads to an increase in the tendency to commit suicide.

Suicidal pact: An agreement between two or more people to die simultaneously by committing suicide.

Suicidal preventative factors, counters, or resiliency factors: A set of factors operating within the individual, family, or society that are likely to reduce the risk of suicide.

SUICIDE CONTEXT: A SIGNIFICANT PUBLIC HEALTH PROBLEM

Suicide is a significant public health problem in the United States today, yet its scope is not generally well understood by either the general public or mental health professionals. Currently, suicide is ranked the 11th leading cause of death in the United States across all age groups and the third leading cause of death among adolescents. There are roughly over 32,000 completed (known and classified) suicides in this country each year (Granello, 2007). To get a mental image of that number, imagine the population of large town completely disappearing each year.

Another way to grasp the raw number of suicides is to realize that 32,637 (2005) equates to about 89 suicides each and every day. Stop and think about that for a minute. Each of those 89 people had a life, had a family (maybe children, a spouse, or a partner), worked, was a member of a church, and was a member of a community. In fact, it has been estimated that for every suicide there are approximately 6 suicide survivors (family, partners, spouses, etc.) that are directly affected by the death. At 31,484 completed suicides annually, that would yield approximately 189,000 survivors who are affected each year.

Table 2.2 provides the most recently available statistics on completed suicides, as reported by the Centers for Disease Control and Prevention. Continually updated statistics on suicide can be found on the American Association of Suicidology webpage (http://www.suicidology.org).

Although the statistics reported in Table 2.2 are enough to warrant concern, in reality the true number of suicide deaths is likely higher than the numbers officially reported. Suicide rates have long been suspect as being underreported or inaccurate (Jobes, Berman, & Josselson, 1987).The actual number of deaths by suicide is thought to be as much as five times greater than the numbers commonly compiled by the Centers for Disease Control Jobes, Berman, & Josselson,1987). This is because it is suspected that many suicides are reported as deaths by other causes (e.g., vehicular accident, alcohol-related fall). MacKinnon, Farberow, and Nelson's seminal 1977 work argued that investigations often, if not always, fail to uncover the true intent of the deceased's action and his predeath thoughts. In other words, without fully understanding what the individual was thinking—whether or not he was intentionally planning on ending his life—the coroner or medical examiner likely cannot make an accurate determination as to whether the death was the result of suicidal intent.

The statistics surrounding suicide in the United States are staggering, and it is very important to familiarize yourself with them. We want to emphasize the importance of not ever forgetting that each suicide statistic represents the life of a real person and his or her family.

TABLE 2.2   Final U.S. Suicide Statistics, 2005

Group	Number	Number Per Day	Rate*
Nation	32,637	89.4	11.0
Males	25,907	71.0	17.7
White males	23,478	64.3	19.7
Black males	1,621	4.4	8.7
Females	6,730	18.4	0.5
White females	6,049	16.5	5.0
Black females	371	1.0	1.8
Other Minority			
Hispanics (both sexes)	2,188	6.0	5.1
Native Americans (both sexes)	392	1.0	12.4
Asian/Pacific Islanders (both sexes)	726	2.0	5.2
Elderly (65+)	5,404	14.8	14.7
Young (15–24)	4,212	11.5	10.0

*Rate is the number of suicides per 100,000 deaths.

Official data source: H.-C. Kung, D. L. Hoyert, J. Xu, & S. L. Murphy. (2008, April 24). Deaths: Final data for 2005. *National Vital Statistics Reports, 56*(10). Retrieved September 17, 2008, from http://www.cdc.gov/nchs/data/nvsr/nvsr56/nvsr56_10.pdf

Each of the client cases that you read about in this text presents the life events of a real individual and a real mental health practitioner; these are not faceless statistics.

The Continuing Social Stigma of Suicide

The stigma surrounding suicide is one reason that it persists as a significant health problem in our society. To date, suicide remains one of the few topics that are taboo in our modern society. The general public in the United States still has significantly negative attitudes toward suicidality, as well as toward those individuals afflicted with mental illness in general. The taboo nature of suicide in the United States derives from the religious, political, social, and legal traditions in Western society. For example, it was not long ago that it was viewed as unacceptable to bury the body of a suicide victim in a consecrated cemetery. In fact, there have been times in history when the body of a suicide victim was placed in a crossroads to be trampled by the carts and horses of others. There were not only strict religious injunctions against suicide but civil laws as well. Often families where not allowed to inherit the property of the individual who had committed suicide, with the property being forfeited to church or state. It is not surprising; therefore, that suicide remains a social taboo.

Suicide is considered a very unpleasant topic and, therefore, not openly or frequently discussed within the general public and even between professionals. One detrimental effect of this lack of open discourse and public education is that inaccurate information, in the form of myths about suicide, continues to be perpetuated. Many of these myths concerning suicide are widespread despite our increased understanding of mental illness. For example, the beliefs that asking someone if she is suicidal will put the idea into her head and that suicide is not a predictable event, so there is no way to stop it, are commonly held. These myths are harmful because they are almost always falsely portray the facts of suicide and

may lead to suicide deaths. As counselors, we need to first educate ourselves and then our clients and the general public. We need to advocate for more education concerning the facts of suicide and defeat the social taboo that allows false myths to persist.

Research on Suicide Risk Factors

Most of the research on suicide to date has focused on the investigation of risk factors that may increase the tendency to attempt or complete suicide. Many different risk factors have been identified for several diverse populations. These risk factors for suicide are genetic, psychological, social, and environmental in nature. This section briefly describes what is known about several of the most important risk factors.

AGE   Suicide risk increases with age across the lifespan. Although children do commit suicide, risk significantly increases in early adolescence and continues to increase into young adulthood. For men, risk dramatically increases after age 65.

GENDER   Generally, males complete suicide at four times the rate of females, whereas females attempt suicide at six times the rate of males. Over 70% of completed suicides are committed by white males.

RACE   White males are overwhelmingly responsible for the most suicides (72%) and are at high risk. Minority populations, especially Native Americans, all have significant suicide rates. The rate for African-American males has increased by 100% in the last 20 years.

ACCESS TO MEANS   Access to lethal means, particularly firearms, increases the risk of suicide. Guns account for 60% of the suicide completions in the United States. Suffocation (usually by car exhaust or hanging), ingestion of poisons, and overdosing are also significant means of completing suicide.

SUBSTANCE ABUSE   The abuse of any substance, especially alcohol, has been connected to an increase in the likelihood of a suicide attempt or completion. The abuse of substances impairs judgment and leads to impulsivity that is often lethal. Alcoholics have a chance of completing suicide that is 40 times greater than that of a nonaddicted individual.

MENTAL ILLNESS   Although the vast majority of people with a mental illness never attempt or complete suicide, it is estimated that 90% of completed suicides are the result of an undiagnosed mental illness. People with mood disorders, anxiety disorders, schizophrenia, and personality disorders have all been shown to be at significantly increased risk for suicide.

PSYCHOLOGICAL CHARACTERISTICS/PERSONALITY TRAITS   Any psychological characteristic that leads to impulsivity (for example, attention deficit disorder) or rigid cognitive structure may contribute to suicide risk. Compromised ability to solve problems or engage in social support systems may significantly increase suicide risk. An interesting personality trait often found in high-functioning individuals, such as graduate students, is perfectionism. Perfectionism has been shown to be related to increased suicide risk.

FAMILY HISTORY   Suicide is not genetically inherited. However, many of the underlying causes of suicide, such as impulsivity or mood disorders, are inherited. A previous suicide in the family of an individual is a significant risk factor for that individual. In addition to the inherited dispositions, there is a reduction in the stigma of or injunction against suicide for the individual when a family member has previously attempted or completed a suicide.

PROXIMAL AND DISTAL STRESSORS   It is important to remember that what an individual perceives as a stressor is based on his internal frame of reference. An event such as the loss of a boyfriend may seem manageable to us but can be overwhelming to an adolescent female who does not have any experience with loss of relationships. Further, stressors can be distal, such as early child abuse, or proximal, such as a recent house fire. It is important when assessing suicidality to inquire about both the proximal and the distal stressors that the individual may have had in his life in the past and in the present.

PREVIOUS SUICIDE ATTEMPT   Unfortunately, one of the best (although still not highly predictive) indicators of suicide risk is a previous suicide attempt. When individuals attempt suicide often, they must always be taken seriously. The number one cause of death among people with borderline personality disorder is suicide. Therefore, even if suicide attempts are used as a method to communicate, avoid, or control others, they must be taken seriously.

Summary

The purpose of this book is not to provide an exhaustive study of suicide but rather to illustrate through a case study approach how clinicians manage suicidal clients in their practices. The information presented in this chapter is a basic overview of suicide, and you are encouraged to pursue additional readings and learning.

References

Granello, D. H., & Granello, P. F. (2007). *Suicide: An essential guide for helping professionals and educators.* Boston: Allyn & Bacon.

Jobes, D. A., Berman, A. L., & Josselson, A. R. (1987). Improving the validity and reliability of medical-legal certifications of suicide. *Suicide & Life-Threatening Behavior,* 17, 310–325.

Nelson, F. L., Farberow, N. L., MacKinnon, D. R. (1978). "The certification of suicide in eleven western states: An inquiry into the validity of reported suicide rates." *Suicide and Life-Threatening Behavior,* 8(2), 75–88.

Suicide Risk Screening

This chapter discusses some of the verbal and written methods used to conduct a suicide screening. Suicide screening is intended to be much like hearing or vision screening. The intent is to determine whether a problem exists to the extent that a more in-depth assessment by a professional with specific expertise is required. Clinical suicide assessments are conducted in more depth than suicide screens and are used to determine what types of placement and treatment an individual should receive. It is our view that while specific advanced training should be sought by clinicians who will regularly engage in full clinical suicide assessments, all mental health clinicians and many other health professionals should be skilled in suicide screening and risk determination, no matter what their practice setting.

SCREENING FOR SUICIDE RISK

Screening for suicide is a process for determining the degree of risk a client exhibits in regard to engaging in suicidal behavior. In order to properly determine if a client is at risk for suicide, many variables must be considered, early foreclosure in decision making must be avoided, and clinical judgment must be used to weigh the variables in developing a risk formulation.

There are three major categories of variables that clinicians should attend to in a suicide risk screening: static risk factors, dynamic risk factors, and protective factors. *Static risk factors* include those variables that are relatively constant for an individual, such as race, gender, age, and family history of suicide. *Dynamic risk factors* include those variables that are not fixed but rather are highly changeable at any one point in time. Examples of dynamic risk factors include suicide ideation, agitation, and hopelessness. *Protective factors* include those variables that ameliorate suicide risk. Examples of protective factors include will to live, coping skills, religiosity, strong social supports, and strong therapy relationship.

The combinations and weighting given to these types of factors vary depending on the population being screened and oftentimes on the specific strategies that a clinician employs. As of yet, there is no one best formula for determining which risk and protective factors have the most predictive ability, and there is still variation among clinicians and the instruments they use for screening individuals for suicide risk. This chapter offers suggestions for

how to organize your approach to suicide screening. Direct questioning, suicide acronyms, and suicide screening checklists are all means to assist you in assessing a full range of risk and protective factors.

DIRECT QUESTIONING

It is a common myth that asking individuals about their suicidality will then put the idea in their heads to complete suicide. This is completely in error. In fact, research shows that asking individuals directly about their suicide intent, ideation, and plans may be one of the most effective ways of helping them (Gould et al., 2005).

The method most commonly used to assess suicide risk is simply to ask. Sometimes beginning practitioners get so caught up in all the complexity of the risk assessment that they forget to ask the question (something like "Have you thought about suicide?" or "Are you considering killing yourself?"). Other times clinicians let their assumptions, rather than their clinical judgment, interfere with assessment.

One student in her practicum told the story of a high school girl who was a very popular student, a cheerleader, and on her way to a top-quality college. As she told the story of the girl's depression, she kept emphasizing how much the girl had going for her—looks, popularity, and intelligence. It was clear, however, that the girl was very depressed, and the practicum student was asked what sort of suicide assessment she had done. The practicum student quickly exclaimed, "Oh, she's not suicidal!"

With some exploration, however, we soon learned that the practicum student simply assumed that a young woman like this—who did not "look" like a candidate for suicide—could never be suicidal, so a suicide risk assessment never entered her mind. If the girl had been less popular, overweight, or sullen in her mood, the practicum student might have made very different assumptions. In this instance, we immediately made plans for a suicide risk assessment, and it turned out that the girl had a very serious and organized plan. She actually was relieved when someone finally asked her. She said it was the first time that someone had looked at her for who she was underneath, rather than through all the trappings of success. Once she felt heard and understood, we could get started on the process of treatment. The "take-home" message is this: *Always ask.*

THE FED INTERVIEW METHOD

In addition to direct questioning, interviewing methods which employ open ended questions can also be used to determine risk when screening for suicide. The severity of suicidality may be determined by using a helpful process for assessment that we refer to as the FED. This acronym indicates the *frequency* of suicidal thoughts, the *extent* of suicide plans, and the *duration* of suicidal thoughts and impulses. As you read the upcoming cases, use the FED to help organize the clients' clinical presentations and the counselors' key concerns. In most cases, whether stated by these counselors or not, the FED factors alerted them that their clients had moved past the point of being considered nonsuicidal (at minimal risk for suicide) to being considered suicidal (at significant risk of self-annihilation).

Let's make the use of this acronym to distinguish the nonsuicidal client from the suicidal client easier to understand by reviewing two brief clinical vignettes. These vignettes will allow us to us compare and contrast the use of the FED in two different situations.

In the first clinical vignette, Maria presents as a nonsuicidal, 23-year-old, female college student who has a few brief and fleeting suicidal thoughts. Maria's fiancé of three years has abruptly ended their marriage plans and proposed to Maria's roommate. Maria's internal thought process might go something like this:

> That jerk promised to marry me. I've done everything to get him through college. I've helped him write his class papers, and I've even put up with his beer guzzling and imbecilic friends. Now, he dumps me for that immature witch. I can't believe he did that! I feel abandoned, hurt, and embarrassed. I'd like to simply vanish and get away from this devastating emotional pain and hurt. Will my pain ever end? My head hurts from crying, and I can't focus on anything except the breakup and pain. I can't believe what he has done to me; I want him to hurt just as bad as me. I want him to be miserable, too. Maybe I should kill myself. If I kill myself, I will be free of this horrible misery, and everyone will hate him for how cruelly he has treated me. That will show him! His parents and family will tell him it was his fault that I killed myself, and he will feel like the true idiot he is. Whoa! Maria girl, that's a dumb idea. Sure, I want him to feel lousy. But the problem with this "killing myself to make him feel miserable thing" is that I'd be dead. He wouldn't care. He never has cared. And my mom and little brother would be devastated by my suicide. I'm not going to kill myself over him! Instead, the way to make him miserable is to finish my degree and find someone better than him. That won't be too difficult. I'll show everyone he was the loser for dropping me. That's it. Instead of ending my life and hurting the people who really love me, I'll complete my degree and become even more successful at what I do. Lots of people will want to be around me, and I'll show him who the real loser is.

In this somewhat stereotypical clinical vignette, Maria has fleeting thoughts about suicide. The thoughts are centered on two distinct issues—her feelings of emotional devastation and embarrassment and her desire to seek revenge or "get back" at her ex-fiancé. Maria considers the option of suicide and quickly realizes that the costs of suicide far exceed the potential benefits.

In this case, Maria's FED is clearly within a normal range. The *frequency* of her suicidal thoughts is minimal. Here, she has considered suicide one time. She is not continually bombarding herself with new thoughts of suicide throughout her waking hours. In other words, she doesn't frequently or constantly think of suicide as a means of coping with or responding to life's continual barrage of stressors.

Next, the *extent* of her suicidal plan is completely missing. In other words, although she thought about vanishing, she never developed an actual suicide plan. Maria's suicidal thoughts did not progress to the next tier of thinking about how she would go about ending her life. Had she begun to create a suicide plan and then extensively elaborate on that plan to ensure her ultimate self-annihilation, the extent or severity of her plan would clearly be outside the normal range.

Finally, the *duration* of Maria's suicide thoughts is exceedingly brief. She does not ruminate on suicide once she has considered the significant costs to both her and her family. In other words, once she has weighed the costs of suicide, she does not pine away her

waking hours thinking how to end her life. Maria's healthy response to her ex-fiancé's disengagement is strikingly different from that of others who dwell on or fantasize about their suicide. For example, others might contemplate in great detail who will attend their funeral and what the funeral attendees will be feeling or saying to themselves about the deceased. However, Maria's suicidal thoughts abruptly end when she realizes her ex-fiancé will not care and understands that the only true victims of her suicide will be her family and herself.

In contrast, let's look at Mark's FED. Mark is a 34-year-old male who, until his termination earlier this week, had worked as an ergonomic seating engineer for one of the Big Three automakers. Throughout high school and college, Mark often had suicidal thoughts. These thoughts typically occurred when he felt stressed over responsibilities or pressing challenges. As a matter of fact, during finals week of his senior year of college, Mark felt so overwhelmed by thoughts of suicide that he was hospitalized for a four-day period. During the last year, Mark has strongly considered suicide on three separate occasions and has made one suicide attempt. He has voiced suicidal thoughts so regularly that friends have begun teasing him about his suicidal statements over what most others would perceive to be trivial offenses. Since being terminated from his job this week, Mark has continually ruminated on how he could kill himself to get even with his supervisor and the company. From the moment Mark awakes in the morning until he fitfully attempts to fall asleep at night, one overwhelming concern occupies his mind: suicide. In contrast to Maria, Mark's internal thought process might go something like this:

> I can't believe it. After three years of dedicated work, they fired me. They are no different from my landlord, my former wife, my neighbors, and my former high school friends Charlie, Robert, Cassandra, and Julia. Since high school, I've thought about killing myself because of how these "friends" treated me. Each time I considered suicide, I wanted to get back at all of them. This time I'm really going to do it. Last year when I tried to kill myself, I used my pain medication to overdose. My botched suicide attempt didn't stop the emotional pain and resulted in my being involuntarily hospitalized. This time I'm really going to do it. I want them to actually see me die. That way they will remember me and wish they had treated me differently. Instead of overdosing at my house, I'm going to buy hollow-point bullets and load them in my gun. Hollow-points will blow a big hole in my head, and I'm certain that this will cause my death. I'm going to leisurely walk into the office at morning break and lock all of them in the break room with me. I'll tell each one how they hurt me and aim the gun at each person when I talk. Just before I pull the trigger, I will threaten to kill all of them. They will think I'm going to kill them and then I will put the gun to my temple and pull the trigger. I will most certainly die. I'll make sure my blood spatters on each of them, and I'll lie in a pool of blood that will forever stain those hardwood floors that the boss was so proud of. To make certain they won't soon forget, I'm going to sign each of them up for one of those prepaid greeting card programs. That way they will receive a card that says "Gone, But Never Forgotten" each month for the next year. I'll make certain to instruct the prepaid card program to send the cards so they arrive on the 19th of each month—the exact day that I kill myself. I'll make certain they never forget me or what they've done to me.

Unlike Maria, Mark has a long-term suicidal ideation history. In other words, he *frequently* has considered suicide as a viable option. According to the vignette, his suicidal ideation began in high school and continues to the present.

The extent of his suicidal plan demonstrates a difference from Maria's clinical presentation as well. Maria considered suicide but did not establish a suicide plan. In contrast, Mark not only has identified the suicide method but even has identified the type of bullets he will use. His intent in using hollow-point bullets is to increase the lethality of his method. Mark has also identified more than a suicide plan. He has decided when he will carry his plan out and how he will ensure that those present will remember him on his monthly suicide anniversary date. He has even described how he wants to impact survivors. These features of Mark's suicidal ideation demonstrate the severe extent of his suicidal ideation.

Finally, with regard to duration of suicidal thoughts, Mark appears to continue his suicidal rumination. He pines away his time thinking about how to ensure that those who hurt him will be forced to remember him.

As you can quickly determine from the above clinical vignettes, the FED helps clinicians determine if clients are presenting with suicidal ideation beyond that considered typical of the general population at large. The components of the FED and the general risk factors discussed in Chapter 2 are important factors to note within each of the cases that follow and can be helpful when assessing a client's immediate suicide risk.

ACRONYMS

Beyond the FED, there are several other mnemonic systems available that make use of acronyms to help clinicians remember the major areas or questions that should be asked in a suicide risk assessment interview. Following are some of the commonly used acronyms:

SLAP

S *What are the specific details? (S = specificity)*

L *How lethal is the plan (e.g., guns, pills, rope)? (L = lethality)*

A *How available is the method of choice? Where is it? (A = availability)*

P *What is the proximity to help? Who will find him/her? How long will it take to be found? (P = proximity)*

PLAID

P *Previous attempts*

L *Lethality*

A *Access*

I *Intent*

D *Drugs/alcohol*

PIMP

P   Plan

I   Intent

M   Means

P   Prior attempt

MAP (Bonner)

M   Mental state for suicidality (thinking)

A   Affective state for suicidality (emotions)

P   Psychosocial state for suicidality (circumstances)

NO HOPE (Shea)

N   No framework for meaning

O   Overt change in clinical condition

H   Hostile interpersonal environment

O   Out of hospital recently

P   Predisposing personality factors

E   Excuses for dying are present and strongly believed

DIRT (Marv Miller)

D   Danger: What is the level of Dangerousness of attempt?

I   Impression: Did the client realize the severity concerning dangerousness of the attempt?

R   Rescue: Was there a chance of intervention? Did the client seek last-minute help?

T   Timing: When did the last attempt occur?

In 2006, the American Association of Suicidology put forth IS PATH WARM? as an acronym that could be useful for clinicians in screening for suicide.

Suicide **I**deation	Does the client report active suicidal ideation? Has she written about her suicide or death?
Substance Abuse	Does the client excessively use alcohol or other drugs, or has she begun using alcohol or other drugs?
Purposelessness	Does the client voice a lack or loss of purpose in life?
Anger	Does the client present with feelings of rage or uncontrolled anger?
Trapped	Does the client feel trapped? Does she believe there is no way out of her current situation?
Hopelessness	Does the client have a negative sense of self, others, and her future? Does the future appear hopeless with little chance for positive change?
Withdrawing	Does the client indicate a desire to withdraw from significant others, family, friends, and society?
Anxiety	Does the client feel anxious, agitated, or unable to sleep?
Recklessness	Does the client act recklessly or engage in risky activities, seemingly without thinking or considering potential consequences?
Mood Change	Does the client report experiencing dramatic mood shifts or states?

CHECKLISTS

In addition to mnemonic acronyms, many clinicians find that having a paper-and-pencil checklist in front of them helps them to make sure they conduct a thorough assessment, addressing all the relevant risk and protective factors.

There are several checklists that are available to guide questioning around suicide risk. Again, just as with the acronyms, these checklists are intended only as a guide for the interview, not as a definitive suicide risk assessment. A caution is necessary: The "objective" scoring of some of the checklists can encourage inappropriate use. Remember, these are general guidelines only. Nevertheless, research shows that mental health professionals who have been trained in the use of such checklists as SAD PERSONS and Adapted SAD PERSONS are better able to evaluate suicide risk than are those who have not had such training (Juhnke, 1994).

SAD PERSONS

Semistructured suicide assessment interviews are frequently used by counselors to assess immediate client suicide risk. One of the most widely used semistructured clinical suicide assessment interviews is the SAD PERSONS Scale (SPS). The SPS was created by Patterson, Dohn, Bird, and Patterson (1983). The SPS was developed to help physicians conduct a detailed investigation into the same three domains (thinking, emotions, and circumstances) identified by Bonner (1990) as critically important when assessing suicide potential. The instrument's

TABLE 3.1   SAD PERSONS Scale

Risk Factor	One Point Given For . . .
Sex	Male
Age	19 years of age or younger or 45 years of age or older
Depression	Depressed
Previous Attempt	Previous suicide attempt has been made
Ethanol Abuse	Substance abuse or substance dependence
Rational Thinking Loss	Rational loss is present (e.g., hallucinations, delusions)
Social Supports Lacking	No close friends, no social supports
Organized Suicide Plan	Well-thought-out and well-constructed plan on how to end one's life
No Spouse	Divorced, never married, separated, widowed
Sickness	Debilitating or life-threatening illness or disease is present

authors created the acronym SAD PERSONS from 10 literature-identified suicide risk factors (i.e., sex, age, depression, previous attempt, ethanol abuse, rational thinking loss, social supports lacking, organized suicide plan, no spouse, and sickness) (Table 3.1). Counselors can use the SPS during the clinical interview process to systematically investigate each of the 10 risk factors. The semistructured format of the scale aids counselors in facilitating an interview based on specific criteria established for each risk factor. Thus, counselors generate questions for each factor pertinent to the specific client.

Absent from the SPS are stock questions that potentially give clients the impression of being interrogated. Instead, the SPS allows counselors to ask multiple questions related to specific risk factors. Questioning continues until sufficient information regarding each factor has been gathered. One point is scored for each factor present; total scores can range from 0 (suggesting very little suicide risk) to 10 (suggesting very high suicide risk). Clinical actions are suggested on the basis of these scores (Table 3.2).

TABLE 3.2   SAD PERSONS Guidelines for Clinical Actions

Total Points	Suggested Clinical Action
0 to 2	Send home with follow-up
3 to 4	Arrange close follow-up; consider hospitalization
5 to 6	Strongly consider hospitalization depending on confidence in the follow-up arrangement
7 and above	Hospitalize or commit

Adapted SAD PERSONS

In 1996, Juhnke adapted the SPS for use with adolescents. The adapted scale (Table 3.3) can be used to screen immediate suicide risk factors and provide general intervention recommendations for school counselors.

In general, even students with low scores on the Adapted SAD PERSONS Scale warrant counseling if they present with mood disorder, alcohol or substance abuse, rational thinking loss, and/or an organized suicide plan.

TABLE 3.3   Adapted SAD PERSONS Scale

Risk Factor	Up to 10 Points Given
Sex	Males = 10 points; females = 0 points
Age	Older students are at higher risk and receive more points
Depression or affective disorder	The more serious the disorder, the more points received
Previous attempt	Recent attempts and more lethal attempts are scored higher
Ethanol/drug abuse	Students using alcohol or drugs are at higher risk
Rational thinking loss	Any student experiencing rational thinking loss is at risk
Social supports lacking	50% of adolescent suicide completers had no close friends
Organized plan	Specificity and lethality increase risk
Negligent parenting	Neglect, abuse, family stress, and suicidal modeling increase risk
School problems	Aggressive behaviors, vandalism, or deterioration of academic performance signals increased risk

Scoring Guidelines

Assign points (0–10) according to severity for each risk factor. Total scores can range from 0 to 100.

0–29   Students perceived to be at risk should be encouraged to participate in counseling services and should be given information about crisis counseling. Counselors should consider a "no suicide" contract.

30–49   Students should be strongly encouraged to receive counseling and close follow-up services. School counselors should contact parents/guardians and make sure a thorough suicide assessment occurs.

50–69   Students in this range should be strongly considered for an evaluation for hospitalization.

70+   Scores in this range suggest both environmental turmoil and severe emotional distress. Scores at this extreme end of the continuum warrant immediate hospitalization. Child Protective Services should be contacted in cases when family turmoil does not allow adequate assurance of care.

FORMAL OR STRUCTURED INSTRUMENTS

Standardized instruments can be useful in obtaining information that helps the clinician get a clearer picture of the client during suicide screening. They also provide additional support for clinical decisions when working with managed care companies (Granello & Granello, 2007a). However, at best they can provide only an estimate of suicide risk and will never ultimately replace clinical judgment.

Standardized instruments that are used for suicide risk assessment are generally divided into two major categories: those that measure suicidal risk directly and those that measure emotional states (e.g., depression, hopelessness, anxiety) that correlate with suicide risk (Granello & Granello, 2007a). Table 3.4 gives some examples of standardized instruments

TABLE 3.4   Examples of Commercially Available Measures of Suicide Risk

Instrument/Author(s)	Population	Publisher/Source
Beck Scale for Suicidal Ideation A. R. Beck & R. A. Steer	17+ years	The Psychological Corporation
Inventory of Suicide Orientation J. D. King & B. Kowalchuk	13–18 years	National Computer Systems, Inc.
Suicide Probability Scale J. C. Cull & W. S. Gill	14+ years	Western Psychological Services
Suicidal Ideation Questionnaire W. M. Reynolds	Grades 10–12 (Suicidal Ideation Questionnaire–Junior, grades 7–9)	Psychological Assessment Resources

that may be used as part of suicide screening. (For a more detailed list, see Granello & Granello, 2007a.)

IMPORTANCE OF SUICIDE SCREENING DOCUMENTATION

The mere act of writing down exactly what was done becomes a built-in checklist for quality care (Granello & Granello, 2007a). Lawsuits that follow a completed suicide are among the highest-paying malpractice cases. It is imperative that clinicians write down in the client's chart all of the efforts that they made to assess and intervene with a client who may be suicidal. Courts understand that clinical judgment is not perfect and will tend to rule on the side of clinicians who have met the standard of care concerning suicide screening assessment and have properly documented their care. When courts find against psychiatrists and other clinicians in suicide-related lawsuits, the cause is usually improper and insufficient documentation.

Summary

Within this chapter, you have learned about suicide screening and clinical assessment. You have learned how to use direct questioning, mnemonic acronyms, and the FED to better understand your clients' immediate suicide risk and intervention needs. You have gained a basic understanding of the SPS—including the 10 literature-identified suicide risk factors that suggest further investigation and intervention are immediately necessary. You also learned about the importance of proper documentation of suicide screening and assessment.

As you read about the suicidal clients in the upcoming cases, make use of the information in this chapter. What specific suicide risk factors do you note? Look for details that might help you evaluate the clients based on the FED and the SPS. Most important, learn how the experienced mental health professionals who contributed these cases both evaluated and responded to their clients.

References

American Association of Suicidology (2006). Is Path Warm? Retrieved March 31, 2008, from http://www.suicidology.org/displaycommon.cfm?an=2

Bonner, R. L. (1990). A "M.A.P." to the clinical assessment of suicide risk. *Journal of Mental Health Counseling, 12*, 232–236.

Brown, G. K. (2002). *A review of suicide assessment measures for intervention research with adults and older adults.* Retrieved March 31, 2008 from http://www.nimh.nih.gov/research/adultsuicide.pdf

Goldston, D. B. (2000). *Assessment of suicidal behaviors and risk among children and adolescents.* Retrieved March 31, 2008 http://www.nimh.nih.gov/research/measures.pdf

Gould, M. S., Marracco, F. A., Leinman, M., Thomas, J. G., Mostkoff, K., Cote, J., et al. (2005). Evaluating iatrogenic risk of youth suicide screening programs: A randomized controlled trial. *Journal of the American Medical Association, 293*, 1635–1643.

Granello, D. H., & Granello, P. F. (2007a). *Suicide: An essential guide for helping professionals and educators.* Boston: Allyn & Bacon.

Granello, D. H., & Granello, P. F. (2007b). Suicide assessment: Strategies for determining risk. *Counselling, Psychotherapy, & Health, 3*(1), 42–51.

Hatton, C. L., & Valente, S. M. (1984). *Suicide: Assessment and intervention.* New York: Appleton-Century-Crofts.

Juhnke, G. A. (1994). Teaching suicide risk assessment to counselor education students. *Counselor Education & Supervision, 34,* 52–57.

Juhnke, G. A., Granello, P. F., & Lebron-Striker, M. (in press). IS PATH WARM? A suicide assessment mnemonic for counselors. *ACA Professional Counseling Digest*

Maris, R. W. (1991). Introduction (Special Issue). *Suicide & Life-Threatening Behaviors, 21,* 1–17.

Motto, J. A. (1991). An integrated approach to estimating suicide risk. *Suicide & Life-Threatening Behaviors, 21,* 74–89.

Patterson, W. M., Dohn, H. H., Bird, J., & Patterson, G. A. (1983). Evaluation of suicidal patients: The SAD PERSONS Scale. *Psychosomatics, 24,* 343–349.

Seldes, G. (1985). *The great thoughts.* New York: Ballantine.

Shea, S. (2002). *The practical art of suicide assessment: A guide for mental health professionals and substance abuse counselors.* Hoboken, NJ: Wiley.

Jenny
An Adolescent Female Inpatient

MARYBETH MCDONALD

EDITORS' COMMENTS

- This case takes place on an inpatient unit for children and adolescents where group therapy is used with the clients.
- One of the highlights of this case is the use of expressive writing techniques as a therapeutic intervention.

INTRODUCTION

Welcome to my world. I work on an inpatient unit. My clinical focus is frequently on suicide. The people I meet are hospitalized because they have very recently attempted suicide or they present with serious suicidal ideation and intent. When I say serious, I mean serious. My clients have secured guns to shoot themselves, tied nooses from which to hang, and purchased enough Tylenol to destroy their livers. Many have written their last wills and testaments. Or they have shot, stabbed, overdosed, or hung themselves. Some have set fire to their homes and stayed inside. Others have deliberately driven cars into trees. Many have left detailed notes describing what they are about to do, and why.

BACKGROUND/REFERRAL

I am a Licensed Independent Social Worker in a large university hospital. I work on a psychiatric unit for children and teens. The young people I counsel are suicidal, homicidal, and/or psychotic. I provide group therapy. The program goal is to provide intense, short-term crisis stabilization. This case began for me when I looked at the new admissions board and learned about 17-year-old Jenny. She broke her back and arm during a suicide attempt. Jenny was originally admitted to a physical rehabilitation center due to her para-suicide—inflicted injuries. Once physically stabilized, Jenny was referred to and entered our adolescent psychiatric unit. Our charge was to address Jenny's immediate psychological needs and ensure her safety.

Prior to actually meeting Jenny, the multiprofessional, interdisciplinary treatment team met to discuss her case and participate in morning rounds. Members of Jenny's treatment

team included a psychiatrist, nurse, occupational therapist, medical resident, medical student, teacher, family therapist–social worker, and me. My specific charge was to engage Jenny in effective group-counseling experiences that would (1) promote appropriate mood stability, (2) reduce her impulsiveness and suicidal behaviors, and (3) help her identify more effective coping strategies.

ASSESSMENT

To better understand Jenny and her presenting needs, the treatment team began the assessment by reviewing information provided by Jenny's referring rehabilitation center. The center's report noted that Jenny had broken her back when she intentionally threw herself down a stairwell. According to the report, Jenny had stated she "attempted suicide" in an effort to "end it all." Jenny's para-suicide was precipitated by intense anger directed at her former boyfriend. When Jenny somehow survived the para-suicide, she gleefully indicated her fall was also used to get her boyfriend's attention.

The rehabilitation center staff indicated Jenny's inpatient psychiatric referral was based primarily on her suicidal behaviors and her continued mood instability and impulsiveness. Most recently, Jenny had repeatedly banged her head against a wall when she was upset with her mother. Given her compromised physical condition due to her recent para-suicide, her head-banging behaviors were viewed as life threatening.

Next, we reviewed the parent data report, completed by her mother and stepfather. The report indicated Jenny lived in a blended family that also included half siblings. Notably, Jenny's indicated last name on the report was strikingly different from that of the other family members with whom she lived.

Mother's data report indicated that mother had struggled with depression as a teenager and had "seriously considered" suicide when she was Jenny's age. However, mother denied previous para-suicides or mental health treatment.

According to mother, Jenny had never been arrested or experienced difficulties with the legal system. Jenny reportedly had no identified learning problems and was expected to graduate from vocational high school at the end of the current academic year. Mother further reported Jenny had no history of physical, sexual, or emotional abuse or of neglect or exposure to domestic violence. As an aside, Jenny's toxicology screen was negative upon entering the psychiatric unit. This supported Jenny's and her parents' claims that Jenny did not use illicit drugs or alcohol.

Jenny's mother and stepfather reported that Jenny's mood and interpersonal problems began at age 15. At that time, Jenny became excessively moody, frequently accused others of attempting to emotionally "hurt" her, and "wildly exaggerated" incidents where she believed she had been wronged. Her parents indicated Jenny had difficulty "seeing other people's points of view" and was overly sensitive. Jenny's parents indicated that Jenny would easily cry when in "a bad mood." Jenny began having trouble maintaining friendships at age 15 as well. Reportedly, longtime friends began to avoid Jenny due to her "moods." According to mother, Jenny viewed her friends' avoidance as an indication of "jealousy." Specifically, Jenny would report to her parents that friends avoided her because "I [Jenny] am so pretty."

Jenny briefly engaged in counseling after she had voiced suicidal ideation. She was 15 years old at the time. However, Jenny discontinued treatment soon afterward. Jenny reportedly discontinued treatment because she believed people were simply making a big deal about "a few comments" she made about ending her life. Jenny denied intentions of

hurting herself at the time she discontinued treatment and reportedly believed that talk therapy "wasn't helping."

Her parents noted significant changes in Jenny's mental health status after she became involved with an 18-year-old male. According to Jenny's mother, the male seemed "nice enough" at the onset of the dating relationship. However, when he attempted to end the dating relationship, Jenny became "frantic." Jenny called him repeatedly, regularly drove past his home, and went to his workplace attempting to reconcile the relationship. Jenny's parents were concerned with her noticeable increase in crying, verbal expressions of hopelessness, and accusations that she had been "wronged" by her boyfriend's ending their dating relationship. Jenny also told others that he would be sorry for ending the relationship.

According to Jenny's parents, the former boyfriend contacted them and reported that Jenny had threatened, hit, bitten, and thrown rocks at him. He believed Jenny was "stalking" him, and he threatened to contact the police if Jenny's behaviors did not stop. According to Jenny's parents, the former boyfriend believed Jenny would harm him or herself. The conversation between Jenny's parents and the former boyfriend occurred shortly before Jenny's para-suicide.

When the team met with Jenny, she was pleasant. Her back brace allowed her to walk. However, the brace prevented her from being able to turn her head. When asked, "What happened?" Jenny reported she had taken a "bad fall." She reported that she was glad her injuries were not more serious. Jenny denied current or past suicidal ideation or intent. Jenny denied ever deliberately hurting herself and reported she did not need psychiatric care. Instead, she briskly requested immediate discharge. Jenny denied any problems at home and stated she got along well with her mother, stepfather, and half siblings. When asked about her boyfriend, Jenny dismissively replied, "We mutually decided to break up" and indicated the breakup was "fine" with her.

According to the psychiatric hospital admissions report, Jenny had screamed, spit, and cursed at staff during the admissions process. When team members queried Jenny about her behaviors at admission, Jenny said she had been "a little upset." According to Jenny, her behaviors were quite understandable—especially given her desire to return home. At the conclusion of the assessment and ensuing treatment team meeting, it was decided that Jenny would be best served if she remained in the hospital for a 14-day minimum stay.

TREATMENT

A client's psychiatric diagnosis typically drives the psychiatric treatment team's plan. This was no different in Jenny's case. Her preliminary psychiatric assessments led to a provisional diagnosis of Mood Disorder, Not Otherwise Specified with a rule-out for Bipolar Disorder. Given Jenny's physical injuries, a physical medicine consultation team created a physical rehabilitation treatment that coordinated with her psychiatric care.

A mood-stabilizing medication was begun in an attempt to help regulate Jenny's significant mood swings. Her treatment plan focused on helping Jenny experience mood stabilization and regulation. This was accomplished via multiple layers, including therapy, medication, and milieu control. Related to milieu control, the unit was locked, and there was no access to computers for patients. Potentially hazardous items such as knives were removed from her environment. Also, visitation was limited to Jenny's immediate family. A daily schedule was imposed in addition to an established bedtime. The milieu of the unit was intentionally created to be calm, with clear behavioral expectations posted.

While housed on the unit, Jenny was required to work daily on her safety and anger management plans. Further, she was required to review these plans daily with unit staff and her parents. Each person involved in the plans, including Jenny, was required to offer written feedback about the plans and also sign the plan, thereby acknowledging that the plans had been discussed and agreed on that day. The plans included questions such as these: How did I come to be in the hospital? What were my stressors? What did I do to harm myself? What could I do differently in the future? What adults can I count on for support? What are their phone numbers?

When Jenny was first given the assignment to write about the behaviors leading to her hospitalization, it was very difficult. Her first assignment required her to write a report responding to the stem "What I did to come to the hospital." She especially had difficulty writing "I" statements. Over the course of treatment, Jenny became increasingly able to write about her inner experiences.

The first day of group therapy for teens is often very difficult. Thus, I anticipated that Jenny would have a difficult time. However, in Jenny's case I anticipated further difficulty because she truly believed she did not belong on the unit. According to Jenny, she had no problems and had nothing of significance to discuss. Like other teens, she also believed that her life was no one else's business and that no one else could understand her.

Our first group session began with members stating their first names and describing something they like doing. Starting with a moderately neutral question lessened Jenny's potential resistance and was intended to help her get to know others within the group. Each group session that Jenny participated had a theme. Group members responded to three basic stems related to each theme during the group experience. On Jenny's first day, the theme was "Influence." The three basic stems related to influence were as follows: (1) "Talk about a time you were positively influenced by someone," (2) "Talk about a time you were negatively influenced by someone," and (3) "Talk about a time you influenced someone else, either positively or negatively."

The other group members had previously participated in group therapy, and most responded to the stems in great detail. Others responded more briefly. When Jenny's turn came, she freely spoke. It was clear that she was interested in her church and her youth group, and she trusted her youth minister. Jenny spoke about the mission trips she had participated in. Reportedly, she enjoyed both the travel and the religious aspects of the trips. As well, she indicated that she enjoyed helping to build things on these trips. According to Jenny, she found school peers a mostly negative influence and did not feel especially close to anyone there. Furthermore, she did not like the social aspect of school. She saw herself as a mostly positive influence at church and felt some social connections there.

Following discussion, we spent time at a table doing a paper-pen exercise related to the group experience theme. Group participants were encouraged to write more regarding their experiences related to "Influence." Jenny wrote about her important personal influences: media, music, advertising, parents, friends, and teachers.

Jenny was also given the opportunity to choose a journal and pen. The journals are provided by a group called "The Friends." This group supports programs for hospitalized children and teens. There was a wide variety of journals from which Jenny was able to choose. She also chose a pretty pen to keep. Bill, another new member, hobbled up to Jenny's table using a walker. He had para-suicided by driving a car into a tree. He chose a black pen. They sat across from each other. Six other teens sat at the table. Several others had para-suicided via ingestion. Together, they talked and wrote.

Bill nonchalantly inquired why Jenny was hospitalized. Jenny claimed her hospital-ization was a just "big mistake." According to Jenny, she fell down a flight of stairs, and her parents mistakenly thought that she had attempted to hurt herself. Bill rolled his eyes and quipped that he had mistakenly been hospitalized, too. In a manner that was gentle but intended to be humorous, Bill reported that he had accidentally run his car into a tree. Another member chimed in. She stated she had "accidentally overdosed." Soon they were appropriately laughing and describing how they had participated in a series of be-haviors that had escalated to the point of their hospitalization and what they "should have" done differently rather than para-suicide. Then, as a group, we helped others iden-tify new coping or responding behaviors that could have been utilized without becoming suicidal.

Later I asked the group why people like "The Friends" exist. "Why would people go out of their way to buy journals for you—especially teens they had never met?" My intent was to generate conversation and expand their sometimes myopic thinking that others "don't care." Concomitantly, my intent was to indirectly address the group members' previ-ous statements that they feel "hopeless" due to others' noninvolvement and nonsupport. The gentle discussion of what "The Friends" did for them provided an opportunity for the group to stop and reflect. I then encouraged the teens to think about others who had helped them at some time in their lives and to consider writing a thank-you note.

Next, I opened the "Words of Wisdom" book. This is a big, impressive binder, with a well-decorated cover. Inside are "words of wisdom" written by previous patients on their last day at the hospital. The last day is a time for them to share with the group, reflect on their experiences and growth since entering the group, and offer encouragement to those entering treatment. Patients write their words and then read them to their peers.

On the first day of Jenny's group experience, Katy was leaving. Katy stood in front of the group and began, "On my first day here, I hated it. I did not want to be here. I thought everyone here was crazy. I thought my parents were crazy for bringing me here. . . ." Katy finished by describing the positive change that she had experienced within herself and the new closeness that she felt with her family. When Katy finished her words of wisdom, she put the book on the table for the group and encouraged those interested to read what she had written. Shortly afterward, when the group members were saying their good-byes to Katy, Jenny thumbed through the book's pages.

I ended the group session as I always do. I asked members to suggest topics for the next day's session. Then I asked group members to give a compliment. Specifically, each member is to look another group member in the eye, use the member's name, and say something nice. For most members, this is their favorite part of the group. When it was Jenny's turn, she struggled and said, "I don't know any one that well." The group silently waited. Finally, Jenny complimented Bill on his drawing.

I purposefully format my groups to encourage sharing within a comfortable setting. Many patients resist attending group on the first day of hospitalization, but they are present the second. Structuring the group in a predictable manner and providing a format that en-courages nonthreatening self-disclosure with opportunities for social skill enhancement help patients gain new confidence and skills. These include being able to introduce themselves and initiate conversations with others, noticing things about others that they can favorably comment on, and learning how to socially engage in general conversation.

The topics suggested by Jenny's group that day included (a) family problems, (b) cliques at school, (c) too much pressure, and (d) mood swings. While counseling Jenny in

the group experience, it became evident she was worried about the future. She was not happy with the vocational program she had chosen and expressed little interest in finishing it. She also voiced little interest in choosing a different program and reportedly did not feel ready to transition from high school. Over time within the group experience, Jenny gained insight about the connection between her mood swings and her relationship stressors.

While Jenny was superficially pleasant, she did not make friends easily. Jenny was generally irritable with other females. This was especially true when other females did not agree with Jenny. On two or more occasions, Jenny was able to coax several male group members to report Jenny's concerns that she was not being treated fairly. However, Jenny always refused to directly address any of these concerns with me.

During my group observations of Jenny, I found that she continually believed others were responsible for her feelings. For example, she often reported that others "made" her mad or "caused" her to become upset. Concomitantly, if you "caused" her to become angry, she believed it demonstrated that you "hated" her. Thus, linking her mistaken beliefs, persons who "hated" Jenny acted in ways that "caused" her to become angry and suicidal.

Over time, as our therapeutic relationship strengthened and Jenny began to trust me, I slowly and gently confronted her faulty thinking. This was done by asking questions and making statements like "So how exactly did his words 'make' you 'throw yourself down the stair case'? I guess I didn't know words could physically 'throw someone' like that. Any chance you could show me how to verbally use words to move these chairs across the room after group because it would be a lot easier than having to physically lift them?" Little by little, Jenny gained the insight that others' words couldn't control or harm her.

As she gained such insights and increased her coping behavior repertoire, Jenny's mood began to stabilize. She was less irritable, and she said she felt better. She slept regularly. She was able to express herself more clearly and had moderate success in modifying her expectation of others.

Jenny denied intent to hurt herself. She agreed to avoid all contact with her previous boyfriend, and she was able to better interact with her parents without feeling that they were "making" her mad.

Jenny also developed a return-to-school plan with the hospital educator and modified her school schedule with a more workable graduation date. She agreed to outpatient treatment and the continuation of her new medications. Concomitantly, she agreed to continue in an outpatient teen group and in family counseling. Her church youth minister, parents, school counselor, and teachers agreed to be actively involved in Jenny's safety plan.

Jenny's parents had several family therapy sessions and received information on how to respond to Jenny as well as resources to help Jenny and their family within the community. Jenny's parents also agreed to safety-proof their home. They removed all firearms from their home and limited Jenny's access to unsecured knives, razors, and medications. They voiced their intent to monitor and supervise Jenny. They were committed to keeping their daughter alive. At last, Jenny was discharged to her parents.

CONCLUSION

At the time of discharge, the crisis had passed. Jenny's brief 14-day hospital stay had provided an opportunity for her to stabilize in a safe environment. She gained important insight and learned ways to practice mood moderation, appropriate self-expression, and relaxation. The hospitalization also provided an important time to determine which

medications would be helpful to Jenny and to get her therapeutic dosage to an effective level prior to discharge.

Yet I am continually frustrated when I see people needlessly suffer. Persons who parasuicide are often very resilient—especially when they have access to necessary medications and experience supports within their immediate milieu. Regretfully, some significant others fail to recognize the suicide signs. Our job must include both helping those who are suicidal and training the public to recognize those who perceive life is not worth continuing.

Case Reflection Questions

Suicide Issue Questions

1. In the case of Jenny, treatment takes place on an inpatient unit. Is this the best place to treat all clients who are suicidal? What are the advantages and disadvantages of treating suicidal clients in inpatient versus outpatient environments? What severity of symptoms warrants an inpatient stay?

2. What do you think is the most effective therapeutic approach for working with a suicidal client? An interpersonal group-therapy modality was used on the treatment unit described in the case. Do you think that group therapy was an effective approach for this client? Would individual therapy or some other approach have been superior?

Skill Builder Questions

1. How might you feel if you were counseling this suicidal client? What is your personal emotional reaction to this client's suicidal behavior?

2. What would you have done in order to ensure this suicidal client's safety? Utilizing the FED, described in Chapter 3, which indicates *frequency* of suicidal thoughts, *extent* of suicide plans, and *duration* of suicidal thoughts and impulses, indicate your assessment of this client's degree of danger to self.

What would you have done to properly assess this client's immediate suicide risk?

3. What important suicide risk factors were present in the case? What unique individual factors or characteristics of this client would be important to your suicide risk assessment? As you read this case, which adapted SAD PERSONS risk factors (sex, age, depression, previous attempt, ethanol abuse, rational thinking loss, social supports lacking, organized suicide plan, no spouse, and sickness) did you find most relevant to this case?

4. What would be your therapeutic approach to treating this suicidal client? What two pieces of information described within this case would be most helpful for your own work in intervening with potentially suicidal clients and their loved ones?

5. How would your approach be the same as or different from that of the clinician in the case? What interventions described in the case did you think were most helpful to the client?

6. How will you care for yourself when working with clients who are suicidal?

7. What strategies will you use to make sure you are competent and prepared to work with high-risk clients?

Marybeth McDonald, MA, is a Licensed Independent Social Worker practicing within a psychiatric unit for children and adolescents in Columbus, Ohio.

Mandy

An Adolescent Female with Recurrent Ideation

Scott W. Peters
Elias Zambrano

EDITORS' COMMENTS

- One of the strengths of this case is that it highlights the importance of collaboration between school and mental health counselors.
- The case also demonstrates multidisciplinary and necessary suicide triage approaches when clients present as suicidal.

INTRODUCTION

Mental health and school counselors that work with children are confronted with a myriad of client concerns. These concerns range from relatively benign issues, such as adjustment disorders and academic concerns, to more serious issues, such as major depression and suicidal ideation. The latter type of life-threatening concerns can be highly distressing for entry-level counselors. This often is due to the extreme impulsivity of these children and their frequent miscalculation related to suicide's danger.

BACKGROUND/REFERRAL

I am a mental health counselor specializing in children at a nonprofit agency in a large southwestern city. The majority of our agency's families are impacted by domestic violence. However, some of our families' parents initiate counseling for their children due to nonviolent concerns. Most of these families have experienced past family violence but have since been separated from their perpetrators. One such family was Ms. Sanchez and her children.

Ms. Sanchez initiated individual counseling for her children because they were having "trouble" adjusting to their reunification with her. Child Protective Services (CPS) had removed mother's four children from her custody following substance abuse, unsafe living conditions,

and failure to protect allegations. Mother and children were reunited after a six-month separation. During the court-mandated separation, mother participated in parenting, domestic violence, and substance abuse classes. Concomitantly, she successfully passed all random drug screens and located an apartment acceptable to CPS. The result was the return of her children.

When originally removed from mother's custody, her four children were sent to separate foster homes; at that time, the children ranged in age from 7 to 15 years. Now, three months after being returned to mother, they were understandably having reunification difficulties. According to the children, each foster home was big and had an abundance of toys and games. The children had personal bedrooms. Upon returning to mother's care, the children lived in a markedly smaller apartment. Food was limited. The children shared toys and slept in the same beds with their siblings. Additionally, mother worked as a home health nurse. Her position required travel, which often brought her home late. When she was home, the children competed for mother's attention. Most important, the children believed their mother's substance abuse, domestic violence exposure, and ultimate divorce from their father caused the CPS-mandated removal. Thus, their perceived resentment was reality based.

ASSESSMENT

I began my assessment by jointly interviewing the children and mother. This allowed me the opportunity to observe the family interactions and provided important background information. Tim was 15, Mandy 13, Chelsea 10, and Daphne 7. At the onset of the interview, I discussed confidentiality and its limits. I then met with each child individually. After three individual sessions, it was evident that Tim, Chelsea, and Daphne were adjusting well to the family reunification. However, Mandy continued to struggle. We spent two sessions allowing Mandy to process her feelings, challenge statements made by others, and find strategies to address her anger. Moreover, I was able to get Mandy into the local Big Sisters program. The intent of the referral was to help Mandy find another female to act as a role model.

TREATMENT

During the initial family session, mother reported that Mandy's birth and developmental history were unremarkable. Mandy had asthma but infrequently needed her inhaler. Mother had divorced her husband when Mandy was seven. Mandy had been a secondary victim, meaning that while she had never been directly abused, Mandy had witnessed father punching, kicking, and choking mother. Mandy's father was alcohol dependent and had a checkered work history. Additionally, father had failed to pay child support. In fact, the Sanchez children could not remember the last time they had seen or heard from father. Mother admitted that she had become crack cocaine dependent two years earlier and had been terminated from multiple employment sites prior to the removal of her children and active recovery. Furthermore, a live-in boyfriend had struck Daphne. While the boyfriend purported that the behavior was an accident, CPS used this as the impetus to have the children removed from mother. Finally, Mandy had not been seen by a mental health professional before seeing me.

Armed with a very good history, I felt well prepared for my individual sessions with Mandy. In the first session, we played cards and darts and did non-counseling-like things. These non-counseling-like things engendered rapport and trust. While playing games, I asked

questions and gathered information without being too intrusive or threatening. Mandy first presented as pleasant, affable, and cooperative. She was an A student who generally interacted well with her peers. Mandy also was very helpful at home. Often she would assume the mother role: making meals, washing clothes, and getting younger siblings ready for school. In subsequent sessions, it became clear that several things were troubling Mandy.

First, Mandy reported being teased at school. The teasing revolved around Mandy's wearing dated clothes. Mandy was also teased by peers for "getting handouts" in the Federal free lunch program at her middle school. Furthermore, she felt "fat" and would often make self-abusing statements about herself and her body image.

Mandy also articulated a profound fear of darkness and reported she would often lay awake at night for hours, fearing falling asleep and being vulnerable to attack. This left her exhausted by the following school day. She related that father's abuse of mother would occur at night and that mother would send the children to their rooms in an effort to protect them. Unfortunately, as is typical with most of the children that I have counseled, she knew when physical abuse occurred regardless of her location in the house. Even with Mandy's physically abusive father removed from her home, Mandy's fears and apprehension would come flooding back at bedtime.

There had also been incidents the previous year when an uncle and cousin inappropriately "touched" Mandy. Although CPS, law enforcement, and the local children's advocacy center investigated the incident, no resolution was made, and Mandy was left with the perception that she was not believed. However, Mandy's final statement was most disturbing. She stated that she felt she would not live very long.

Prioritizing and Intervening

My foremost concern was Mandy's reported fatalistic attitude toward living. No matter if you are an intern, a new counselor, or a seasoned counselor, it can be unsettling when a client such as Mandy reports a desire to die and presents several treatment concerns. Hospital emergency rooms utilize a *triage* method to decide who receives services first. This method is based on the seriousness of each patient's complaints. When a client presents with multiple concerns, I use a similar triage method to sort out the most pressing concerns first.

For Mandy, it was apparent that her thoughts and feelings about dying should be addressed first. Specifically, I queried Mandy's mother about Mandy's desire to die. Her mother was unaware of her daughter's statements but seemed unconcerned. At this point, I felt a suicide assessment was critically important. Specifically, I utilized Juhnke's (1996) Adapted SAD PERSONS Scale (A–SPS). This scale was created for suicidal children and adolescents and provides counselors a risk score with general clinical intervention guidelines. The scale is comprised of 10 suicide risk factors: sex; age; depression; previous attempt; ethanol/drug use; rational thinking loss; social supports lacking; organized plan; negligent parenting, significant family stressors, or suicidal modeling of parents or siblings; and school problems. Once scored, this scale graphically illustrates a child's or adolescent's risk level. The A–SPS scale for Mandy demonstrated she was at mild to moderate risk. However, during the remainder of the session, I began to understand just how serious her situation was.

Mandy enjoyed playing darts, so as we began the game, I asked when she had initially begun considering "shortening her life." According to Mandy, these thoughts began when she heard "a meteor smash into us." As I probed further, Mandy began to cry. Then she stated,

"I just want to kill myself." When queried about her suicide plan, Mandy reported, "I would stab myself in the chest." Given Mandy's agitation level and mother's noted lack of concern, I asked Mandy's permission to bring mother into the room. Once permission was granted, I asked Mandy to express her suicidal feelings to her mother. Again, Mandy began to cry and stated her she wanted to die. Mandy's statements in conjunction with her emotionally charged behaviors made it clear to mother that Mandy was a significant danger to herself. I expressed my concerns regarding Mandy's safety and reported Mandy's need for a more restrictive care level to ensure Mandy's safety. It was decided that Mandy would be admitted to a local behavioral health facility for children and adolescents. The basis for this admission included Mandy's present suicidal ideation and specific suicide plan.

Mandy spent five days in the behavioral health unit but continued to articulate her suicidal ideation and plan. She was then transferred to the local state hospital and stayed there for two weeks. Mandy was diagnosed with Major Depressive Disorder and placed on a low dose of Prozac. Additionally, she was prescribed Trazedone at bedtime to address her sleeping difficulties.

Mandy and I began counseling upon her hospital discharge and continued counseling together for several months. On three separate postdischarge occasions, Mandy presented with suicidal ideation and plans that necessitated my readmitting her to the hospital. I found myself becoming frustrated with her repeated suicidal ideation. Specifically, I believed her recurrent suicidal ideation and hospital readmission increased the likelihood of her hospitalization at a state-operated facility that specialized in chronically and severely mentally disordered children and adolescents. Additionally, I was concerned that her younger sisters might begin to imitate Mandy's statements. Furthermore, Mandy's mother was struggling. The demands of being a single mother, working full-time, and maintaining her sobriety were already overwhelming challenges. The additional financial and emotional strain resulting from Mandy's suicidal ideation and readmissions was negatively impacting this already fragile family. Thus, I needed to come up with a plan to address Mandy's continued suicidal ideation.

Counselors confronted with clients such as Mandy can experience feelings of fear, frustration, anxiety, and helplessness. I hypothesized that her recurrent statements were an effort to gain attention. From a behavioral perspective, her behaviors were doing just that. At home, her role was that of surrogate mother. When her mother was home, Mandy was often the last to get any "me and mom time," as she called it. At school, Mandy was a very good student. Therefore, she received very little teacher attention. Additionally, it was often very hard for Mandy to end our session. Lastly, while she would refer to suicide, her affect was strikingly incongruent. Thus, I decided that her school counselor might provide just the solution to tackle this problem. I obtained the necessary consent from her mother to speak with Mandy's school counselor.

When I called Mandy's school counselor, Mr. Zambrano, I learned Mandy's situation was not uncommon. Mr. Zambrano was very appreciative of my call and quite informative. Specifically, he indicated that more effective treatment occurred when school counselors and mental health counselors worked together with suicidal students. Mr. Zambrano reported that when students have previously had positive experiences with mental health counselors, they often understand the potential benefits that can result from the counseling relationship. He also believed that responsiveness to suicidal students' issues is more easily facilitated when these students have a previous successful counseling history with a mental health professional. He further noted that parents often are more understanding and accepting of their children's need for professional support when their children have had positive experiences with mental health counselors.

Because Mandy had such a positive treatment history, her mother trusted the therapy, and an immediate referral to her school counselor occurred. Mr. Zambrano quickly built on the positive mental health history that Mandy and I had established. Thus, Mr. Zambrano and Mandy began to build similar levels of confidence, trust, and respect.

Addressing the Needs of Suicidal Students in the School

Professional school counselors plan and use many strategies to respond to students' immediate concerns (American School Counselor Association [ASCA], 2005). Whether a student self-refers or, as in Mandy's case, is referred via another source, school counselors select from a broad continuum of counseling strategies. This continuum can include consultation, "individual and group counseling, crisis management and suicide prevention" (ASCA, 2005, p. 42). In Mandy's case, we conjointly identified and intentionally selected several strategies that would address her immediate needs as well as securing other indirect services that would build a support web.

Mr. Zambrano often utilized multiple opportunities to develop positive, supportive, and caring relationships with his students. The school where he worked had a comprehensive guidance program. Therefore, students became familiar with their school counselors via classroom guidance presentations and individual student planning sessions. These sessions were designed to address students' personal, academic, and career goals. Through such student-centered activities, Mr. Zambrano and his staff had established relationships with many students. However, because Mandy was new to the school, she did not yet have such a strong personal relationship with Mr. Zambrano.

Interestingly, Mandy knew her counselor from classroom and other guidance activities, and she did not indicate surprise or alarm when Mr. Zambrano and I met with her to discuss how we planned to jointly address her counseling needs. As Mr. Zambrano invited Mandy to share her concerns, she quickly disclosed past suicidal thoughts and feelings. Mr. Zambrano gently asked questions but did not force Mandy to talk. By allowing Mandy the time to share her thoughts and feelings and the ability to control the session's purpose and cadence, Mr. Zambrano created a helpful and safe counseling environment.

Specifically, Mandy reported the session as helpful and desired to schedule another session with Mr. Zambrano. Hence, Mr. Zambrano, Mandy, and I agreed that Mr. Zambrano would work with Mandy to help her address her needs within the academic milieu. My charge would be more specific to Mandy's recurrent and chronic suicidal ideation. However, Mr. Zambrano and I discussed how issues at school could impact issues related to Mandy's home life and suicide. Conversely, we discussed how issues related to suicide and home life could impact school. Therefore, we described how we both would be working together to ensure Mandy's concerns were best addressed (ACA, 2005). Mandy was also informed that this school-based service was not intended to replace her sessions with me (ASCA, 2004). The limits of confidentiality and other professional issues were described. Mandy then expressed approval of this arrangement and was assured that she would be at the epicenter of these discussions.

Consultation with Mandy's Teachers

Like other students in the school, Mandy's experiences with teachers could greatly impact her day. Thus, Mr. Zambrano knew it was important to include Mandy's teachers in building

a web of support (ASCA, 2005). Mandy's school utilized a teaming approach in scheduling students, so Mr. Zambrano was able to quickly call a meeting with Mandy's team of teachers. With regard for student and family confidentiality at the center of the discussion, he provided teachers with relevant information about Mandy's presenting concerns. Mr. Zambrano and the teachers also discussed Mandy's need to be a child and not a surrogate parent, her need for peer acceptance, and the family's many stressors.

Mr. Zambrano used the strength of the multidisciplinary team (McGowan, 2006) to brainstorm strategies to assist Mandy. Her teachers agreed that Mandy should have access to Mr. Zambrano when needed. Additionally, they decided to provide tutorial sessions to assist her with remediation of academic skills missed while she was hospitalized. At the same time, this would allow the teachers opportunities to give her individualized attention. They also assigned her a classmate who was friendly, accepting, and acknowledged as a class leader to be her "buddy" and to influence acceptance among her peers. Finally, the group agreed that a conference involving the teachers, Ms. Sanchez, and Mr. Zambrano would facilitate a coordinated plan of action to better assist Mandy.

Consultation with Ms. Sanchez

When Mr. Zambrano and I met with Ms. Sanchez, we outlined the roles that we were assuming and asked for input. Ms. Sanchez was enthusiastic and welcomed the incorporation of both school-related and mental health–related services. Given mother's existing stressful life, Mr. Zambrano offered flexible meeting times for both mother and Mandy (Lee, 2001). Thus, at mother's request, meetings were scheduled for early morning before she went to work and late afternoon at the conclusion of her workday.

Daily communications between mother and school were also critical. Mr. Zambrano provided mother daily opportunities to communicate with teachers regarding Mandy's academic, emotional, and social progress. Additionally, Mr. Zambrano wanted to facilitate biweekly face-to-face meetings between mother and Mandy's teachers. In preparation for the first meeting, Mr. Zambrano provided Mandy's teachers sufficient information to create an understanding of Mandy's presenting issues. Mother met before school with Mandy's teachers.

Mr. Zambrano began the meeting by informing mother and staff that the purpose of their time together was to communicate openly and in a caring manner regarding Mandy's school-related behavior and peer interactions. Teachers described Mandy as a responsible student who worked hard, made good grades, and interacted well with classmates. Mother described Mandy as someone who loved school, yet had been teased about her dated clothing and her family's low income. Mother tearfully indicated that such teasing and other family stressors had proven too much for Mandy, resulting in Mandy's suicidal thoughts. In response to Ms. Sanchez's words, the teachers offered expressions of understanding, support, and concern.

Discussion then turned to strategies the teachers would use to capitalize on classroom opportunities to praise Mandy as a person of worth in addition to praising her for her efforts as a student. The teachers also committed to more closely monitor and intervene if they observed peer teasing. Mother indicated a strong desire for Mandy to attend school and participate in extracurricular activities. The team of teachers and Mr. Zambrano were heartened to learn of mother's desire and agreed to have a follow-up meeting to assess progress.

A support web had been established for Mandy via work with her teachers and Mrs. Sanchez. The groundwork for a counseling relationship had also been laid with Mandy, Mr. Zambrano, and me. With clarity and distinction between my role and that of her school counselor established, Mandy and Mr. Zambrano began using the first few scheduled sessions to explore Mandy's needs. Mandy expressed the need for a quiet and private place she could go when she felt low, sad, and alone. She also expressed the need to know how to respond to teasing that she experienced from peer group members, which contributed to her feelings of sadness and aloneness. Mandy also expressed a need to discuss stressors from her home environment.

During each session, Mandy expressed her thoughts and emotions. Using a behavioral-cognitive theoretical framework, Mr. Zambrano guided her exploration of thoughts and emotions associated with these areas of need. One such discussion led to the brai storming, selection, and practice of strategies for responding to teasing. With Mr. Zambrano's assistance, Mandy practiced deflecting words and attitudes, building stronger connections with identified real or potential friends, and increasing and practicing positive self-talk. As a result of these sessions, Mr. Zambrano suggested to Mandy that it might be helpful if he and I communicated with some frequency. In this way, Mandy and I could further explore identified experiences and emotions during our counseling sessions. Mandy agreed.

Mandy and Mr. Zambrano also agreed to meet daily for a brief check-in, at least initially. They used this brief time to assess and monitor the state of her feelings and thoughts and to identify strategies for building emotional resilience during the school day. Mr. Zambrano maintained a log of the words Mandy used during this time and later reported the themes he identified to me. This daily ritual also provided Mandy with special time for daily recognition, a need I had earlier identified and communicated. With time, Mandy expressed the desire to reduce daily visits to every other day and then to once a week, a positive sign of movement toward improving emotional health.

CONCLUSION

Mandy continued counseling with Mr. Zambrano and me for several more sessions. Some sessions involved Mandy's mother and revolved around topics such as self-esteem, coping strategies, and boundary setting. The combination of our sessions eliminated her recurrent suicidal ideations. I was able to assist Mandy in more directly expressing her needs to her mother. I worked with Mandy and her mother to "de-parentify" Mandy. In addition, Mr. Zambrano provided Mandy with the support, encouragement, and skills she needed to succeed in school. Eventually, Mandy's depression lifted, and the Prozac and Trazedone were discontinued. Currently, Mandy is doing quite well and reports increased life satisfaction with no suicidal ideation.

Mandy's case illustrates how complicated and potentially life-threatening situations can confront counselors, both novice and seasoned. Clients who present with recurrent suicidal ideation can provoke anxiety and frustration in nonprofessionals as well as professionals. I was very troubled and had many sleepless nights thinking about Mandy's safety. Fortunately, I was able to consult with her school counselor, who provided just the answer: a bridge between our sessions that allowed her to remain out of the hospital, to be monitored by other professionals, and to help her develop the skills necessary to abate her suicidal ideations.

Case Reflection Questions

Suicide Issue Questions

1. This case raises the issue of clients who present with suicidal ideation. What factors concerning the type or severity of the client's ideation have to be considered when selecting potential treatment approaches? Are all clients with suicidal ideation representing "imminent danger" to themselves?

2. A school counselor and a mental health counselor collaborated to help Mandy. What are the advantages of taking a collaborative approach to working with a suicidal client? Are there any potential disadvantages?

Skill Builder Questions

1. How might you feel if you were counseling this suicidal client? What is your personal emotional reaction to this client's suicidal behavior?

2. What would you have done in order to ensure this suicidal client's safety? Utilizing the FED, described in Chapter 3, which indicates *frequency* of suicidal thoughts, *extent* of suicide plans, and *duration* of suicidal thoughts and impulses, indicate your assessment of this client's degree of danger to self.

What would you have done to properly assess this client's immediate suicide risk?

3. What important suicide risk factors were present in the case? What unique individual factors or characteristics of this client would be important to your suicide risk assessment? As you read this case, which SAD PERSONS risk factors (sex, age, depression, previous attempt, ethanol abuse, rational thinking loss, social supports lacking, organized suicide plan, no spouse, and sickness) did you find most relevant to this case?

4. What would be your therapeutic approach to treating this suicidal client? What two pieces of information described within this case would be most helpful for your own work in intervening with potentially suicidal clients and their loved ones?

5. How would your approach be the same as or different from that of the clinician in the case? What interventions described in the case did you think were most helpful to the client?

6. How will you care for yourself when working with clients who are suicidal?

7. What strategies will you use to make sure you are competent and prepared to work with high-risk clients?

Scott W. Peters, MA, LPC–S, is the children's counselor at Family Violence Prevention Services in San Antonio, Texas. He is currently a doctoral student in Counselor Education and Supervision at the University of Texas at San Antonio. He is also a member of the Psychiatric Assessment Team for the Methodist Healthcare System in San Antonio, Texas. You can reach Scott at scott.peters@utsa.edu

Elias Zambrano, MA, is a retired certified school counselor. He worked as a professional school counselor for 23 years. Additionally, he served as the Safe and Drug Free Schools and Communities Program Coordinator and then Director of Guidance Services for Northside Independent School District in San Antonio, Texas. He is currently a doctoral student in Counselor Education and Supervision at the University of Texas at San Antonio. You can reach Elias at Elias.zambrano@utsa.edu

References

American Counseling Association. (2005). *ACA code of ethics 2005*. Retrieved March 6, 2006, from http://www.counseling.org/Resources/CodeOfEthics/TP/Home/CT2. aspx

American School Counselor Association. (2004). *Ethical standards for school counselors*. Retrieved July 7, 2005, from http://www.schoolcounselor.org

American School Counselor Association. (2005). *The ASCA national model: A framework for school counseling programs* (2nd ed.). Alexandria, VA: Author.

Juhnke, G. A. (1996). The Adapted SAD PERSONS: A suicide assessment scale designed for use with children. *Elementary School Guidance & Counseling, 30*(4), 252–258.

Lee, C. L. (2001). Culturally responsive school counselors and programs: Addressing the needs of all students. *Professional School Counseling, 4*(4), 257–261.

McGowan, M. (2006). Assessing "risk" vs. promoting resilience. *Therapy Today, 17*(1), 27–28.

Popenhagen, M. P., & Qualley, R. M. (1998). Adolescent suicide: Detection, intervention, and prevention. *Professional School Counseling, 1*(4), 30–35.

Stephanie

A Lonely and Hopeless High School Student

Jeremy R. Sullivan

EDITORS' COMMENTS

- This case points out the importance of not minimizing suicidal thoughts or feelings.
- Teaching coping skills is also highlighted in this case as a method of working with suicidal clients.

INTRODUCTION

I have chosen to talk about a case encountered during my internship at the end of my doctoral training. As a doctoral candidate in School Psychology, I was required to complete a one-year predoctoral internship in professional psychology. I attended a well-established internship program at an urban/suburban school district with over 75,000 students, located in a large southwestern U.S. metropolitan area. I chose this specific site anticipating that such a large student population would expose me to students presenting with many different types of problems and backgrounds. I was right.

I worked in the school district's Department of Psychological Services, which was separate from other district departments, such as Special Education and Student Support Services. Thus, the interns and district psychologists functioned somewhat differently from what is typical for school psychologists. Our role included conducting psychological and behavioral evaluations, providing consultation to parents and teachers, providing individual and group counseling services to students, and responding to crises within the schools. As an intern, I worked at two elementary schools, one middle school, one high school, and the district's alternative school. Needless to say, my intern colleagues and I were spread pretty thin and usually went to multiple campuses each day.

BACKGROUND/REFERRAL

One February day, toward the end of the fourth six-week period, I was counseling one of my assigned middle school students. I received a page from one of our department secretaries, who informed me that a counselor at my high school campus needed to talk to me about a potentially suicidal student who had come to her office. I called the counselor, and

she described a 14-year-old, female, ninth-grade student named Stephanie. This was not one of the students with whom I met on a regular basis. In fact, I had never known or heard about Stephanie. The high school counselor also did not know Stephanie, so this student was unfamiliar to both of us. It is important to note that in the state where I completed my internship, mental health service providers such as school counselors and psychologists are legally permitted to talk to minor students without their parents' permission when circumstances suggest these students are suicidal.

Over the phone, the counselor indicated that Stephanie was sent to her office by a teacher because Stephanie was crying in class and passively refused to complete her work. Once at the counselor's office, Stephanie made several indirect statements suggestive of suicidal ideation. These statements included "I wish all of this would just end" and "Everyone would be better off if I was gone." However, Stephanie resisted the counselor's attempts to explore the reasons for these feelings. Because this student was unfamiliar to both of us, we were unaware of any relevant student background information or the specific context within which to interpret her statements.

It happens that this was a new counselor in her first year at the high school. She was skilled enough to recognize that these indirect statements should be taken seriously. However, she wasn't sure how to handle the situation in terms of assessing the student's level of risk and determining whether some immediate intervention would be necessary in order to protect the student. Thus, the counselor wanted me to come to the school and meet with Stephanie so we could then decide what to do next. Given the circumstances, including the potential seriousness of Stephanie's statements, the lack of previous contact with this student, and the counselor's limited experience with suicidal students, I decided that it would be a good idea for me to meet with Stephanie in order to gather more information about her feelings. The counselor agreed to keep Stephanie in her office until I got to the school.

ASSESSMENT

When I arrived at the high school, approximately two hours were left in the school day. I went to the counselor's office to meet Stephanie and take her to my office. The counselor introduced me as someone who worked at the school who talked to students about different types of problems. I immediately noticed that Stephanie appeared sad and listless. She did not seem very excited about accompanying me to my office. Still, she came willingly.

Consistent with Poland's model of suicide intervention in the schools (Poland, 2004; Poland & Lieberman, 2002), I saw my immediate duty to determine the level of actual risk posed by the student. That level of immediate risk or danger would then drive my decision regarding what to do next. In conducting the risk assessment, I did not use any norm-referenced or formal assessment instruments. Rather, my risk assessment process involved a series of interview questions addressing factors such as the frequency of Stephanie's suicidal thoughts, whether she had made previous suicide attempts, whether she had developed a specific plan for committing suicide (e.g., method, time, place), whether she had the actual means of following through with her plan, her awareness of more positive alternatives to suicide, and her available support system. These questions were generated by combining questions, risk factors, and models of intervention discussed in a variety of resources (e.g., Juhnke, 1996; Poland & Lieberman, 2002; Sattler, 1998).

I began the interview session by asking Stephanie about the statements she made to the counselor. She responded by revealing that she wanted to hurt herself. I asked whether she

had thought *how* she might hurt herself. Stephanie then described a plan to take some of her mother's pills when she got home from school that day. Stephanie took the bus to and from school, and she explained that she would be alone when she got home, since her parents wouldn't be home from work yet. As Stephanie described her plan to take her mother's pills, she maintained her depressed affect and matter-of-fact delivery; she did not appear to be describing her plan in an attempt to "get a rise" out of me. Many of us have worked with adolescents who say things for shock value or for the purpose of getting a reaction from us. Stephanie's plan, and her commitment to complete it, seemed quite genuine.

During the interview, Stephanie indicated that she had thought about hurting herself before but had never actually attempted suicide. I was distressed to hear that this was not the first time she had considered suicide, but at the same time, I was somewhat encouraged by the fact that she had never attempted (according to her self-report, at least). Out of everything, I was probably *most* alarmed by Stephanie's sense of hopelessness and loneliness. She openly admitted to feeling unhappy and alone most of the time and did not seem to think that her life would get better. Further, she had been thinking of suicide more and more often lately, and this was starting to seem like a good idea and the best solution to her problems.

Next, I asked a series of questions about what was happening in Stephanie's life to make her feel so hopeless and sad. She described her relations with classmates as "nonexistent" and reported that nobody at school liked her or wanted to hang out with her. She also reported that she didn't feel like an important member of her family because she perceived her parents as being overly punitive. When asked what kinds of things she was getting punished for, Stephanie described several acting-out and risk-taking behaviors, such as drinking beer and liquor that she got from her house, sneaking out at night, skipping class, and taking pills that she got at school. Her parents responded to these behaviors by grounding her and restricting her access to TV and other activities. Thus, although her parents' disciplinary methods seemed appropriate to me, Stephanie felt that they were being unreasonable, and this suggested to her that they didn't care about her. To Stephanie, who was probably hypersensitive to rejection as a result of being rejected by peers, the punishments were seen as another indicator that nobody liked her or cared about her. Stephanie was alienated from peers at school, and her acting-out behaviors were resulting in punishment from parents, which made her feel alienated from her family as well. She felt like she didn't really "fit in" anywhere.

Next, I wanted to get an idea of Stephanie's coping and problem-solving skills. I asked how she handled all the different things in her life that were causing her stress. She stated that she used alcohol and pills to feel better and that she cried to herself because she didn't really have anyone to talk to about things that were bothering her. She didn't have any friends, and she didn't want to talk to her parents; she was usually arguing with her parents anyway. Stephanie also reported that lately she had been cutting herself as a way to make herself feel better. While self-mutilation behaviors alone do not necessarily suggest that an adolescent is suicidal, I felt that, in Stephanie's case, these behaviors may have contributed to her risk when combined with other factors.

As noted above, Stephanie reported that she had thought about suicide in the past and that these thoughts were becoming more and more frequent. I asked what had stopped her from actually attempting to hurt herself when she experienced suicidal thoughts. She responded that she didn't want to hurt her parents. But now it almost seemed like one of the reasons she wanted to hurt herself *was* to hurt her parents—to get "payback" for what she perceived as excessive punishment for her behaviors. It seemed as though the factor that

had protected her from hurting herself in the past was no longer protecting her; now she wasn't worried about causing her parents pain.

Typically during the risk assessment interview, the student is asked to sign a "no suicide" contract, in which the student agrees not to harm herself and agrees to tell an adult if she is having suicidal thoughts. In my experience, students usually are willing to sign a "no suicide" contract. Stephanie, however, refused to sign. I interpreted this as a sign that she could not guarantee that she wouldn't hurt herself. In my eyes, this refusal certainly added to Stephanie's level of risk. When I tried to communicate that I, as well as many others, cared about her and about what happens to her, she said, "How can you care about what happens to me? You didn't even know me until like an hour ago."

Given the presence of multiple risk factors, I considered Stephanie to be at a high level of risk. I explained to Stephanie that I needed to call her parents because I was concerned about her safety and because I had an obligation to protect her from harm. While I was somewhat worried about how she would react to this news, she did not argue or offer any resistance. In fact, she sat with me as I talked to her mother over the phone. I wanted to keep her in my sight because I thought that constant supervision was critical, given my assessment that she posed a genuine risk to herself. Had I wanted to make the call in private, I could have asked the counselor or someone else to closely supervise her for a few minutes.

By this time, there was only about an hour left in the school day, so I was hoping that I would be able to reach one of Stephanie's parents quickly. Given my concern about constant supervision, combined with Stephanie's specific plan to take pills once she got off the school bus, I had decided not to let her leave campus when the school day was over. Fortunately, I was able to immediately reach Stephanie's mother at work. I explained the circumstances leading to my involvement with Stephanie and my impressions based on the risk assessment interview.

Unfortunately, parents sometimes discount or minimize the importance of suicide threats (e.g., "He always says that, but he'll never do it"; "She just says that to get our attention"). But Stephanie's mother was very concerned about her daughter and seemed surprised that Stephanie was feeling so sad, hopeless, and alone. I explained that I believed Stephanie's threat was genuine, that she needed immediate intervention, and that I didn't think she should be left alone for any period of time. Stephanie's mother left work and came to the school immediately. She reported that she did, in fact, have some potentially lethal pills in the medicine cabinet at home. I advised her to secure the pills in a safe location, along with any weapons, lethal household products, and anything else that Stephanie could use to hurt herself. We also discussed my impression that Stephanie seemed to be making a cry for help: What she was really saying was "I'm unhappy and I want something to change." We talked about the importance of finding the root of her unhappiness, what she wanted to be *different* in her life.

Stephanie and her mother interacted very little during all of this. I was able to convince Stephanie's mother that the potential for self-harm was great enough to warrant a psychiatric evaluation and that Stephanie was desperately seeking help. Stephanie's mother agreed to take her to an emergency psychiatric hospital at the large medical center downtown; this facility was a frequent referral source for the school district when students were suicidal. Finally, I asked Stephanie's mother to sign a district form to document that she had been notified that her child was suicidal and that she had been provided with information about where she could take her child for psychological/psychiatric consultation within the community. I was relieved that Stephanie's mother seemed appreciative of my involvement and took the suicide threat seriously.

Stephanie returned to school the following week. I talked to Stephanie's mother that week and explained that I wanted to offer school-based counseling services for Stephanie as a way to (a) continue to monitor her emotional functioning and suicide potential and (b) help her to learn more adaptive ways of handling problems and stressors. At the same time, I wanted to facilitate access to assistance beyond what the school was capable of providing, so I recommended family counseling to address Stephanie's behaviors at home and her feelings of unimportance within her family. I provided Stephanie's parents with a list of mental health service providers within the community.

During this conversation, Stephanie's mother reported that Stephanie had spent several days at the psychiatric facility because staff were concerned about her safety if she was allowed to return home right away. While at the facility, Stephanie was diagnosed with a mood disorder and was prescribed Zoloft for depressive symptoms. Stephanie's mother stated that Stephanie's conduct problems, school difficulties, and symptoms of depression were not really apparent until the current school year; she had been relatively happy and a good student until coming to high school. She also explained that she perceived many of Stephanie's current emotional, behavioral, and academic problems as a result of her difficulty with fitting in and making friends with other teenagers at her school. This perception was consistent with my conceptualization of Stephanie's difficulties, based on my interview with Stephanie. I obtained signed consent from Stephanie's mother to allow me to provide continued counseling services at school.

Key Suicide Risk Assessment Factors

The initial interview with Stephanie revealed that she exhibited many of the risk factors for suicide identified in the suicide research literature (e.g., Evans, Hawton, & Rodham, 2004; Miller & McConaughy, 2005), such as depression, a sense of hopelessness, current suicidal ideation and intent, a specific plan (and the means to carry it out), recent school failure, substance use, problems in relationships with peers, and oppositional-defiant behaviors. Stephanie also refused to sign the "no suicide" contract, which elevated her risk for suicide.

In addition to the presence of multiple risk factors, Stephanie did not appear to have many protective factors working in her favor. For example, given her reliance on self-mutilation and substance use to cope with her problems, she did not seem to have very adaptive coping skills. And given her limited relationships with peers and tumultuous relationship with her parents, she was likely to perceive that she had no social support.

Often when we work with suicidal adolescents, we are able to identify a precipitating event that serves as a catalyst for the suicide threat or attempt, such as losing an important relationship, having an intense argument with parents, or getting in serious trouble at school. In Stephanie's case, however, I was unable to identify a *single* precipitating event. Rather, her threat seemed to be a culminating response to a *gradual accumulation* of stressors.

Stephanie had few trusting relationships with adults or peers; she was experiencing neglect from peers and regular arguments with parents. Over time, this lack of positive interactions with others left Stephanie feeling lonely and disconnected at both home and school; in Stephanie's eyes, both of these environments were threatening and unrewarding. As a result of Stephanie's loneliness and emotional isolation, her performance in school deteriorated, and she engaged in acting-out and risk-taking behaviors, as she didn't see the importance of doing well in school or staying out of trouble. These behaviors ultimately resulted in Stephanie being even more isolated from others because she was grounded in her room most of the time. She tried to make herself feel better by cutting herself, drinking, and taking pills,

and she didn't feel like she had anyone to talk to that she could trust. Suicide started to become an attractive solution. This *combination* of factors led me to believe that Stephanie should be considered at high risk for suicide completion.

TREATMENT

I conceptualized Stephanie's suicide threat as a cry for help. I believed her initial threat to be genuine, but I also thought that she truly wanted to be helped and cared for. She felt alone and insignificant, and I saw the primary goal of intervention as helping her to feel important, needed, and part of a group. I also wanted to help Stephanie develop more adaptive coping skills for dealing with the stressors in her life. I tried to use a two-pronged approach in addressing these concerns. The first involved manipulating the school environment to make it more supportive; the second involved providing counseling services to work on coping and problem-solving skills. Both approaches are described below. I would also like to note that while Stephanie's relationship with her parents was certainly a concern, I left the decision to pursue family counseling to her parents after I provided them with referral information.

Counselors and psychologists working in the schools often have opportunities to be creative and design environmental or systemic interventions that complement more-direct counseling interventions. Thus, we had the opportunity to use the school environment to provide Stephanie with more social support. For example, Stephanie's counselor and I set up a system where Stephanie could access me on any day that I was at the campus, and if I wasn't there, she could access the counselor at any time.

As an alternative, we also gave her a pass to a special classroom in the school. This classroom was designed for students who were receiving special education services due to emotional disabilities, but a few students in general education also used the classroom. Stephanie could access this classroom at any time, as long as she presented her pass to her teachers. The classroom was staffed by a certified special education teacher and an aide, both of whom were quite gifted in communicating with adolescents in a caring but noninvasive manner. Students accessed the classroom when they were feeling overwhelmed in their regular classrooms. The teacher helped students process their feelings and create a plan for solving whatever problems they were facing. This was not a place where students could come simply to escape a stressful environment; they were required to formulate a plan and return to their regular classroom environment as soon as possible. The purpose of these interventions was to provide Stephanie access to *immediate* support and assistance when she needed it and to enhance the resources that she could access when feeling stressed out or overwhelmed.

We informed Stephanie's teachers of these interventions so they knew it was alright for her to leave class to talk to me or the counselor or to access the special classroom, as long as she asked appropriately. We also took Stephanie to the special classroom and introduced her to the teacher and aide because we figured she would be more likely to access this resource if the setting and people were familiar to her. We recognized that Stephanie's use of these support systems would need to be monitored in order to ensure that she wasn't taking advantage of or using them as a way to skip class and avoid work. As it turned out, she didn't access any of these resources excessively, though she did access each of us from time to time. Perhaps simply knowing that these support systems were available was enough to help Stephanie feel more nurtured and capable of handling her problems.

In addition to the environmental approach, I used a group counseling approach with Stephanie. Once I had obtained parental consent, I met with Stephanie for a follow-up

session. I saw this session as having three purposes. First, I wanted to maintain my rapport with Stephanie and give her an opportunity to describe her experience after she left school and went to the psychiatric hospital. Stephanie actually thanked me for taking her threat seriously, and she explained that the medication the doctors prescribed was helping her feel better about things. She almost seemed surprised that everyone took her threat seriously and that her mother was so worried that she took her to the hospital. Second, I wanted to gauge Stephanie's current level of suicidal ideation and risk. She reported no current ideation, and since she seemed to be much happier and appeared to be touched by the amount of support she had received, I considered her to be at a low level of risk. Third, I saw this as an ideal time to offer Stephanie the opportunity to participate in a small counseling group with three other ninth-grade girls I had been seeing for individual counseling every two weeks or so. I had not started this group yet, but I thought this would be a good way to address Stephanie's feelings of social alienation, while also providing her with another source of support. She readily agreed to participate in the group.

For the rest of the school year, Stephanie was seen for counseling in this group with the three other girls and was quite comfortable with opening up to the other members. None of the girls knew each other when we started the group, but all of them were surprisingly willing to share their experiences and offer each other different perspectives on their problems. The other members had been experiencing difficulties and significant distress related to depression, self-mutilation, social anxiety, substance use, suicidal ideation, limited coping skills, and family issues (e.g., one girl's mother was incarcerated, another girl's parents had moved back to their home country and left her with an older sister); in all cases, these difficulties were interfering with the students' ability to function academically.

The group was open with regard to themes and topics. It focused on helping members process their feelings regarding a number of issues, such as effective and ineffective coping skills, relationships with parents, the importance of social support, emotional expression, and school stressors. The group met every two weeks for about 45 minutes. Stephanie seemed to develop a close friendship with one of the members, and I often saw them together during the school day.

As a school-based practitioner, I often used a combination of cognitive-behavioral and solution-focused approaches when working with adolescents. I found these approaches to provide a nice fit with the focused and time-limited nature of interventions in school settings. These approaches also were conducive to teaching the problem-solving process, which was one of the skills that I wanted Stephanie to learn as a result of participating in the group. Students who are chronically depressed or hopeless may turn to suicide or other maladaptive coping methods (e.g., substance use) because they are unable to generate alternative solutions to their problems. Part of our group sessions, therefore, involved working together to brainstorm multiple possible solutions to specific problems or issues faced by the students.

Many variations of the problem-solving process have been presented in the literature on adolescent coping and problem-solving skills (e.g., Forman, 1993; LeCroy, 1994); these models often differ somewhat in the details of the problem-solving steps. The approach that I used in our group counseling sessions included five steps that are common across many of the problem-solving models described in the literature.

The first step of our process involved *identifying the problem*. We discussed how problem identification or recognition often results from dissatisfaction with the current state of affairs. We discussed how our dissatisfaction motivated us to find a label for the problem. Once we could name the problem we could then explore it further in our second step. The second

step of our process involved *gathering information about the problem.* When faced with a problem, students were taught to think about what they had learned and experienced in similar situations. Then students were taught to gather additional information by asking others to share their perspectives of the problem based on their own experiences. This is where I thought the group counseling format would be most effective for Stephanie and the other members, as they all were willing and able to share their experiences with similar problems and to discuss what worked and what didn't work for them. In this way, the group counseling format took advantage of the perspectives and experiences of everyone in the group.

During the third step of our process, the group members learned how to *brainstorm a variety of solutions.* After students identified the problem and gathered information about the problem, they listed all the solutions they could think of, without evaluating the merit of those solutions. The students also were instructed that it was appropriate to ask others, such as peers, a parent, or a teacher, for assistance as they brainstormed possible solutions. Stephanie and the other members struggled with this step at first; out of all five steps, this one required the most involvement and instruction by me. I interpreted this difficulty as resulting from a previous overreliance on maladaptive coping methods. That is, the girls had established a pattern of automatically jumping to dangerous solutions such as suicidal ideation, self-mutilation, or substance use when faced with a problem, and they weren't used to generating other potential solutions. This was a new experience for them.

The fourth step in the process involved *choosing a solution and trying it out.* After generating a list of possible solutions, the group members were ready to evaluate the potential effectiveness of each solution at solving the identified problem and then choose one to implement. We discussed the fact that our choice of solutions to implement may be influenced by our past experiences: We are likely to choose a solution that has been helpful or effective in the past, and we are unlikely to choose a solution that has not been helpful in the past. The group members were encouraged to seek the perspectives of others when contemplating the possible positive and negative consequences of different solutions. It was fun to watch the group members hypothesize about possible outcomes of their different solutions and to see them engage in the process of reality testing until they finally decided on one solution to implement.

The fifth and final step in our problem-solving process involved *evaluating the solution.* After the group members chose a solution and tried it out between group sessions (this was their "homework"), they determined whether their chosen solution was effective in solving the identified problem. If they determined that the solution was effective, we discussed what they needed to do in order to make sure the solution continued to be effective. If they determined that the solution was ineffective, we discussed which solution should be tried next; then the group members would try the new solution and evaluate it. This process was repeated until an effective solution was found.

This step-by-step process was used during our group sessions to help members deal with feelings of depression, social anxiety, and suicidal ideation in addition to other issues such as failing grades and conflict with parents and peers. While the group members had relied on maladaptive methods (e.g., substance use, cutting, suicidal ideation) for coping with stressors in the past, the group counseling sessions showed them that a specific problem-solving process could be used to generate more-adaptive solutions to their problems. It was my hope that by teaching the group members how to use the problem-solving steps to solve a specific problem, I would enable them to generalize the process to new problems when they encountered them.

Once the group members were familiar with the steps of the problem-solving process, I often found that I had to say very little during our group discussions. After introducing and practicing the steps, my role shifted to that of a facilitator who kept everyone on track and moved the discussion along. This process gave the students the chance to learn from one another, and I figured they would be more likely to accept a solution devised by a peer than a solution offered by me. Further, as the group members brainstormed solutions to another member's problem, they gained practice in generating alternative solutions to *their own* problems. Another attractive feature of the problem-solving process is that it is fairly generic; the same process can be applied to many different types of problems and stressors. The idea behind using the process with this particular group of students was to introduce a way to think about options other than suicide and similarly maladaptive coping methods. I also felt that the group counseling helped Stephanie and the other members to express feelings of unhappiness *verbally* rather than *behaviorally* (e.g., by acting out or abusing substances).

CONCLUSION

Throughout the remainder of the school year, Stephanie did not make any additional suicide threats. She began making As, Bs, and Cs and demonstrated significant improvement in her behavior. She still had a few discipline referrals at school, but these were primarily related to skipping classes to hang out with friends. Once Stephanie became an important part of a group and realized the vast amount of social support that was available to her, it seemed like her ability to cope with stressors improved. When faced with a problem or stressor, she was able to think through several possible solutions and also sought advice and ideas from others. As noted previously, Stephanie did not visit the school counselor's office or special classroom very often, nor did she come to my office outside of the group meetings, except for a few occasions. When Stephanie had issues that she needed to discuss, she was usually able to wait until our group sessions. This suggested that she especially valued the other group members' interactions and perspectives.

Stephanie's parents continued accessing psychiatric services throughout the school year, and Stephanie maintained her use of Zoloft. At the end of the school year, her parents had chosen not to pursue private counseling or psychological services outside of the school setting. Consistent with my department's policy regarding students in regular education seen by interns, I asked Stephanie (and the other members of our group) whether she would like to participate in counseling the following school year. She replied that she didn't think she would need counseling next year but agreed to meet with next year's intern at the beginning of the school year to determine how she was doing. Stephanie's file was given to the supervising psychologist, to be passed on to the next group of interns.

By no means do I take credit for Stephanie's apparent turnaround. I believe her improved functioning was the result of a group effort to create a more supportive environment at school. Stephanie's relationship with her parents also seemed to become more positive as a function of her improved academic performance and behavior. Since Stephanie began making better grades and significantly reduced her oppositional-defiant behaviors, her parents only rarely found it necessary to punish her. Still, I regret that I was not able to convince them to access family counseling services.

I learned a lot from working with Stephanie and from going through the stressful process of assessing suicide risk, contacting parents, recommending psychiatric intervention, and then

providing school-based counseling services. I have never experienced a referral of a potentially suicidal student that did not cause some amount of anxiety because I always knew that my response to these situations would have important implications for the student. After going through the process several times with several different students, however, I began to feel more comfortable with the process itself, which allowed me to focus more attention and energy on the individual student sitting in front of me. Thus, while intervening with suicidal students never became "easy" for me, it did get easier for me to listen to students and determine their needs without worrying as much about following each step of the risk assessment process or asking the right questions in a cookbook-type fashion. Once the *content* of the process becomes second nature, more attention can be focused on the *student.*

As a final thought, I would like to commend the teacher who sent Stephanie to the counselor's office rather than to the assistant principal's office with a discipline referral. Remember, Stephanie was initially referred because she was sitting in class crying and passively refusing to work. The distinction between true emotional pain and defiant, manipulative behavior is not always an easy one to make, and this teacher made the right call. Clearly, Stephanie was making a cry for help. Had she never reached the counselor's office, where the intervention process began, her cry may have gone unanswered.

Case Reflection Questions

Suicide Issue Questions

1. The importance of listening to and not dismissing clients' "cries" for help is highlighted in this case. What type of training should counselors and other "gatekeepers" who work with at-risk populations receive so that they can better identify potentially suicidal clients?

2. A major focus of the treatment provided was teaching Stephanie a problem-solving approach in a peer group setting. Why do you think that such an approach may be particularly helpful to a potentially suicidal client? What other cognitive or behavioral interventions might you consider when working with a client like Stephanie?

Skill Builder Questions

1. How might you feel if you were counseling this suicidal client? What is your personal emotional reaction to this client's suicidal behavior?

2. What would you have done in order to ensure this suicidal client's safety? Utilizing the FED, described in Chapter 3, which indicates *frequency* of suicidal thoughts, "*extent* of suicide plans, and *duration* of suicidal thoughts and impulses, indicate your assessment of this client's degree of danger to self.

What would you have done to properly assess this client's immediate suicide risk?

3. What important suicide risk factors were present in the case? What unique individual factors or characteristics of this client would be important to your suicide risk assessment? As you read this case, which Adapted SAD PERSONS risk factors (sex, age, depression, previous attempt, ethanol abuse, rational thinking loss, social supports lacking, organized suicide plan, no spouse, and sickness) did you find most relevant to this case?

4. What would be your therapeutic approach to treating this suicidal client? What two pieces of information described within this case would be most helpful for your own work in intervening with potentially suicidal clients and their loved ones?

5. How would your approach be the same as or different from that of the clinician in the case? What interventions described in the case did you think were most helpful to the client?

6. How will you care for yourself when working with clients who are suicidal?

7. What strategies will you use to make sure you are competent and prepared to work with high-risk clients?

Jeremy R. Sullivan, Ph.D., is an assistant professor in the Department of Counseling, Educational Psychology, and Adult and Higher Education at the University of Texas at San Antonio (UTSA). He received his doctoral degree in School Psychology from Texas A&M University in 2003, and he is a Licensed Psychologist, Licensed Specialist in School Psychology, and Nationally Certified School Psychologist. Prior to joining the faculty at UTSA, Jeremy worked as a school psychologist in Houston. You can reach Jeremy at jeremy.sullivan@utsa.edu

References

Evans, E., Hawton, K., & Rodham, K. (2004). Factors associated with suicidal phenomena in adolescents: A systematic review of population-based studies. *Clinical Psychology Review, 24,* 957–979.

Forman, S. G. (1993). *Coping skills interventions for children and adolescents.* San Francisco: Jossey-Bass.

Juhnke, G. A. (1996). The Adapted SAD PERSONS: A suicide assessment scale designed for use with children. *Elementary School Guidance & Counseling, 30*(4), 252–258.

LeCroy, C. W. (Ed.). (1994). *Handbook of child and adolescent treatment manuals.* New York: Free Press.

Miller, D. N., & McConaughy, S. H. (2005). Assessing risk for suicide. In S. H. McConaughy (Ed.), *Clinical interviews for children and adolescents: Assessment to intervention* (pp. 184–199). New York: Guilford.

Poland, S. (2004). School crisis teams. In J. C. Conoley & A. P. Goldstein (Eds.), *School violence intervention: A practical handbook* (2nd ed., pp. 131–163). New York: Guilford.

Poland, S., & Lieberman, R. (2002). Best practices in suicide intervention. In A. Thomas & J. Grimes (Eds.), *Best practices in school psychology IV* (pp. 1151–1165). Bethesda, MD: National Association of School Psychologists.

Sattler, J. M. (1998). Clinical and forensic interviewing of children and families: Guidelines for the mental health, education, pediatric, and child maltreatment fields. San Diego, CA: Author.

Nancy

A Native American Youth

KENNETH M. COLL
BRENDA J. FREEMAN
PATTI THOBRO

EDITORS' COMMENTS

- This chapter highlights the importance of cultural considerations when working with suicidal clients.
- Internalized anger at oppression can play a part in depression and suicide ideation and attempts.

INTRODUCTION

I have provided consultation, clinical supervision, and outcome evaluation for a number of years at a 50-bed, Joint Commission for the Accreditation of Health Care Organizations (JCAHO)–accredited therapeutic community with a fully accredited middle and high school in a Rocky Mountain state. A treatment issue that has arisen over the last few years relates to effective approaches with American Indian (AI) youth. Recently, the agency has received an increasing number of referrals of AI youth who present with depression and active suicidal ideation. Most of these AI youth are referred from reservations in the region. The professional staff (counselors, teachers, nurses, and administrators) have been puzzled about how to best serve these youth, and especially how to include cultural identity development as part of therapeutic care. In response to this identified challenge, the community's leadership team—consisting of six counselors, six administrators, and myself—agreed that I should search existing literature and draw on my clinical experiences with this specific population to identify and develop a thorough treatment guide. This treatment guide would then be disseminated to the community's professional staff and discussed during in-services.

Working With AI Youth

Previously, I had worked with Substance Abuse and Mental Health Services Administration (SAMHSA) projects (called Circles of Care) that focused on reforming mental health services for American Indian and Alaska Native (AI/AN) children and families. Drawing on this experience,

I developed the following information and disseminated it to professional staff through in-services and written material.

Adolescents who are most at risk of harm to self and others tend to display high levels of other risk factors, such as chemical abuse/addiction, lack of parent-child closeness, family conflict, beliefs and attitudes favorable to criminality, early childhood aggressiveness, antisocial behavior, and poor peer acceptance (Hawkins et al., 2000). Huizinga, Loeber, Thornberry, and Cothern (2000) note the cooccurrence or overlap of self-harm with drug use and other mental health problems.

The AI/AN populations in particular report a high occurrence of such risk factors (Manson, 2001). Beals (1997) compared the mental health disorders of AI/AN youth with those of nonminority children and found that AI/AN youth were more likely to report significantly higher rates of depression, alcohol and other drug (AOD) abuse, and suicidal acts. Garrett (1999) notes that many of the current problems that the AI/AN populations have with depression and suicidal behaviors can be tied back to historical cultural trauma—most notably, genocide, the land grabs based on the Dawes Act of 1867, the outlawing of Native religions, and the massive federal program designed to relocate reservation Indians to urban areas.

The history and political context surrounding depression and suicidal behaviors among AI and AN, especially adolescent girls, emphasize the need to direct more attention and resources toward the AI community (Hawkins, Cummins, & Marlatt, 2004). Within the general adolescent population, boys usually have higher rates of drug use and suicide completion; however, within the AI population, there does not appear to be a significant difference between boys and girls (Hawkins et al., 2004).

Residential therapeutic community (TC) placements are common for depressed and AOD-abusing adolescents, including AI/AN youth (LeCroy & Ashford, 1992; Libman, Lyons, Kisiel, & Shallcross, 1998; Lyons, Kisiel, Dulcan, Cohen, & Chesler, 1997). Indeed, MacKenzie (1999) found that out-of-home placements for adolescents grew 51% between 1987 and 1996. Bauman, Merta, and Steiner (1999) observed that youth in residential treatment scored significantly higher on baseline depression and substance abuse measures than did students in alternative high schools. Similarly, Manson (2001) found that AI/AN youth in therapeutic communities reported significantly elevated levels of AOD abuse and depression upon admission. However, only a small amount of treatment case data has been found for AI/AN youth exhibiting these problems in these settings. Such case data could prove beneficial in treatment planning and intervention.

Adolescents treated in TC programs are more likely than are those in outpatient programs to have a history of drug abuse and more-severe depression problems, such as one or more suicide attempts (Hanson, 2002). Despite being more difficult to treat, adolescents in TC environments typically exhibit significantly improved outcomes, including reduced drug use and criminal activities and improved school performance and psychological adjustment (Hanson, 2002). One of the emerging "best" practices with AOD-abusing adolescent offenders in therapeutic communities is to establish specific and integrated individualized treatment based on their AOD abuse cooccurring with other risk factors (e.g., depression) (Burdsal, Force, & Klingsporn, 1990; Grimley et al., 2000). Bauman, Merta, and Steiner (1999) assert that the first step in treating adolescent AOD abuse is comprehensive risk assessment.

Professional staff enthusiastically received this information, and it was decided that the next AI youth entering the TC would be asked to be a case study. This approach was deemed valuable to the agency in its effort to determine how to best help AI youth. I was asked to coordinate this case study approach in an attempt to find a clear example that would provide

insight to the agency in treating depressed AI youth. The purpose of using this approach is not to offer generalizable conclusions; it is to provide an accounting of the experience

BACKGROUND/REFERRAL

The next AI youth entering the TC was Nancy, an adolescent mandated through the CHINS (Child in Need of Supervision) provision into our treatment program for a period of no less than 30 days. A clinical treatment team (consisting of the clinical director, myself, the counselor assigned to Nancy for individual and family counseling, and the two counselors to be working with Nancy in group counseling) began gathering information from Nancy. She belonged to a Northern Plains tribe and came from a rural Indian reservation. Her age at admission was 14 years, 6 months. Nancy's grandmother had referred her to the state's Department of Family Services. Her grandmother reported to the treatment team that Nancy would not get out of bed on most days, was irritable, and was drinking alcohol and smoking marijuana on a regular basis.

ASSESSMENT

Nancy was administered cognitive and academic assessments. Her results revealed an above-average IQ; and her academic achievement at a ninth-grade education level. During the first two weeks after Nancy's admission, the treatment team completed the Youth Comprehensive Risk Assessment (YCRA), which assesses multiple risk factors (including risk to self and substance abuse). A brief description of the YCRA follows.

    The YCRA was developed for use in clinical evaluations. It is a structured interview process that allows trained professionals to systematically gather information and make clinical judgments related to six risk areas: (1) risk to self (e.g., risk for suicide, self-harm, risk taking, and victimization), (2) risk to others (e.g., aggression, sexually inappropriate behavior, and destruction of property), (3) social and adaptive functioning (e.g., developmental disorders, disabilities, cognitive disorganization, and social skills), (4) substance abuse/-dependency, (5) family resources, and (6) degree of structure needed (e.g., frequency of out-of-home placements and need for supervision). The YCRA has met or exceeded all of the rigorous quality criteria for inclusion on the JCAHO list of approved performance measurement systems, including those covering sampling, standardization, monitoring, documentation, feedback, education, and accountability (JCAHO, 1998). The YCRA uses a non-equal interval Likert scale of 1 to 4×2 (8), with 1 being slight, 2 being mild, 3 being moderate and 4×2 (8) severe. Lyons et al. (1997) noted that objective assessment process is particularly important because many youth offender measures rely on ratings that are often influenced by subjective and idiosyncratic approaches.

    The YCRA has proven to be valuable for treatment planning in various studies with youth offender populations. For example, one investigation using the YCRA provided evidence that effective identification and treatment of depression and self-harm can reap benefits in reducing other risks, such as substance abuse (Coll, Thobro, & Haas, 2004). Another study indicated that the YCRA was useful in guiding and validating successful addictions treatment with young offenders (Coll, Juhnke, Thobro, & Haas, 2003).

    During the initial risk assessment period, Nancy openly discussed with me and other members of the treatment team the fact that over the last year she had been in a group home for three months and had spent two weeks in a psychiatric hospital related to a suicide

attempt. In accord with past records, Nancy, during a structured series of interviews using the YCRA, reported that she has a long history of depression, beginning at age seven, and has repeatedly and recently threatened to kill herself. She attempted to hang herself during the last six months. Nancy also discussed being been teased and picked on by peers at school—describing comments referring to her as "an Indian from a bad family."

Nancy described her mother (currently serving a long prison sentence) as having a history of severe alcoholism. Nancy had no information about her father other than that he was an American Indian. Nancy revealed that her grandmother has raised her over the last several years in a generally nurturing and supportive environment. Nancy indicated that she gets along well with and is helpful toward her six-year-old sister. Nancy also indicated that her brother died in a car accident last year at the age of 16. During the initial assessment phase, Nancy appeared motivated to dig herself "out of this hole, at least for grandma and little sister's sake," and demonstrated sadness about the losses in her life. She cried when discussing her mother, her brother, and how much her grandmother loves and cares about her.

Key Suicide Risk Assessment Factors

Using the information from Nancy's interview and her YCRA scores, the treatment team developed a treatment plan. The treatment team also requested that I present this information, with Nancy's permission, to professional staff, framing Nancy's issues in a cultural context based on the professional AI literature when possible. The risk assessment was performed during the first month of Nancy's stay

Of the six YCRA scales, there were notable elevations related to the Risk to Self scale. This scale includes categories risk for suicide, self-harm, risk taking, and victimization. It reflects an individual's tendency to put himself or herself in harm's way, by either direct behaviors (e.g., suicide attempts) or indirect behaviors (e.g., AOD abuse).

A moderate risk score on the Risk to Self scale is 9; Nancy's score of 15 was considered very high. As indicated, Nancy entered the TC with an extensive history of depression, including suicide ideation and one significant attempt. She also had significant environmental stressors and serious grief and loss issues (involving her mother and brother). This high Risk to Self score is in keeping with literature regarding the internalization of anger in populations that have been the victims of racism and subsequent trauma (Beiser, 1997). The cycle of racism and trauma suggests that oppression becomes internalized, often due to external messages (Manson, 2001). In some situations, it is viewed as unsafe to express anger toward the dominant culture, so anger is often turned inward (Sue & Sue, 1999).

Related Risk Assessment Factors

The Degree of Structure scale includes categories such as "intensity of interventions (e.g., child in residential and/or criminal justice system)," "frequency of placements (e.g., number of out of home placements)," and "need for supervision (e.g., runaway history)." This scale reflects an individual's ability to function well independently (moderate risk score = 9). Nancy entered the TC showing less need for structure (score = 5). She had a history of multiple out-of-home placements, yet with no serious violations of parental rules.

The Social and Adaptive Functioning scale includes categories such as "cognitive disorganization (e.g., poor reality testing)" and "social interpersonal skills (e.g., prone to conflict with others)." This scale reflects an individual's ability to function well socially. Scores below the moderate risk score of 16 indicate lower risk. Nancy showed positive social and

adaptive functioning (score = 10). She entered the TC with no extensive risk history in this area. Nancy's lower score on social and adaptive functioning is consistent with literature on the relational worldview of many tribal peoples (Garrett, 1999). The relational worldview concept accents interpersonal relationships and highly respects responsibility toward others.

Nancy was rated as a very high risk in relation to substance abuse. Risk scores below 3 indicate lower risk. Nancy's Substance Abuse scale score was 8, indicating the highest risk rating. Nancy's responses evidence extensive alcohol and other abuse, problems with impulsiveness, low frustration tolerance, detached feelings, and difficulty accepting the significance of substance abuse in her life. Studies show that the use and abuse of alcohol and other drugs to cope with current circumstances and trauma are much more prevalent among American Indian youth than among non-American Indian youth (Hawkins, Cummins, & Marlatt, 2004).

During the initial assessment period, Nancy was cooperative and indicated that she felt much despair and that life had little meaning. She said she felt sad about her mother and brother and saw little she could do to change things.

TREATMENT

Based on the information gathered, the treatment team directed Nancy to the drug education class, which describes the costs of addiction, and to the AOD group, which follows the rudimentary 12-step process. Both the class and the group meet weekly for $1\frac{1}{2}$ hours and have recently been infused with content related to other high risk factors, such as self-harm. Two licensed counselors cofacilitate both the drug education class and the AOD abuse group.

Consistent with the current research base, the weekly one-hour individual counseling sessions with Nancy incorporated motivational interviewing (MI) as part of Motivational Enhancement Therapy (MET). This individual counseling supported self-efficacy, with Nancy's Change Plan Worksheet serving as ongoing follow-up (Miller, 1993). Nancy's goals, as set out on her worksheet, included academic success, social skill development, extended family connecting, and positive peer relationships. The treatment team also developed a plan with the school that encouraged Nancy's involvement in active classroom instruction, emphasized interactive teaching and cooperative learning, and used tutoring.

Other individual counseling goals used to help Nancy deal with her depression and suicidal thinking focused on increasing her sense of self-worth, reducing her isolation, teaching stress management, encouraging better communication and problem-solving skills, and helping promote inner directedness (through journaling) (Jongsma, Peterson, & McInnis, 1996). The agency's psychiatrist determined that Nancy needed psychotropic medication based on a genetic condition and/or early trauma. Such medication has been proven effective with adolescents (Jongsma, Peterson, & McInnis, 1996).

Nancy's social adaptability was noted as a strength on which we could help her build. For example, after encouragement by other treatment team members and me, Nancy decided to volunteer at the school and began tutoring younger residents with great success.

Nancy's grandmother was included in all decisions about Nancy's treatment plan and was consulted, along with Nancy, via a biweekly conference call. This focus is consistent with the recommendations for family-centered treatment of adolescents made by Brendtro, Brokenleg, and Van Bockern (1998) and by Burden, Miller, and Boozer (1996).

In addition, and *specifically for Nancy as an AI youth,* our treatment team and Nancy's grandmother adopted the philosophy that Nancy could be best understood when viewed within her cultural context. The treatment team questioned Nancy extensively about her

wishes concerning culturally specific healing. As Manson (2001) noted, traditional healing is common in many AI/AN communities, with ethnographic studies indicating that traditional healing does indeed help such problems as depression and substance-related disorders. Moreover, traditional healing approaches frequently operate in cooperation with Western psychotherapeutic interventions (Csordas, 1999; Guilmet & Whited, 1989). The treatment team helped Nancy become involved with traditional healing services from her community. Services that were coordinated by the TC and accessed by Nancy included sweat lodge purification, smudging, and other ceremonies (e.g., the offering of food).

As a treatment team, we drew on the work of Garrett (1999), who indicated that many AI/AN children tend to define themselves less by possessions and more by family ties and traditional customs and beliefs. He noted that with such a strong cultural emphasis on one's relationship with others (especially with extended family), AI/AN children are susceptible to encountering a variety of difficulties (including depression and suicidal thinking) in a society that emphasizes individualism, competition, and achievement over contrasting values of group harmony, cooperation, and sharing.

The staff at this facility responded to this knowledge and understanding by promoting and expanding extended family involvement and participation in the development of AI/AN youth. For example, in cooperation with and with approval from Nancy's tribe, the treatment team added a sweat lodge on-site. A tribal elder is currently coordinating the sweat lodge process. The purpose of the sweat lodge is to cleanse and purify the body, while the prayers heal the spirit.

Nancy was reassessed after six months using the YCRA, and her scores indicated that she had made significant therapeutic progress, with impressive reductions in risk to self, increased social and adaptive functioning, reduced substance abuse risk, and decreased degree of structure. The most notable change for Nancy was in risk to self. In her responses on standardized tests and during her exit interview, Nancy reported a much stronger sense of purpose, much lower despair, less likelihood to act out her depressed feelings, and greater resolution of negative feelings. Nancy indicated that her attitudes and behaviors around substance abuse also seemed to change. She reported more insight about her reasons for using in the past, and she went home on two unsupervised visits and did not use. The tribal elder also reported that Nancy seemed to have a much stronger identity and had new perspectives on what she could give back to her community.

It seemed likely that through cultural and traditional AI connections and family-centered treatment planning and implementation, Nancy would be able to move home and continue a nurturing and facilitative relationship with her grandmother and sister. For Nancy, following general treatment best practices and infusing treatment programming with traditional spirituality, language, teachings, and ceremonies (Beiser, 1997; Garrett, 1999) produced a 28-point reduction in overall risk behaviors on the YCRA (from 60 to 32). After she experienced culturally appropriate and family-centered treatment opportunities, Nancy's risk-to-self behaviors and attitudes noticeably decreased, resulting in less treatment time and an appropriate and supportive home placement.

CONCLUSION

Nancy made improvements overall and especially in the area of risk to self, most likely due to the intense involvement of her grandmother in treatment and the specific culturally sensitive interventions that were employed. AI/AN youth have often been painted in the literature as

being "sicker" than non-AI groups (Manson, 2001). The results for Nancy do not support this notion. Indeed, a reasonable conclusion is that in spite of high risk, this youth, with culturally sensitive treatment, was able to make great gains. This supports the growing literature emphasizing the strong resiliency of AI/AN populations (Manson, 2001). The treatment team shared these results and recommendations with all professional staff. Consequently, treatment planning for AI youth has incorporated the protocols described with similar promising results.

These positive results suggest the possibility that treatment approaches for AI youth could be adapted to build strength and resiliency for non-AI youth. For example, with group work, the relational worldview could be reinforced as a model for all youth struggling with social skills. The treatment team is now exploring the value of such ideas.

Case Reflection Questions

Suicide Issue Questions

1. American Indians, as a cultural group, have very high rates of suicide. What are the special cultural considerations that should be taken into account when working with a suicidal American Indian? How would you modify your treatment approach with an American Indian client, given these cultural considerations?

2. The counselor in this case utilizes formal paper-and-pencil assessments in addition to clinical interviews to evaluate the suicidality of clients. What are the possible advantages and disadvantages of using suicide assessment instruments? How do you know that the suicide instrument you are using is psychometrically accurate?

Skill Builder Questions

1. How might you feel if you were counseling this suicidal client? What is your personal emotional reaction to this client's suicidal behavior?

2. What would you have done in order to ensure the suicidal client's safety? Utilizing the FED, described in Chapter 3, which indicates *frequency* of suicidal thoughts, *extent* of suicide plans, and *duration* of suicidal thoughts and impulses, indicate your assessment of this client's degree of danger to self. What would you have done to properly assess this client's immediate suicide risk?

3. What important suicide risk factors were present in the case? What unique individual factors or characteristics of this client would be important to your suicide risk assessment? As you read this case, which Adapted SAD PERSONS risk factors (sex, age, depression, previous attempt, ethanol abuse, rational thinking loss, social supports lacking, organized suicide plan, no spouse, and sickness) did you find most relevant to this case?

4. What would be your therapeutic approach to treating this suicidal client? What two pieces of information described within this case would be most helpful for your own work in intervening with potentially suicidal clients and their loved ones?

5. How would your approach be the same as or different from that of the clinician in the case? What interventions described in the case did you think were most helpful to the client?

6. How will you care for yourself when working with clients who are suicidal?

7. What strategies will you use to make sure you are competent and prepared to work with high-risk clients?

Dr. Kenneth M. Coll PhD is Professor and Chair in the Department of Counselor Education at Boise State University, **Dr. Brenda J. Freeman PhD** is Professor and Chair in the Department of Counselor Education at Northwest Nazarene University, and **Patti Thobro MS** is Clinical Supervisor at Cathedral Home for Children. You can contact Dr. Coll at Boise State University, 1910 University Drive, Boise, Idaho 83725; (208) 426-1821; kcoll@boisestate.edu

References

Bauman, S., Merta, R., & Steiner, R. (1999). Further validation of the adolescent form of the SASSI. *Journal of Child & Adolescent Substance Abuse, 9,* 51–70.

Beals, J. (1997). Psychiatric disorder among American Indian adolescents. *Journal of the American Academy of Child & Adolescent Psychiatry, 36,* 1252–1259.

Beiser, M. (1997). Mental health and the academic performance of first nations and majority–culture children. *American Orthopsychiatric Association Journal,68,* 455–467.

Brendtro, L. K., Brokenleg, M., & Van Bockern, S. (1998). *Reclaiming youth at risk.* Bloomington, IN: NES.

Burden, C. A., Miller, K. E., & Boozer, A. E. (1996). Tough enough: Gang membership. In D. Capuzzi, & D. R. Gross (Eds.), *Youth at risk* (2nd ed., pp. 283–306). Alexandria, VA: American Counseling Association.

Burdsal, C., Force, R., & Klingsporn, M. J. (1990). Treatment effectiveness in young male offenders. *Residential Treatment for Children & Youth, 7,* 75–88.

Coll, K. M., Thobro, P., & Haas, R. (2004). Relational and purpose development in youth offenders. *Journal of Humanistic Counseling, Education, & Development, 43,* 41-49.

Coll, K. M., Juhnke, J., & Thobro, P., & Haas, R. (2003). A preliminary pilot study using the Substance Abuse Subtle Screening Inventory–Adolescent Form as an outcome measure with youth offenders. *Journal of Addictions & Offender Counseling, 24,* 11–22.

Csordas, T. J. (1999). Ritual healing and the politics of identity in contemporary Navajo society. *American Ethnologist, 26,* 3–23.

Garrett, M. T. (1999). Soaring on the wings of the eagle: Wellness of Native American high school students. *Professional School Counseling, 3,* 57–64.

Grimley, D., Williams, C. D., Miree, L. L., Baichoo, S., Greene, S., & Hook, E. (2000). Stages of readiness for changing multiple risk behaviors among incarcerated male adolescents. *American Journal of Health Behavior, 24,* 361–369.

Guilmet, G. M., & Whited, D. L. (1989). *The people who give more: Health and mental health among the contemporary Puyallup Indian tribal community.* Denver: University Press of Colorado.

Hanson, G. D. (2002). *Therapeutic community* (National Institutes of Health Publication No. 02-4877). Bethesda, MD: National Institute on Drug Abuse.

Hawkins, E. H., Cummins, L. H., & Marlatt, G. H. (2004). Preventing substance abuse in American Indian and Alaska Native youth: Promising strategies for healthier communities. *Psychological Bulletin, 130* (2), 304–323.

Hawkins, J. D., Herrenkohl, T. I., Farrington, D. B., Brewer, F., Catalano, R. F., Harachi, T. W., et al. (2000, April). Predictors of youth violence. *Juvenile Justice Bulletin,* 1–11.

Huizinga, D., Loeber, R., Thornberry, T. P., & Cothern, L. (2000, November). Co-occurrence of delinquency and other problem behaviors. *Juvenile Justice Bulletin,* 1–7.

Joint Commission on Accreditation of Healthcare Organizations (1998). *Technical Implementation Guide.* Oakbrook Terrace, IL: Author.

Jongsma, A. E., Peterson, L. M., & McInnis, W. P. (1996). *The child and adolescent psychotherapy treatment planner.* New York: Wiley.

Libman, L. N., Lyons, J. S., Kisiel, C., & Shallcross, H. (1998). *Understanding the mental health needs of children and adolescents in residential treatment.* Chicago: Northwestern University Medical School.

Lyons, J. S., Kisiel, C. L., Dulcan, M., Cohen, R., & Chesler, P. (1997). Crisis assessment and psychiatric hospitalization of children and adolescents in state custody. *Journal of Child & Family Studies, 6* (2), 2–18.

MacKenzie, L. R. (1999, September). Residential placement of adjudicated youth, 1987–1996. *Fact sheet.* Washington, DC: U.S. Department of Justice, Office of Justice Programs, Office of Juvenile Justice and Delinquency Prevention.

Manson, S. (2001). Behavioral health services for American Indians. In Y. Roubineaux & M. Dixon (Eds.), *Promises to keep: Public health policy for American Indians and Alaska Natives in the 21st century* (pp. 174–185). American Public Health Association Publications.

Miller, W. (1993). *Motivational Enhancement Therapy manual.* Rockville, MD: U.S. Department of Health and Human Services.

Sue, D. W., & Sue, D. (1999). *Counseling the culturally different* (3rd ed.). New York: Wiley.

Mike

A Depressed Adolescent Male

SAMUEL C. WOLFE

EDITORS' COMMENTS

- This case illustrates the importance of probing clients for information concerning their suicidal intent.

INTRODUCTION

I am the supervising counselor in the office of a psychiatrist. I have been working with adolescents and adults for the past 15 years. I have spent 8 years working in community mental health and 7 years in private practice. I have worked with adolescents in mental health settings, as a volunteer with programs in the community, and also in school settings.

BACKGROUND/REFERRAL

Mike is a 16-year-old, Caucasian male in the 11th grade. He was referred to me for counseling by his primary care physician and brought to the initial sessions by his mother. Mike's mother reported that Mike had been very withdrawn from the family setting, was feeling like he had no friends at school, and was not participating in any extracurricular activities at school. She further reported that Mike had taken an overdose of Tylenol and said he wanted to "sleep." After the overdose, Mike was treated in the emergency room (ER) and released with a plan for a follow-up appointment with the family doctor. He was referred to me for counseling for a suicide attempt and depression.

Mike agreed with everything his mother said except he continued to deny he wanted to kill himself. Mike denied being depressed but admitted he had been withdrawn from family activities such as meals, recreation, and television. Mike also admitted he had spent a great deal of time in his room and had not been involved in activities at school. He and his mother agreed that his grades had not dropped.

I began seeing Mike weekly as an outpatient in our office. Mike came with his mother, who would participate in the session for the first 10 minutes and then go to the waiting room for the remainder of the session. During our second session, I pointed out to Mike my concerns regarding what I heard from him and his mother about the events leading up to his taking the

Tylenol. Mike had been withdrawn, and there was a change in his behavior with his family. He had been withdrawn from school friends and was not participating in the activities he had enjoyed in the past. He admitted to feeling overwhelmed with all the things he had to do in school. He also admitted there was a troubled relationship with a girlfriend.

After identifying these things, Mike admitted he had been having thoughts about being "better off dead" but denied that taking the Tylenol was a suicide attempt. Since Mike understood my concerns, he was willing to develop a safety plan with me. The safety plan included these provisions: (1) Medications, both prescribed and over the counter, would be moved to his mother and father's bathroom, (2) he would meet weekly with me in counseling, (3) he would call the after-hours telephone number for our office if he needed to check in about his emotions, and (4) he would begin journaling regarding his emotions.

ASSESSMENT

Family Information

Three months before the Tylenol incident, Mike had moved to our small midwestern town from a larger city in another state. The towns were close enough for him to stay in touch with his girlfriend and a few of the friends he had in his old high school; however, his mother wanted him to make new friends and become a part of the high school he attended now. Mike was not interested in making new friends because he was very angry that he was forced to move. The family moved here because of his father's job transfer. Mike was candid in session about how he felt about the move but expressed very little about his feelings to his father.

Mike's father and mother had been married for 22 years. Mike had a 19-year-old brother, who was a freshman in college. Mike described his relationship with his brother as being very close until his brother left for college. Mike reported he was "without an ally" now. His brother seldom came home other than on holidays because he did not "get along with dad." Mike also had a 12-year-old sister. He did not spend much time with his sister other than being around the house on weekends.

Mike's mother was the one to describe the overdose episode in the counseling session. I never met his father until I asked for a family meeting to talk over the safety plan. Mike's father was cooperative but distant, and he came only to the one session. Mike described him as "determined and pushy" and said "he wants to make decisions for you." Mike's mother was very involved and expressed concern over all aspects of Mike's life. I found out from Mike's mother that she and her husband had been in counseling for a short time but that there had been no change in their strained relationship.

Mike's girlfriend was one year older than Mike. Mike described their relationship as being "serious" and "long lasting." He would go back to his previous town and see his old friends and his girlfriend as often as possible. Mike thought his relationship with his girlfriend was serious enough to think about marriage some day. They had already talked about college but were not planning to attend the same college. Mike reported his parents would not let him go to the same college as his girlfriend. He stated that his parents liked his girlfriend but that they thought the relationship was too serious at this point.

Current Health Status of Client

Mike suffered from migraine headaches and was taking Topamax for them. He was also diagnosed with vasovagal syncope and was taking Fludocortisone for that. The migraines

started shortly after the family moved to their current home, and the syncopy was diagnosed a month later.

Mike's mother was insistent that Mike be assessed for Attention Deficit Disorder (ADD). She believed some of his school struggle was due to ADD, which she had read about on the Internet. I gave Mike the National Institute of Children's Healthcare Quality (NICHQ) Vanderbilt Assessment Scale for his mother and one of his teachers to complete. This scale is a simple screen to show how his mother and his teacher evaluated Mike's attention to detail. Both the Teacher Informant Scale and the Parent Informant Scale indicated Mike had no problem with focus or attentiveness to details.

Mike's mother continued to insist ADD was to blame for his lack of motivation and feelings of being overwhelmed with school. At his mother's request, Mike's physician gave him a trial on Adderall XR. There was little change, and Mike was switched to Concerta. Mike continued to perform well in school but also continued to express his feelings of being overwhelmed with the amount of schoolwork he had to do. The Concerta was discontinued after Mike complained that it did not help or change things.

Psychosocial History

Mike described himself as always feeling awkward in groups. He reported feeling very good with his girlfriend, but even when she would have parties, he would stay with her and a small group of friends during the course of the evening. Now that he had moved to a new town and new school, he reported feeling even more "left out" and expressed feelings of being an "outsider" in his school.

Mike had always made good grades. He received As in all but one of his courses. Mike reported making a C in that course on his interim report because he has failed to complete multiple assignments. He hoped to remedy the situation by completing the assignments within the next two-week period. Mike was enrolled in two advanced placement (AP) classes. The remainder of his courses consisted of upper-level classes in his grade. Mike admitted feeling "lost" in the AP math class. When asked about the math class, Mike reported, "I just don't get into it." However, this course was one in which he was receiving a grade of A.

Mike's mother expressed concern over his involvement with his girlfriend. Prior to moving, Mike's parents had "discovered" a letter written by Mike's girlfriend. According to Mike's parents, Mike and his girlfriend had been "too intimate for young people their age." Mike's parents did not try to end the relationship. Mike was not involved in sports; however, he had played in the band at his former high school. Mike was certain he would be able to participate in the marching band at his new high school and planned to enroll in the marching band the next academic year. He expressed hope that this would afford him new friendships at school.

Behavioral Observations

Mike was tall, thin, and athletic even though he did not participate in sports. He was quiet and cooperative as we talked. At the beginning of each session, when his mother was present, he would always look at her before he answered. He seldom contradicted her but would sometimes later clarify something she had said during the preliminary session time. Mike would sit with very little movement during sessions, and he seldom even crossed his legs. He would think before he would answer but just for a second or two. I never had the impression he was screening his answers, but he did seem to think about his answers before he spoke. He would usually give short answers without much elaboration.

During the time Mike was on Adderall and then Concerta, he did become more talkative during sessions. His speech patterns were the same, but he would elaborate more on the answers when he would talk. I pointed that out to him, and he just smiled about it.

Diagnostic Impressions

Mike displayed symptomatology consistent with Major Depressive Disorder. He was withdrawn, he had feelings of hopelessness and helplessness, he felt down more days than not, and he had a suicide attempt with recurring feelings of being better off dead. Mike had a decrease in appetite and an increase in sleep. Anhedonia was present, and he had moved away from one part of his primary support system. He had experienced a major change in his life, and he was helpless to do anything about it.

TREATMENT

The first thing we did was complete the safety plan. Once that was in place, I began working with Mike using a cognitive behavior therapy (CBT) approach. Mike believed he did not fit into his new school and would not be able to gain new friends. I worked with him to begin identifying automatic thoughts about himself and his abilities and how they might contribute to his procrastination on schoolwork. He was able to describe how he would begin with thoughts about himself and then say to himself that he could not do the work.

Mike viewed himself as being "weird" or somehow "not fitting in" at his new school. We worked on his self-concept and used cognitive restructuring to focus on who he really is as a person. If he sees himself as being "weird," then he will feel uncomfortable when he is around his peers. This will become a self-fulfilling prophecy with respect to how he is treated.

Sessions 1–3

We spent our time talking about the initial incident, family relationships, how he was responding to the transition from his hometown to here, and the safety plan we developed with his parents. Mike was willing to talk about some of his personal life by the third session. We had begun to build a therapeutic alliance, and he was willing to disclose some of the struggles with his family.

SAM: So tell me how your dad has responded to this whole transition.

MIKE: Well, he doesn't know too much about how I feel about the move.

SAM: Why not?

MIKE: Well [pause], he thought everyone was okay with it because it was his work. He thinks the whole Tylenol thing has to do with school stuff. I really haven't talked to him about not liking to be here.

SAM: So who would you talk to about these kinds of struggles?

MIKE: Well, I used to talk to my brother, but he is away at college. We were really close.

SAM: How about now? If you had a problem, would you talk to mom, or would you talk to dad?

MIKE: [Pause] I'd talk to my mom. I just talk surface talk to dad, you know, how school went, dinner, stuff like that.

SAM: How did dad react when you were in the ER?

MIKE: [Pause] I feel like I'm talking bad about him.

SAM: I'm not wanting you to talk bad about him. I need you to give me a picture of what's happening at home and how it affects you.

MIKE: Well, dad was pretty mad. He wanted me to snap out of it and get this whole schoolwork stuff under control. He started talking about going to the principal and getting a tutor and stuff like that. He just didn't get it.

Mike identified two major stressor areas: (1) his perceived loss of support from his former friends back in his hometown and (2) his lack of support from and communication with his family. These identified stressors provided an opportunity to note where the primary issues of concern were and how we could effectively respond. Concomitantly, Mike was able to admit and explore his hopeless and helpless feelings.

Sessions 4–6

We talked about his various school relationships and his relationship with his girlfriend. He admitted they were having some very "intimate" emails and instant messages. Mike also admitted feeling very guilty after these interactions over the Internet. He would be apologetic with his girlfriend, and then she would get upset with his lack of consistency about their relationship. This sequence of events and the outcome typically caused Mike to feel insecure.

We also discussed his school friendships and relationships. Mike and I explored the idea of being "weird" and what that was like for him.

SAM: So tell me about this idea that you are viewed as being weird by your friends at school.

MIKE: I had this thing happen when we were choosing teams for a game. I overheard one of the other students say, "Do we want him? He's a little weird."

SAM: How did you respond?

MIKE: I just blew it off and didn't say anything.

SAM: But what happened to you inside, I mean, you know, in your head?

MIKE: I just said to myself, "I really don't fit in here no matter what I do."

SAM: Do you have those thoughts on a regular basis?

MIKE: Yeah, pretty much!

Mike interpreted these negative peer experiences as reinforcement for his existing perception of being "weird." We talked through the circle of other students' perceptions of him and of his actions in response to what he already believed.

Because I was using a CBT approach, Mike's goals and interventions were based on cognitive and behavioral techniques. Mike developed two long-term goals and three short-term goals. His first long-term goal was to examine his self-concept and focus on the truth about who he is and what he wants to do. He would identify his positive traits and talents in order to increase his self-esteem. The second long-term goal was to identify his negative automatic thoughts. He would work on replacing these with positive, truthful self-comments.

Mike's first short-term goal was to focus on his schoolwork and make sure his grades did not suffer during this period of transition. His second short-term goal was to select some extracurricular activity in which he would like to participate and begin taking action steps to be involved. He decided he would be involved in the band at school and he would join a swim team at the local YMCA. Mike's third short-term goal was to coconstruct reasonable boundaries in order to avoid the guilt feelings in his relationship with his girlfriend.

The interventions I used with Mike were formulated to assist him in reaching his goals. I built trust with Mike by using active listening and acceptance that helped him increase his ability to identify and express his feelings. I encouraged Mike to use journaling to keep track of his negative automatic thoughts.

CONCLUSION

This case is an example of what is happening in many adolescents' lives. Mike was doing all the right things. He was making good grades, he was going to school, and he was showing up to most things in his life. However, he was not expressing his life struggles to people of significance to him. No one was aware of his depression until his suicide attempt.

Thus far, Mike and I have had 10 counseling sessions. Mike's involvement in school activities has helped him feel more like a member of his current school. He no longer sees suicide as an option, and although he still struggles with issues related to this transition, he has been able to take appropriate action steps. Our therapeutic alliance has been developed, and Mike is able to express his feelings and emotions about various subjects in our sessions. At our 10th session, his mother reported Mike was handling his stress better, he was "less withdrawn," and he was expressing less negativity about various aspects of his life.

I have not been able to solve the issue of a clear diagnosis on the ADD. I do not believe Mike's academic struggle is due to ADD. However, his mother is convinced that this is the problem. Mike is taking a very heavy academic course load and admits that he still feels overwhelmed at times. He has talked to his teachers, and he has been able to identify course constructs that he does and does not understand. Mike is not forgetful. He is not disorganized. And he remains focused for one to two hours on his homework material without a break. Frankly, Mike maintains his schedule very well. He is not exhibiting the typical symptomatology expected with an ADD diagnosis. My plan is the use further assessment tools in an attempt to clarify this issue.

Case Reflection Questions

Suicide Issue Questions

1. Depression is the most frequent underlying mental disorder related to suicide. How do you determine whether the clinical focus should be on managing a suicide crisis or on treating the underlying mental and emotional disorders that may be the basis of that crisis?

2. This client's move to a new high school was a significant proximal stressor for him. What are the distal or chronic stressors in this that may contribute to his current feelings? Why is it important to assess both types of stressors when working with suicidal clients?

Skill Builder Questions

1. How might you feel if you were counseling this suicidal client? What is your personal emotional reaction to this client's suicidal behavior?

2. What would you have done in order to ensure this suicidal client's safety? Utilizing the FED, described

in Chapter 3, which indicates *frequency* of suicidal thoughts, *extent* of suicide plans, and *duration* of suicidal thoughts and impulses, indicate your assessment of this client's degree of danger to self. What would you have done to properly assess this client's immediate suicide risk?

3. What important suicide risk factors were present in the case? What unique individual factors or characteristics of this client would be important to your suicide risk assessment? As you read this case, which SAD PERSONS risk factors (sex, age, depression, previous attempt, ethanol abuse, rational thinking loss, social supports lacking, organized suicide plan, no spouse, and sickness) did you find most relevant to this case?

4. What would be your therapeutic approach to treating this suicidal client? What two pieces of information described in this case would be most helpful for your own work in intervening with potentially suicidal clients and their loved ones?

5. How would your approach be the same as or different from that of the clinician in the case? What interventions described in the case did you think were most helpful to the client?

6. How will you care for yourself when working with clients who are suicidal?

7. What strategies will you use to make sure you are competent and prepared to work with high-risk clients?

Samuel C. Wolfe, MA, LPCC–S, is a licensed professional clinical counselor in the state of Ohio. He works in a private practice setting in the office of a psychiatrist. He is also a third-year Ph.D. student at The Ohio State University (OSU). Samuel is current serving as the clinical supervisor for the Counselor Education/Community Counseling Program at OSU. He has 15 years of counseling experience in community mental health and in private practice. Prior to beginning the doctoral program at OSU, he taught for five years in an undergraduate human services and social work program.

Tori

A Survivor of Sexual Violence

LISA HINKELMAN

EDITORS' COMMENTS

- One of the most important aspects of this case is its illustration of how Posttraumatic Stress Disorder and childhood abuse can impact a client's mood and suicidality.

INTRODUCTION

As a counselor in an urban community mental health agency, I have had the opportunity to work with a very diverse group of clients, children as well as adults, who were dealing with serious mental, familial, and interpersonal issues. In my city, community mental health agencies tend to have long waiting lists for client intake appointments, very needy clients who have few options for their mental health care, and staff who work heavy caseloads with few resources. While many counselors find community mental health to be a frustrating environment to work in, I found it to be exhilarating and rewarding. At any one time, I worked with children in the child welfare system, foster families, couples, and adult clients, all struggling with various types of mental health issues.

BACKGROUND/REFERRAL

The agency where I worked had a referral system and a full-time intake coordinator. This person would meet with each client for an initial intake interview and determine suitability for counseling. She would gather available records and documentation on the client and would start the initial insurance or Medicaid precertification process so that the client could begin treatment as soon as possible. Based on her assessment of the client, the intake coordinator would assign the case to a specific counselor in the agency. Generally, the assignment was based on the area of expertise of the counselor, although it was often the case that the client was assigned to any counselor who had an open appointment! It was not unusual to come to work and find that you had been assigned a new client who would be arriving at your office that day. This structure did not give you much time to learn a great deal about the client, and what little information that was available was based on the initial

intake and the supporting paperwork the intake coordinator may have received from the referral agency.

One day, when I arrived at the office, I found a new file in my box, detailing a new client that I would be meeting with that day. Tori, a 19-year-old African American woman, was referred to the community mental health agency by her family physician. Her initial paperwork indicated that her family physician had diagnosed her with Major Depressive Disorder, severe with psychotic features, and reported that she was currently having difficulty with suicidal ideation and anxiety. This is the extent of the information that I had available prior to my initial meeting with Tori.

ASSESSMENT

Tori arrived on time for our session and was accompanied by her mother. Tori was casually, yet appropriately dressed in name-brand clothing consisting of athletic shorts, a windbreaker jacket, tennis shoes, and a baseball hat. Her weight was proportionate to her height, she wore short hair and glasses, and she had on little make-up. She wore several pieces of jewelry, including several rings, earrings, and bracelets, and had long, manicured nails.

Upon our initial introduction, Tori appeared disorganized and panic stricken as she attempted to quickly finish filling out her paperwork. When told she could finish her papers after our session, she appeared to calm down and collect herself, and she seemed prepared to begin. Tori remained cooperative and compliant throughout the initial session, with a notable amount of physical agitation. She often moved around in her seat and seemed to have difficulty getting comfortable. Her speech was normal and her thought process intact; however, she reported short-term memory deficits. She described her mood as depressed and anxious, which was congruent with her affect.

Tori stated that she had some health problems, including migraine headaches and asthma; however, they currently were not debilitating in any way. She had a history of chemical-dependency treatments, and approximately three years earlier, she had received inpatient treatment for five days at a local substance abuse treatment center. She had been sober for over two years and attended Alcoholics Anonymous meetings regularly. Tori smoked approximately one pack of cigarettes a day.

Initial Presenting Concerns

Tori's chief complaints included anxiety, nervousness, and exhaustion. She reported feeling "edgy" and as though her heart was "racing," and she had a positive startle response. She reported sleep continuity disturbance as well as early morning awakening. Tori described herself as having several symptoms of depression, including a decreased energy level, a decreased appetite, anhedonia, and positive suicidal ideation. She told me she often thinks of suicide and believes that the most painless way to kill herself would be to take "all of my pills." Despite her reported plan, Tori did say she currently did not intend to suicide. She was able to effectively contract for safety and agreed to have her mother manage her medications and lock up any other medicine that was in the home.

Tori stated that this current episode of depression had been present for several months and was precipitated by a recent breakup with her boyfriend of two years, Steven. Tori reported having difficulty coping with his intense anger and physical violence and

stated "I feared for my life." She reported that her relationship with her ex-boyfriend was rather hostile and that he would get angry with her and "beat up on her." She stated that she was in love with him and that he was the first "guy who ever cared about me."

Tori claimed some responsibility for the abuse and felt that she, at times, provoked the physical rage that she experienced at the hands of Steven. When pressed about this, Tori reported that she would often accuse Steven of seeing other girls or cheating on her until he would get so mad that he would shove her against the wall or hit her in the arms or back. She said he would threaten her if she didn't have sex with him when he wanted, so she usually gave in so he would leave her alone for the rest of the night.

Tori reported that her mother had been pressuring her to leave Steven for months, but said "I just couldn't because he really did love me." Tori stated that her mother "made" her move out of Steven's apartment after he pushed her down the stairs and she broke her leg. She told me that Steven had tried to contact her over the last several months and had threatened her through voice mail, email, and instant messages. She said she often has nightmares of these events and wakes up in the middle of the night with her heart racing and her sheets damp with sweat.

Evolving Presenting Concerns

After further talking with Tori, it became apparent that the diagnosis of depression from her family physician was not capturing the scope of all of the symptoms that she was experiencing. Her anxiety was clearly a tremendous problem based on her startle response, nightmares, and replaying of the abusive events. I was not convinced that Tori was experiencing psychosis; I believed that her fears about being attacked by Steven were real, not delusional thinking. I diagnosed Tori with Posttraumatic Stress Disorder and scheduled an evaluation with the agency psychiatrist. Her medications were changed to include an anxiety medication, Ativan, in addition to her antidepressant, Prozac, and she was taken off her antipsychotic medication, Seroquel.

Social History

Tori is an only child. She has two elderly parents. Both were alcoholics during her childhood and adolescence. In our second session, Tori revealed that she experienced verbal and sexual abuse by her father and "felt like I was a bother to my mother." Tori stated that she and her parents have always had a difficult relationship, and she often felt very alone while growing up. Her father currently had heart problems, which had been anxiety provoking for Tori. She clearly had mixed emotions about her relationship with her father, although she made attempts at maintaining some type of relationship with him. Her mother was generally healthy, but they had a strained relationship. Tori said her mother is supportive at times. However, Tori reported that her mother still treats her like she's 15 and tries to run her life. She reported telling her mother several years ago about the sexual abuse she experienced as a child and her mother told her, "Daddy would never do that to you. You're his little girl."

Tori stated that she continued to communicate with her parents on a superficial level because she felt guilty about not being available to them in their advanced years. When her mother asked her to come over and spend time with her father, she obliged even if she had other things to do. Tori told me that she always felt terrible after spending time with her parents because she felt guilty for hating her father when he was an old man who probably didn't have much time left to live.

TREATMENT

Tori was an adult victim of childhood sexual abuse and of later sexual violence. While these two things might initially appear to be separate incidents, they are, in fact, inextricably related (Messman-Moore, Long, & Siegfried, 2000). Research indicates that children who experience sexual abuse are twice as likely to be revictimized at a later time in life (see Messman-Moore & Long, 2003, for a review). Professionals in the field believe that the relationship a child has with a sexual abuse perpetrator has a tremendous impact on the way the child thinks about himself or herself and learns to relate to others (Filipas & Ullman, 2006). The abuse that takes place stunts proper child development and negatively impacts social and interpersonal skill development, self-esteem, and self-concept. Abuse theorists assert that individuals who are abused as children learn inappropriate ways to relate to others, define love and affection primarily through sexual relationships, and blame themselves for the abuse. Additionally, many theorists believe that abusive men will seek out certain women whom they perceive as vulnerable and will further abuse them (Filipas & Ullman, 2006).

The physical and psychological effects of sexual violence are often devastating to the victim. Those who have experienced sexual violence report tremendous difficulties following an assault, including Posttraumatic Stress Disorder, nightmares, difficulty sleeping, suicidal thoughts, alcohol and drug use and abuse, difficulty with sex and intimacy, an increased startle response, and fear of triggering another incident (Bass & Davis, 1988). Ongoing symptoms can include fear and avoidance of particular situations, affective constriction, depleted self-concept and feelings of self-efficacy, and sexual dysfunction (Koss, 1990). Because Tori had experienced sexual abuse as a child and continued to be victimized as an adult, the issues she was dealing with were even more complex. Throughout her childhood, Tori learned how to please others but not know how to stand up for herself. She was rewarded for doing as she was told and punished for telling others how she felt. Essentially, Tori needed to learn how to interact with others to get her own needs met, to see herself as important and valuable, and to develop new ways to respond to others in threatening or manipulative situations.

I utilized a cognitive-behavioral therapeutic approach in my work with Tori. Cognitive therapy is an active, directive, and structured approach (Beck, Rush, Shaw, & Emery, 1979). It is based on the theory that an individual's affect and behavior are determined primarily by the way he or she structures the world. An individual's cognitions are based on attitudes or assumptions that develop from past experience (Beck et al., 1979). Behavioral therapy is designed to replace ineffective or dangerous behaviors with structure and positive new behaviors. Behavioral techniques allow a patient to test maladaptive cognitions and assumptions and to develop and try out new behaviors in a safe and supportive environment. Tori needed to unlearn her current way of interacting and reacting and to learn new, healthier patterns of interacting with others.

Tori had learned through her relationships with her father and her boyfriend that in order to demonstrate love to another person, she must do what that person tells her to do sexually, or she will be punished. She reported having very few times when she felt she was on an even footing with her father or her ex-boyfriend and feeling intimidated and scared by them both. She told me that one of her greatest fears is that she will see her ex-boyfriend out somewhere and he will threaten her and she will freeze up and not be able to do anything. She said this is the nightmare that wakes her up almost every night.

During our third session, Tori revealed that she spent time with her parents over the weekend and that she wanted to make peace with her father. She told me that in order to do this, she really wanted to tell her father about her feelings of being abused by him as a child. When she brought it up in a conversation, her father called her a "lying bitch," and her mother forced her out of the house. She was feeling increasingly helpless and was tearful throughout our entire session. She kept saying that she was "stupid" for even thinking about talking to her father about the abuse and that she "should have known better." She said, "It would just be easier for everyone if I wasn't here. I can't stand this anymore."

Throughout the session, Tori became increasingly agitated, and her suicidal ideation increased. She informed me that she did have a plan to kill herself and that she was not sure she would be safe if she left. We talked about safety planning and whom she could call if she felt unsafe or scared. At this point, she could not identify one person in her life she could call if she was feeling imminently suicidal. I quickly realized that I could not let Tori leave my office in this state and talked with her about her options. After consulting with my clinical supervisor about the situation, I ended up driving Tori to the local 24-hour mental health crisis center that was just a few miles down the street. We stayed there for the next four hours while Tori was evaluated by a crisis counselor and a psychiatrist.

This experience was exhausting and frustrating for Tori, and I think she realized that despite her intense pain, she did not really want to die. She almost seemed surprised that I took her threats so seriously and stayed with her throughout the process. I later wondered whether Tori thought I would simply leave her there to fend for herself. After her evaluation, Tori promised the crisis center personnel and me that she would be safe and asked whether she could go home. After much discussion, Tori decided that she could call her neighbor if she felt unsafe or if she needed someone to talk to. She knew all of the crisis and emergency numbers and told us that she would use them if she needed to. I set an appointment to see Tori again in three days, and after their assessment was finished, the crisis center personnel released her from their care.

Goals of Treatment

Based on this last event, it became clear to me that Tori's confrontation of her abuser was not an empowering experience for her and that perhaps she would never get the validation that she was desperately seeking from her parents that this abuse did occur. She and I spent some time in counseling talking about what might happen if she limited her interaction with her father. What would that mean about her as a daughter? What would that mean about her as a woman? I wanted Tori to begin to think about herself and the importance of her feelings and reactions to the decisions she was making. Tori was very good at pleasing others. However, she struggled immensely to think of herself as a priority in her own life.

As we worked together on Tori's treatment plan, we first identified the symptoms of anxiety that Tori was experiencing and then selected three initial areas where we would focus specifically on symptom management. She reported that her sleep problems were the most disturbing symptom. She had difficulty falling asleep because she knew she was going to have a terrible nightmare and wake up in a panic. Then she would feel terrible the next day because she hadn't gotten an adequate night's rest. Together we set a treatment goal around managing her symptoms of anxiety at bedtime. She said that before bed she usually lies down and then her mind starts to focus on the nightmares that she is going to have and the violent situations with her ex-boyfriend; at times, it takes her hours to fall asleep.

Tori began to devise a new "nightly routine" that included healthy and calming behaviors (i.e., taking a bubble bath, having a cup of tea, reading a pleasant book, and listening to calming music before bed), which allowed her to spend time caring for herself. Tori would learn relaxation techniques, including progressive muscle relaxation, and would spend time throughout her day practicing these techniques in order to minimize her symptoms.

The second focus of Tori's treatment plan was to develop new coping skills to manage her symptoms of depression and anxiety. By learning techniques such as self-monitoring, thought stopping, and thought replacement, Tori would be able to begin to realize how often she was giving herself negative messages and also would be able to stop the downward spiral of self-deprecation.

Coming to terms with the childhood sexual abuse, our third focus was very important in Tori's ability to move forward. She had not spent much time exploring the impact of the abuse on her life, her relationships, and the way she interacted with the world. Through the use of journaling and homework assignments, Tori would begin to process the impact of the abuse on her life and on the way that she currently related to others. She would be encouraged to examine how her abuse impacted her intimate relationships.

The fourth and fifth areas of Tori's treatment focused on the acquisition of new behaviors and attitudes. The fourth area was to improve Tori's assertiveness through participation in assertiveness training. Because this was the fourth focus of Tori's treatment, it would not be part of the therapeutic process until Tori was more stable, had her symptoms under control, and was more confident.

Assertiveness has been defined as showing respect for oneself and others by stating one's opinion and letting others know individual feelings, wants, and needs (NiCarthy, Gottlieb, & Coffman, 1993). It is standing up for one's personal rights and freely expressing ideas, feelings, and opinions (Twenge, 2001). Assertiveness requires a person to attempt to ensure her rights or to "actualize an internalized view of self thorough interaction with others" (Morokoff, 2000, p. 307).

According to NiCarthy et al. (1993), an assertive person demonstrates the following traits: "Uses give and take in conversation; Listens and talks; Speaks with moderate voice volume and tone; Looks the other person in the eye; Does not intrude into another's physical space, nor shrink away" (p. 157). Assertiveness training encourages women to stand up for their rights, challenge their stereotypes, speak for themselves, and adopt new behaviors (Enns, 1992).

Assertive speech provides a foundation for conflict management, as it disrupts cycles of victimization and unhealthy power dynamics that exist in social and personal relationships (Strain, 2001). Assertive verbalizations require an individual to tell, not ask, other individuals to change their behavior and are free of excuses, apologies, and explanations (Telsey, 1988). The difficulty for many women in developing assertive skills lies in the fact that they are not accustomed to articulating clearly what they want and need (NiCarthy et al., 1993). In Tori's case, this was especially true.

The fifth and final goal of my work with Tori was to positively impact her self-efficacy. Self-efficacy theory addresses an individual's belief about his or her ability to produce desired results in specific situations (Bandura, 1997). This is a key construct in Tori's situation because it hones in on the socialized belief that she cannot stand up for herself or be successful in situations or relationships. Individuals who believe strongly in their ability to be successful when engaging in a difficult task are more likely to attempt the task and will experience less anxiety than do individuals who have low efficacy beliefs (Bandura, 1997).

Using enactive mastery experiences, such as practicing skills in an in vivo situation, Tori would learn ways to interact with her father, if she chose to, and also develop skills for the confrontation that she was anticipating with her ex-boyfriend. By role-playing this behavior with me in our sessions, Tori would have the opportunity to successfully engage in a specific behavior, thereby producing stronger efficacy beliefs (Bandura, 1997). Enactive mastery processes produce stronger and more generalized efficacy beliefs than do other types of instruction. Vicarious instruction, cognitive simulations, and verbal instruction are all secondary to personal performance successes. The perception of self-efficacy is a measurement not of the actual skills that individuals possesses but rather of their belief about what they can do in different circumstances with the skills that they possess (Bandura, 1997).

The Working Stage

Tori and I spent the next three months working together—initially weekly, then biweekly—on the aforementioned areas. As her medications got to a therapeutic dose and her mood lifted somewhat, she found she was able to engage fully in the counseling process, and she truly began to take control of her depression and anxiety by developing new skills and behaviors.

Tori's nightmares continued for a few weeks after she began to implement the relaxation strategies. She found she would fall asleep, have a nightmare, wake up, and then have difficulty returning to sleep, sometimes tossing and turning all night. However, her persistence paid off, and she began to report five nightmares a week instead of seven, then three nightmares a week, and then one nightmare every two weeks. As she tried out these new behaviors, she found out what did and did not work for her. Perhaps I would suggest a book of poetry and some classical music, and she would try that out and hate it! Tori learned to modify her "homework" to suit her needs and her personal style. My role was to push her to continue to try new behaviors and to encourage and support her in this difficult process of thought and behavior change.

Working with Tori to process her sexual abuse history was a challenging and emotional experience for both of us. For Tori, she was facing demons of her past and working through very intense emotions, such as hatred for her father, disappointment in her mother, and guilt and shame for herself. For me, pushing Tori to face her past, while encouraging and fostering her hope in the future, was a delicate task. My personal belief is that an individual does not have to forgive his or her abuser in order to move on and to heal, and for Tori, forgiveness was not on her mind. She was angry and felt betrayed. She did not have the need to seek forgiveness, and in fact, I think she garnered strength from realizing that she could heal and become strong in spite of her father. If I would have pushed her to forgive her father or to continue to seek out his acknowledgment of the abuse, I think I would have stymied the therapeutic process.

Learning to be assertive was extremely challenging for Tori, and using her own voice to stand up for herself was a skill that she had to work very hard to develop. After several weeks of working together, Tori and I began to practice assertive responses. We would engage in various role plays of situations in which she would have to stand up for herself. The situations began with scenarios that were somewhat innocuous, such as her friend borrowing five dollars and not paying her back. Tori practiced asking her friend for the money back. Next, we moved to a slightly more serious situation, such as her mother asking her to come and visit her father. Tori's homework would be to engage in one assertive response during the week and come back and report on how it went, how

she felt emotionally and physically when she engaged in this type of behavior, and what the response of the other person was. As a young woman who had a very difficult time making others upset and who was a compulsive "pleaser," any type of an assertive response was a victory for Tori!

As noted earlier, Tori and I worked on skill acquisition through role playing and enactive mastery processes. Her greatest fear was running into her ex-boyfriend and freezing up or not knowing what to do or what to say. Tori anticipated how this meeting would take place, and her scenario always ended with her getting beaten up, yelled at, degraded, or humiliated in some way. She had difficulty seeing the scenario with a different, successful ending. We worked together on developing a more positive ending for this imagined scenario and then truly created that scenario in the counseling office. Tori developed a script of what she would like to say and how she would like to handle this situation, and through ongoing rehearsal of the components, we worked on the development of her skills so she would be able to say assertively and confidently, "Leave me alone! I want you to go away!"

CONCLUSION

While Tori made excellent progress during the time we worked together, the nature of community mental health is such that you can't continue in treatment for a very long period of time. I was amazed at this young woman's spirit and resolve and at her dedication to charting a different course for her life. I believe that when we terminated our counseling relationship, Tori's progress was amazing! While I fully understand that any type of behavior change takes time to be reinforced and generalized, I felt positive about Tori's trajectory and her confidence in herself and her abilities.

Tori came to the therapeutic relationship as a young woman who was completely hopeless and lacked confidence and self-worth, and she left as a woman of increasing strength and pride—this is perhaps a counselor's greatest moment.

Case Reflection Questions

Suicide Issue Questions

1. This case illustrates how feelings of worthlessness, shame, anger, or guilt can drive a client's suicidal ideation. Dr. Hinkelman uses a multipronged therapeutic approach to empower the client. What would your approach be to help a client process these intense feelings?
2. Suicidal clients have often been the victims of painful trauma or life circumstance. How comfortable are you in asking and discussing difficult life questions concerning sex, loss, and death?

Skill Builder Questions

1. How might you feel if you were counseling this suicidal client? What is your personal emotional reaction to this client's suicidal behavior?

2. What would you have done in order to ensure this suicidal client's safety? Utilizing the FED, described in Chapter 3, which indicates *frequency* of suicidal thoughts, *extent* of suicide plans, and *duration* of suicidal thoughts and impulses, indicate your assessment of this client's degree of danger to self. What would you have done to properly assess this client's immediate suicide risk?
3. What important suicide risk factors were present in the case? What unique individual factors or characteristics of this client would be important to your suicide risk assessment? As you read this case, which SAD PERSONS risk factors (sex, age, depression, previous attempt, ethanol abuse, rational thinking loss, social supports lacking, organized suicide plan, no spouse, and sickness) did you find most relevant to this case?

4. What would be your therapeutic approach to treating this suicidal client? What two pieces of information described in this case would be most helpful for your own work in intervening with potentially suicidal clients and their loved ones?

5. How would your approach be the same as or different from that of the clinician in the case? What interventions described in the case did you think were most helpful to the client?

6. How will you care for yourself when working with clients who are suicidal?

7. What strategies will you use to make sure you are competent and prepared to work with high-risk clients?

Lisa Hinkelman, Ph.D., LPC is the Executive Director of The Interprofessional Commission of Ohio at The Ohio State University. She developed and coordinates the ROX- Ruling Our experiences empowerment program for girls and researches, publishes, and lectures on issues related to adolescent girls' development, urban education, mental health issues in schools, women's career development, leadership development in girls and women, sexual harassment and sexual violence prevention, resiliency, and non-school factors that impact academic achievement. Previously, Dr. Hinkelman was a faculty member in the Counselor Education program at The Ohio State University, where she continues to teach Legal, Ethical, & Professional Issues and Counseling Children. Dr. Hinkelman is a Licensed School Counselor and is also licensed as a Professional Counselor. She has worked as a counselor in a school for adjudicated adolescent girls, as an outpatient community agency counselor, as a program assistant in a rape education and prevention program, and as a sexual harassment educator. She earned her Bachelor's degree in Psychology and Elementary Education at Chatham College in Pittsburgh, PA and her Master's and Doctorate degrees in Counselor Education at The Ohio State University.

References

Bandura, A. (1997). *Self-efficacy: The exercise of control.* New York: W. H. Freeman.

Bass, E., & Davis, L. (1988). *The courage to heal.* New York: HarperCollins.

Beck, A. T., Rush, A. J., Shaw, B. F., & Emery, G. (1979). *Cognitive therapy of depression.* New York: Guilford.

Enns, C. Z. (1992). Self-esteem groups: A synthesis of consciousness-raising and assertiveness training. *Journal of Counseling & Development, 71,* 7–13.

Filipas, H. H., & Ullman, S. E. (2006). Child sexual abuse, coping responses, self-blame, posttraumatic stress disorder, and adult sexual revictimization. *Journal of Interpersonal Violence, 21*(5), 652–672.

Koss, M. P. (1990). The women's mental health research agenda: Violence against women. *American Psychologist, 45*(3), 374–380.

Messman-Moore, T. L., Long, P. J., & Siegfried, N. J. (2000). The revictimization of child sexual abuse survivors: An examination of the adjustment of college women with child sexual abuse, adult sexual assault, and adult physical abuse. *Child Maltreatment, 5*(1), 18–27.

Messman-Moore, T. L. & Long, P.J. (2003). The role of childhood sexual abuse sequelae in sexual revictimization: An empirical review and theoretical reformulation. *Clinical Psychology Review, 23*(4), 537–571.

Morokoff, P. J. (2000). A cultural context for sexual assertiveness in women. In J. W. White (Ed.), *Sexuality, society, and feminism.* Washington, DC: American Psychological Association, 299–319.

NiCarthy, G., Gottlieb, N., & Coffman, S. (1993). *You don't have to take it!: A woman's guide to confronting emotional abuse at work.* Seattle, WA: Seal Press.

Strain, P. (2001). *Teaching self-defense core skills: Self-defense teacher's text for self-defense educators, facilitators and instructors.* Union, MI: Mona Lisa's Sword.

Telsey, N. (1988). *Self-defense from the inside out: A woman's workbook for developing self-esteem and assertiveness skills for safety.* Eugene, OR: Breaking Free.

Twenge, J. M. (2001). Changes in women's assertiveness in response to status and roles: A cross-temporal meta-analysis, 1931–1993. *Journal of Personality & Social Psychology, 81*(1), 133–145.

Megan

A University Student

WENDY CHARKOW BORDEAU

EDITORS' COMMENTS

- This case illustrates the importance of developing a client safety plan.
- The case demonstrates that not all suicidal clients need to be hospitalized.

INTRODUCTION

Working as the counseling director, as well as the only full-time counselor, of a small university, I experienced many situations in which I felt unable to provide clients with optimal mental health services without using referrals or seeking further assistance. However, residential college students are often reluctant to seek treatment. This is particularly true when that treatment requires them to travel off campus. Their reluctance may be related to the difficulty of securing transportation, lack of independent health insurance and/or unwillingness to disclose the need for insurance coverage to parents, stigma related to accessing counseling, unfamiliarity with the local community, and plain old fear or lack of knowledge about self-care. I vividly remember one student who provoked a great deal of anxiety for me. Specifically, she offered all the above reasons for not seeking help despite the fact she was in need of intensive treatment related to suicidal, or least para-suicidal, risk.

BACKGROUND/REFERRAL

Megan first presented to our counseling center as a first-year college student with relationship and academic concerns. During the initial phone intake, I was able to garner the following information. Megan had come to the university as an out-of-state 19-year-old Caucasian female. Her family residence was approximately a four-hour drive away. Megan's older sister, Lori, also resided on campus as a junior. Megan's social network mainly included Lori and her friends. Though Megan had a roommate with whom she got along, she indicated that her roommate went home most weekends and that they rarely socialized.

Megan was unclear about her academic and career direction; like many students, she knew that she didn't want "a nine-to-five desk job" but expressed few interests. She was

currently enrolled in her general education courses and was maintaining a C average in most. Megan indicated that she "did enough work to get by and nothing more." Interestingly, Lori was a "star student" and was majoring in biology with a premed concentration. Megan indicated that she had always admired Lori for knowing what she wanted and working to make it happen but that she herself "didn't have that kind of drive." Additionally, Megan said she was not very close with her parents and had no other siblings.

Megan initially presented to counseling on Lori's recommendation after Lori's sorority had participated in an eating disorders workshop with me. Megan reported that Lori thought it might help her with figuring out a major and getting more involved on campus. Based on the overtly innocuous nature of this case, Megan was referred to Lynn, a part-time counselor in the university counseling office.

Megan participated in an intake session and one additional counseling session with Lynn over the course of the next few weeks. According to Lynn in case conferences, she and Megan were working on building rapport and facilitating self-expression, and Megan appeared mainly receptive to the counseling process, though slightly more reserved than other college student clients. Megan had also been referred to career services for career assessment and exploration and agreed to attend a meeting of her residence hall council to meet more people and to start socializing with her own peer network. Megan's provisional diagnosis, Phase of Life Problem (V62.89, Rule Out Adjustment Disorder with Depression), was a standard for college counselors who often work with developmental issues and do not need to bill insurance companies that pay only for established Axis I diagnoses.

One morning as I walked into my office building, I was met by the dean of student life, who requested that I join him immediately for a conference in his office. The director of residence life, Mike, was also in attendance. Apparently, there had been an emergency the night before. One of the students had made a suicide attempt. According to the residence assistant (RA) on duty, a resident had pounded on her door at 1:30 A.M. that morning. The resident was visibly shaken and said that her roommate had swallowed a bunch of pills and was acting "really weird." When the RA went to the room to investigate, the student in question was lying in her bed mumbling to herself. It was impossible to discern what she was actually saying. Next to her bed were empty pill bottles for Percocet and Xanax. The resident cried as she told the RA that those were actually her prescriptions that she kept in her nightstand. The resident also indicated that she had just gotten to the room after spending time with her boyfriend, who lived in another residence hall.

The RA followed protocol and both called for an ambulance and alerted Mike about the situation. Mike, the RA, and the roommate stayed with Megan at the hospital as she underwent triage, physical and psychological assessment, and gastric lavage. Megan was sent back to the university after it was determined that she had not suffered any lasting damage from the pills and she had denied current suicidal ideation or intent. Mike indicated that he still did not feel comfortable leaving Megan alone. Megan did not have any classes that day until late afternoon, so Mike asked her to spend some time with one of the resident directors in her on-campus apartment. Megan agreed to do so, and he came to the dean's office immediately thereafter.

After listening to Mike, the dean of student life turned to me and said, "The student said she was in counseling here. Did you not see this coming?" I informed the dean that I couldn't talk about whether or not she was a client at this point without her consent but that I would do everything in my power to help with the situation. We then decided that Mike would escort Megan to my office, I would assess the situation, and we would reconvene

afterward to determine a plan to ensure the student's safety as well as evaluate whether she could remain on campus.

ASSESSMENT

Mike and Megan arrived at my office about 15 minutes later. In that time, I was able to reschedule my other appointments for the morning. Megan presented as an average college female, casually dressed and visibly nervous, as indicated by her continual foot tapping and nail biting. She also tended to look at the floor rather than in my eyes when responding to questions. I started off by asking her to take a seat and make herself comfortable. I informed her that I would be talking with her over the next hour or so to make sense of what had happened the previous night and to help her make a plan to keep herself safe. I also added that her primary counselor, Lynn, was not on campus today but that I would appreciate Megan's consent for me to talk with Lynn about her case. She readily agreed and then took a deep breath before saying, "I know what I did last night was really stupid. You would think I would have learned my lesson by now. You guys don't have to worry about me doing that again."

That gave me a good opportunity to establish rapport by indicating my appreciation of her honesty and concern for the college staff as well as to probe about past history. Megan indicated that she had had a hard time in high school and had engaged in para-suicidal behavior several times. Most notably, she had twice cut herself on her arms in response to fights with her parents and had taken a small overdose of over-the-counter sleeping medication after she was rejected by a boy in her school. The incident with the pills and one cutting episode went unnoticed; however, her sister had noticed the cuts on her arms the second time and had threatened to tell her parents or someone at school. Megan begged her not to, and Lori agreed after Megan swore to never "do anything that stupid again." Megan said that her parents would have "freaked out" and "never let me out of their sight again." Megan also reported that her parents didn't understand what it was like to be a kid or a teenager and that all they cared about was that she got good grades.

In terms of psychosocial history, Megan denied previous counseling or psychiatric treatment. She said that she was in the process of taking an introductory course in psychology and thought she might have some symptoms of depression, such as not eating much, feeling hopeless, lacking concentration, and not wanting to go out and meet with people. Megan also stated that she once tried to talk to her mother several years ago about being depressed but that "she blew it off as typical teenage drama." When asked whether she had shared this history with Lynn, Megan softly stated, "I thought I was through with all this stuff, and I didn't want to talk about it any more." I thanked her for being open with me and indicated that discussing one's psychosocial history when presenting for an intake session is important even if the problems appear to have passed. I also sensed that she was embarrassed, and I tried to normalize her experiences as possibly related to depression, while also emphasizing the significance of any acts of self-harm, whether they are conducted with the intent of suicide or as an act of coping with intense emotional pain. This then led to and allowed me to naturally ask about her current suicidal ideation and intent.

I asked, "Megan, do you have thoughts about killing yourself?" She said, "No, not really. . . . I just get so tired of having to deal with the same old problems over and over again." I then inquired specifically about the thought pattern and emotional process that accompanied her para-suicide the prior night. Megan reported that she had just had a very upsetting call with

her parents back home. Apparently, her parents had asked about her grades and academic performance. Megan said she tried to avoid the question but they kept "badgering" her. Finally, Megan told them the truth. She said she was obtaining mostly Cs, and "my father had a 'fit.' He said I was going to have to come back home and that they weren't going to waste all their money on me if I was just going to blow it off." Megan started crying as she said, "I can't go back home."

Key Suicide Risk Assessment Factors

Megan's case was puzzling to me, as she presented mostly as low risk, but several "red flags" were nagging at me. In using the SAD PERSONS Scale (see Chapter 3), key factors that I considered included age (late adolescence is a high-risk period for suicide), depression (it appeared that she qualified for some previous and possibly current episodes of major depression and/or possibly dysthymia), and lack of social support other than her sister. I had inquired about substance use, and Megan had reported that she "had a beer or two at a frat party but never anything more. I can't stand the taste or how it makes me feel." I also asked about other substances, such as prescription medications, and Megan reported that the only time she felt she had misused medication previously was in high school when "I went on a diet craze and started taking diet pills with my friend." She denied being on a diet or taking any pills or substances currently. "In fact," said Megan, "I think it is weird that I am not really that interested in eating. I just don't feel as hungry as I used to."

After discussing Megan's eating patterns, I went back to specifically addressing suicidal intent and plan with a question about how she came to the point of taking her roommate's pills. According to Megan, it was the first thing she could think of, since she had seen her roommate, who apparently had recent surgery, put them in her night table when they first moved in. She denied any other access to pills or any other plan or true desire to kill herself, especially now that she had experienced the discomfort associated with the gastric lavage.

I was also concerned by the fact that she had not been forthcoming regarding past and current difficulties in counseling with Lynn and that she had reneged on her earlier promise to her sister about not committing further acts of self-harm. She also appeared somewhat evasive, and I doubted that I was getting the full story. If I had been seeing Megan within a community agency setting and she was living at home, I would have had fewer concerns, as I could have included her parents in a safety plan and family counseling. However, Megan was living away from home with little desire to speak with her parents. I also had to consider the welfare of the college and the other students around her. Simply stated, was it safe for Megan to remain at our college as a residential student?

TREATMENT

My first major concern for intervention related to Megan's immediate living arrangements and whether it was feasible for her to remain on campus. In addition, I felt pressure from the administration of the university to ensure that a student lives on campus only if he or she will not endanger others or put the welfare of the institution on the line. At this point, it seemed that the university was the place for Megan to stay, especially as her para-suicide was triggered mainly by thoughts of leaving. Furthermore, research indicates that young adults attending a residential college are statistically less likely to attempt and/or commit suicide than are their counterparts not living on a college campus.

However, I had to think about both the short-term and the long-term implications of a decision for Megan to remain. For example, would Megan's roommate still be willing to live with Megan, especially as Megan had stolen her medication for her para-suicide? Furthermore, was it safe for Megan to continue living with a roommate with accessible medication? If Megan's roommate was not able or willing to continue living with Megan, was it appropriate or wise to have her room with someone else, or even by herself? This would have to be addressed in consultation with the roommate as well as with Mike, the director of residence life mentioned earlier.

Second, what about the issue of contacting Megan's parents? Megan was legally an adult but was still considered a minor and financially dependent by her parents. In addition, Megan's parents were the only people consistently in Megan's life and living with her when she was not on the university campus, such as during semester breaks and holidays. Would it be safe, or ethical, to withhold this information? I also remembered that Megan indicated a belief that her parents wanted her to come home based on their last phone call. Was this threat a melodramatic gesture fueled by momentary anger and disappointment or a potentially realistic occurrence? If Megan's parents were already seriously considering withdrawing their daughter from college, would the news of a para-suicide only add to their belief that she could not handle college?

This led to the third question: Is our university really the right place for Megan? She stated that she could not imagine leaving and wanted to stay. Yet she had not connected academically or socially to campus life—despite encouragement and support from her sister and a counselor. Is it possible that she would be better off elsewhere, either at home or at another college, though she did not see that as a realistic option at the moment?

If Megan was to remain at the university, there would be several other matters to address. Would she be mandated to continue counseling? She had already come voluntarily before the para-suicide, yet it did not appear that she was honest about her level of depression or her past history. Additionally, she had not been forthcoming about her family patterns. Was this lack of attention to these important issues due to the lack of a working alliance with Lynn, her assigned counselor; the lack of time to develop a strong therapeutic bond; or simply the fact that counseling had been focused more on solutions and developmental issues, without as much attention given to clinical history and possible psychopathology? I told Megan in my first session with her that I would need to contact Lynn, as Lynn was her primary counselor, to notify her of the para-suicide as well as to gather additional information that might be helpful in developing a plan for Megan. Megan consented readily to this and quickly said, "It's not her fault. She didn't know how bad I felt, and I always felt a little bit better after talking to her."

If Megan was to stay on campus and was mandated to counseling, would it be better for her to see a therapist off campus, as the university counseling center had a 12-session limit per student per year and was not open on weekends, holidays, or college breaks? If so, would she use her parents' insurance to help pay for the counseling, and what implications would this have for an already shaky family dynamic? If she was to continue counseling in our center, should she continue to see Lynn because Lynn, as a part-time counselor, had even less availability? These were all questions floating around in my mind as I worked with Megan in that first session and afterward.

After Megan disclosed the content of and emotions related to the telephone call with her parents right before the para-suicide, I empathized with her fear of losing what she had at the university and her uncertainty about where she belonged. I also asked Megan to talk

a little bit more about her relationship with her parents and how it had gotten to the present state. Megan reported that she and her parents had never been particularly close and that she felt like she was a disappointment, especially to her father. Apparently, Megan felt that in his eyes she could never measure up to her older sister, Lori, a straight-A student and accomplished athlete. Megan also indicated that she had dated someone pretty seriously in high school and that her parents disapproved of this relationship. According to Megan, "Brian [the ex-boyfriend] seemed like he really liked and understood me. But my parents drove him off by being rude and were ridiculous about not letting me go anywhere with him, so he ended it. I always think about how things could have been if they wouldn't have just treated me like a baby and let things happen between us. It just seems like they can't ever let me be happy."

After empathizing with her frustration about her relationship with her parents, I gently asked whether she truly felt that they did not care about her happiness or welfare. She thought for a moment and said, "I don't know. . . . I guess they want me to be happy. But their idea and my idea of happiness are very different." This created the perfect opportunity for me to ask Megan how she viewed happiness and how she would like her life to turn out. After some silence, she stated that she wasn't sure but that she wanted to find someone to love who really loved her, and if that happened, then all the rest would probably fall into place. Although I wouldn't normally endorse a rather unempowered view of the future that was so dependent on the actions of others, I was optimistic in that she could at least talk about the future. When I inquired about her perception of hopefulness that this future would pan out, she indicated that she thought it would, as long as "I don't do anything stupid again to mess it up."

At this point in the session, I felt like I had gotten enough information about and "flavor" of this client to move forward to action. I shared with Megan that I thought she was depressed and would need to be treated for this regardless of whether she stayed on campus. I indicated that treatment would probably involve not only short-term solution-focused counseling but also a deeper look at some of the underlying issues relating to her relationship difficulties and lack of life direction as well as an evaluation for psychiatric medication. As a constructive-oriented therapist, I did not want to impose a plan on Megan; rather, I wanted to collaborate with her to develop something safe and workable, so I asked her how she felt we should proceed from this point forward. She shrugged and said, "I don't know. What do you think?" I looked at her and said, "Megan, this is your life. I have only just met you. Ultimately, I will have some power to help you make a short-term decision, but this decision and how you want to live your life are really in your hands. You must have at least some idea of what you want to do, even if you are worried about how to make it happen." Megan sighed, remained silent for a minute, and said that she really wanted to stay at school and that she did not want her parents to find out about the events of the previous night.

We then drew up a written plan that outlined the stipulations of Megan's remaining on campus. If Megan was to remain on campus, she would have to agree to twice weekly counseling appointments with full and honest disclosure, a psychiatric evaluation, and a safety plan that required her to contact either myself or the crisis center at the local community mental health facility (or call 911 if it was after hours or if she should not have the correct numbers with her), should she have any thoughts of hurting herself. If she was remiss in any of these obligations or if it appeared that she was in need of further support, her parents would have to be notified and consulted regarding her treatment plan and disposition. Of course, Megan would be involved in this notification as much as possible if it was needed,

to the point where she would hopefully make the first call. I also indicated that long-term treatment would probably involve family counseling at some point. Finally, I said that the dean of student life would need to know that Megan was in counseling and that he would be contacted if Megan did not fulfill her responsibilities.

Megan agreed to all of these stipulations and indicated that she would prefer receiving counseling and psychiatric services on campus. She also agreed to switch to my caseload, as I was on campus full-time and was more readily accessible in case of an emergency. In terms of the 12-session limit, I told her that we might be able to work around that but that we would seriously evaluate after a few sessions whether she would be better served here or off campus and would make a decision at that point.

Once this had been settled, I wanted to address the issue of the roommate. I asked Megan whether she felt as though living with her current roommate, Kendra, was a good idea. Megan once again expressed concern that Kendra would be blamed for having the medication available. I pointed out that although she was concerned about others being blamed, these were her actions, and portioning out blame was irrelevant. It was not her roommate's unspoken duty to safeguard her medication or to protect Megan from painful feelings or experiences, though it would be nice for the two of them to have a friendly relationship and good living arrangement.

Megan indicated that she liked her roommate and that she would like to stay with her in the same room if Kendra "wasn't too weirded out." I then requested Megan to call Kendra and ask her to talk with us about their living arrangement. Megan agreed and used her cell phone to call Kendra, who was just getting out of class. I told Megan that I would first want to talk with Kendra alone, as Megan had had the opportunity to talk about what she wanted to without worrying about offending others and I felt Kendra should be afforded the same right. Megan said she understood. As I did not have a traditional waiting room, being in a single office within the student life building, I called Mike and asked if he would take Megan to lunch while I spoke with Kendra and then bring her back so the four of us could work out the living arrangement.

Kendra was a pleasant, young African American woman. She immediately expressed concern about Megan and asked what she could do to help. I first indicated that this experience must have been scary for her, and I wanted to give her a chance to talk about what had happened and how she was feeling, if she was willing, before moving to Megan. Kendra's account of the incident was similar to what others had already been told me, and she expressed both guilt and apprehension about her involvement. I indicated that Megan's actions were certainly not caused by anything Kendra did or had and that everyone appreciated how quickly Kendra acted in getting help. I then said that Megan's plan was to stay on campus but that we were unsure regarding the exact living arrangement. I asked Kendra if she would be up to discussing the future or rooming with Megan and how she felt about it. Kendra said, "I like Megan, I really do...but I feel bad because I have my own life and I am never really around to hang out with her. Maybe she would be better off with someone else from out of state."

I then asked Kendra how she would feel if she were placed with another roommate, as it was November and unlikely that she would be able to go the whole year without being assigned another. Kendra sighed and said, "I don't care...but I really don't want anyone who is going to have a lot of issues, and Megan and I seem to get along." Finally, I told Kendra that one measure that would most likely have to be taken would be to lock up her medications in a cabinet to which only she had the key. She agreed to this and also said that she

would bring the postsurgery medicine back home, as she was no longer using it. Of course, I had to go on her word about this, but she appeared sincere and gave me no reason to doubt her truthfulness.

At this point, I asked Kendra if it was OK for me to invite Megan and Mike in and we would get this ironed out. She agreed. I also emphasized that what we had discussed regarding Megan was confidential and that it was important for her not to discuss it with anyone else. I asked her what she had said and what she might say to people who had heard about what happened. Kendra shrugged and said, "So far I've just said that Megan had to go to the hospital. I mean I told my mom and my boyfriend, but they won't spread it around." I validated this response and was pleased to hear that at this point the rumors hadn't started, and hopefully wouldn't start, to spread. I knew this was something else that I would have to be prepared to deal with.

The interaction among Megan, Mike, Kendra, and me was cordial, and it seemed that everyone was willing to work with each other. Kendra gave Megan a hug when she walked in and asked how she was feeling. Megan apologized to Kendra for going into her property and worrying her so. After this exchange, I presented the proposed living arrangement, to which everyone agreed. Mike said he would get a safe with a key in which Kendra could keep her medications. Megan denied having any of her own medications, including over-the-counter medications. We agreed that if she was to need any medication in the future, she would bring it to the health center and register it there. Megan and Kendra gave permission for Mike to do random checks for medication, and this became another stipulation in Megan's treatment contract.

Over the next few weeks, Megan upheld her agreement for the most part. She was a few minutes late to one session, and I was wondering if this would be it for her, but she rushed in and apologized, indicating that a professor had stopped her in the hall and wanted to talk with her about her paper. Our counseling centered at first on referring her to the on-campus consulting psychiatrist and exploring her feelings about depression as well as taking medication. She also had blood work done to ensure that no other condition, such as thyroid deficiency, was contributing to her current mood. Her medication did appear to "kick in" over the next month, as selective serotonin reuptake inhibitors take about three to four weeks to take effect, and she displayed a much higher level of energy. Fortunately, she and her sister had planned on staying at a local family friend's house for the Thanksgiving holiday, and she was not to see her parents until after the semester ended. She brought her sister, Lori, in for a few sessions, and Lori agreed to slowly back off of caretaking, especially socially, so Megan could find her own way. She also agreed to assist with Megan's treatment contract, particularly when school was out of session.

Another large focus of Megan's counseling was her relationship with her parents. It did appear that Megan had overreacted to her parents' threat to withdraw her, as that never materialized. Over the winter holiday break, Megan told her parents that she had been diagnosed with depression and was working with both a therapist and a psychiatrist. Her parents appeared a little suspicious as to whether Megan truly had a mental illness but said they were happy if it was helping her. They were also pleased to see that her grades were on an upswing. Megan and I discussed some of her past experiences with her family in an effort to provide a corrective emotional experience that would compensate for some of the emotional needs she felt were never fulfilled as well as to help her gain empathy regarding her parents' perspective and choices. By the end of the school year, she was talking to her parents more and said that their relationship seemed to be improving now that she was taking more

initiative to communicate with them. I pointed out that perhaps they saw her acting as more of an adult and therefore were more willing to treat her as such.

In terms of social, academic, and vocational goals, Megan did form a study group with some of the students in her introductory psychology class and socialized with some of them outside of school. She was interested in a young man living in her building, but he did not seem to feel the same way. This was a concern to me, as I remembered that dealing with rejection led to a previous para-suicide. However, she appeared to cope better and said, "I am starting to realize that it is OK if I don't get everything I want because something better may be out there for me." Academically, she was making more progress and expressed interest mainly in her psychology and anthropology courses. It appeared that she liked the social sciences and was encouraged to take a few more classes before she had to decide on her major. Megan also agreed to visit with her advisor and discuss career plans, as well as academic advising, with her.

CONCLUSION

In reading this case, it may seem that Megan made an amazing amount of progress in a short amount of time. However, that statement, while partly true, would also be an oversimplification. Though Megan did not engage in any further para-suicides, she still dealt with similar struggles, especially those related to self-confidence, self-care, and assertiveness. What made the major difference, in addition to the treatment for depression, was that she was able to have more patience and develop a healthier perspective for coping—using self-awareness, an understanding of the need to work with rather than denying or running away from emotions, cognitive restructuring, and proactive problem solving.

That being said, it took a good amount of time, and I sometimes wondered, particularly around holidays and other stressful times in the school year, whether we would need to revisit some of the alternative options to the treatment plan. I also took some time to read up on self-mutilation and was sometimes concerned that perhaps something in her past had affected her more than we realized. I expressed this concern to her, along with my clinical opinion that at this point, she seemed to be progressing without getting overly mired in the past. However, I also shared that this was simply my clinical stance, based mainly in an integrated existential and cognitive model of therapy, and may not be how other therapists would work with her. Megan said she understood this.

Megan finished her first year with an improved grade point average and attitude toward her own life. Of course, we talked a great deal about the summer and how to maintain those gains. Megan was planning to go home for the summer, and her sister was going overseas on a study-abroad program. She was concerned about being home with her parents without the normal buffering provided by Lori. She obtained a job at a local summer camp and took the phone numbers I had gotten for several counseling practitioners in her area.

Unfortunately, I moved that summer, and Megan had been made aware that I would not be back in the fall. I was disappointed that the next counseling director had not yet been hired, as I would have left in a more comfortable state if we could have done at least one transition session. I left a detailed termination summary and instructions for Lynn, who was staying on as a part-time counselor, to make the new director aware of Megan's situation and to look out for her when school started back up next fall. Megan consented to this and expressed appreciation and sadness at the termination of our relationship. I reminded her that this was only the beginning of her new approach to life's inevitable twists and turns and that I hoped

she would continue what she and I had worked on as a team. At this point, I am unaware of her disposition, but I hope that she has continued to make self-care a top priority.

Case Reflection Questions

Suicide Issue Questions

1. Would you have let Megan stay on campus as the clinician in this case did? What about your liability and reputation if the student had attempted suicide again?
2. How would you work to keep a student/client safe? It is widely thought that suicide safety contracts are valid only if there is a significant therapeutic relationship. How would you develop a suicide safety plan with a client? What components would you include?

Skill Builder Questions

1. How might you feel if you were counseling this suicidal client? What is your personal emotional reaction to this client's suicidal behavior?
2. What would you have done in order to ensure this suicidal client's safety? Utilizing the FED, described in Chapter 3, which indicates *frequency* of suicidal thoughts, *extent* of suicide plans, and *duration* of suicidal thoughts and impulses, indicate your assessment of this client's degree of danger to self. What would you have done to properly assess this client's immediate suicide risk?

3. What important suicide risk factors were present in the case? What unique individual factors or characteristics of this client would be important to your suicide risk assessment? As you read this case, which SAD PERSONS risk factors (sex, age, depression, previous attempt, ethanol abuse, rational thinking loss, social supports lacking, organized suicide plan, no spouse, and sickness) did you find most relevant to this case?
4. What would be your therapeutic approach to treating this suicidal client? What two pieces of information described within this case would be most helpful for your own work in intervening with potentially suicidal clients and their loved ones?
5. How would your approach be the same as or different from that of the clinician in the case? What interventions described in the case did you think were most helpful to the client?
6. How will you care for yourself when working with clients who are suicidal?
7. What strategies will you use to make sure you are competent and prepared to work with high-risk clients?

Wendy Charkow Bordeau, Ph.D., LPC currently teaches in the counseling program at Georgian Court University in Lakewood, NJ. She also works part-time as an child and adolescent therapist and has been a practicing counselor for eleven years.

Amanda

A Hispanic Woman with Relational Disconnection and Cultural Pain

THELMA DUFFEY

EDITORS' COMMENTS

- Although the author does not provide a full explanation of Relational-Cultural Theory, it is interesting to notice that her treatment of the suicidal client is grounded in a specific theoretical approach.
- The counselor in this case was sensitive to the client's cultural issues as well as her treatment issues.

INTRODUCTION

This case highlights the appropriate use of culturally sensitive theory, along with the importance of the quality therapeutic relationship in counseling.

BACKGROUND/REFERRAL

Amanda was 28 years old when she presented for therapy. She was a strikingly beautiful woman with curly, short, dark brown hair and expressive blue eyes. She was well groomed, poised, and articulate. Amanda was referred to me by her priest, from whom she had sought counsel days earlier. She described feelings that caused her shame. Specifically, she wanted to die. Smiling apologetically through her tears, Amanda described how she had experienced suicidal feelings throughout much of her life. However, Amanda quickly added that she had no intention of acting on her feelings. Half humorously, Amanda suggested that she would do the world a big favor if only she had the courage to take her own life. In the next breath, she worried that I would think she was "crazy" and reassured me that although she had these thoughts, she would never put herself in a position to suicide. She added:

> I am not going to hurt myself, and I feel ashamed even talking about this. But I'm here on the chance that I can do something about these feelings—these thoughts. Really, I love my life and the people in it. And I am proud of many of the things I have accomplished.

And I love my family more than anyone could ever know. I'm just haunted by this feeling of dread—of pain that washes over me sometimes—and when I feel it, all I want to do is die. And when I feel like this, I can't help but think that my family would be so much better off, once they adjusted to the situation.

ASSESSMENT

I sat with Amanda and told her I was glad she had come. We exchanged smiles. I left my writing pad on the floor got comfortable in my chair, and simply said, "Amanda, I'd love to hear more about you—about your family—about the things you enjoy—about anything you'd like to tell me." I wanted to learn about her from *her* perspective. I also wanted her to feel comfortable telling her story. In her words:

I come from a very supportive family. My parents are wonderful and my brother and sister are, too. I am the oldest. My brother, Eddie, is 18 months younger than I am, and my sister, Bertita, is three years younger than me. Eddie is outgoing, funny, and smart. He can fix anything you put in front of him. When we were little and a telephone would break, he would take it apart and try to fix it. And sometimes he did! And Bertita, well, she is the cutest, funniest thing you've ever seen. You can't be around her without laughing.

Amanda continued:

My parents are great. My dad is self-made. He worked so hard all of our lives to give us everything he could. He owns a small business selling textiles, and I am so proud of him. My mother is wonderful. She, too, has worked very hard and has helped my father in his business. She does the books. I am amazed at how good she is with numbers. And she has such a knack for a good look. His building is small, but, boy, is it beautiful! You would think you were walking into a New York store, except it is warm and friendly, and it feels good.

Amanda's mood shifted as she described her family. She appeared genuinely proud of and connected to them. I commented on how her face brightened when she talked about her family. She laughed and said, "Yes, they're great." Then she added somberly, "They would be horrified if they knew I was here—feeling the way I do. They wouldn't know what to think. I don't even know what to think."

Wanting to see the degree of authentic sharing she had with her family, I asked, "Does anyone in your family know how hurt you can feel and how hard things can be for you?" Taken aback by this question, she shook her head. According to Amanda, she couldn't tell them. It would hurt them too much. Amanda would appear ungrateful, and they might see her differently. She did not want things to change in her relationships with them. She liked things as they were. They weren't the ones with the problem—she was. Telling them about her shame and suicidal feelings would only make them her family's problems, too.

In this session, several things became clear to me. Amanda was very bright, motivated, and successful. She appeared to have friends and family whom she loved. She was single and appeared to be comfortable with her single status. Amanda had two degrees and was embarking on an exciting career. At the same time, Amanda could not identify the source of

shame and guilt that seemed to permeate her being, and she felt badly enough about herself that she thought the world would be better off without her.

Amanda had consulted with a psychiatrist twice and had tried various antidepressants without success. She was no longer interested in taking medications and was instead looking for more intrapsychic forms of healing. She did not feel her problems were simply chemical, although depressive symptoms were certainly at play. Rather, she felt that overcoming her utter sense of worthlessness, even in the face of so much contradictory evidence, was her greatest challenge.

Key Suicide Risk Assessment Factors

In making a suicide risk assessment, one of the factors I assess is relational support. Whom does my client identify as "safe to talk to?" How much isolation is she feeling? Is there someone who can give context to her feelings and serve as a mirror for her experience, someone with whom she shares a reciprocal experience? Relational-Cultural Theory (RCT) posits that growth-fostering relationships are essential to psychological development and that the source of our psychological problems is chronic disconnections (Jordan, 2001). In contrast to traditional models of development that identify separation, independence, and autonomy as hallmarks of psychological development, RCT suggests that human development involves growth through mutually empowering relationships (Jordan, 2001).

With that context in mind, I asked Amanda if she had close friends. Amanda nodded and described how she had always had good friends. In fact, she had one friend living in another town who had been part of her life since first grade. With this, I asked Amanda whether her friends knew how badly she could feel about herself and about her thoughts of self-harm. She reported that some friends knew of her suicidal feelings. However, she also reported that she felt uneasy speaking to friends about her suicidal feelings and therefore rarely talked about the topic. Interestingly, Amanda added that some of her friends had also shared their past suicidal feelings. With that, I felt relieved that Amanda indeed had an outlet for her feelings and a place where she could be herself, and we proceeded.

However, in the next breath, Amanda described a friendship where her self-disclosure had backfired. According to Amanda, her friend knew "too much" about Amanda's emotional challenges and used the information in ways that hurt Amanda professionally. Amanda regretted the way she had "let her guard down" and had become so vulnerable. Given that this was the first negative experience she discussed, I wanted to hear more. Perhaps it could shed light on Amanda's situation.

A Relational Betrayal

Amanda described how her friend Julie was fun, supportive, and charming. Julie liked to "live on the edge" and would entrust the details to Amanda. Even though Amanda recognized a number of red flags early on, something inside her drew her toward the friendship. She genuinely loved her friend and liked her colorful nature. Julie could say things Amanda could only think. At the same time, Amanda was conflicted when Julie would behave toward others in insensitive, duplicitous ways. Julie's competitiveness scared Amanda, and Julie did not like admitting she was wrong. Still, like a moth attracted to a flame, Amanda pursued the friendship, a friendship that over time Amanda grew to fear. Just recently,

Amanda had learned that Julie had talked negatively about her to someone in a position of power. Amanda believed Julie's negative conversation about Amanda had resulted in at least one promotion loss.

By her account, Amanda tried to address her concerns with Julie, but Julie would not participate. According to Amanda, Julie remained quiet, deflected responsibility, and refused to discuss the situation. Further, Amanda described how Julie turned the situation around and blamed Amanda. In time, Amanda came to see that she had invested in a high-risk relationship, one that reinforced her belief that she needed to self-protect, pull back, and hide aspects of herself. This, in turn, created more isolation. Amanda's feeling of isolation was at a peak when she came to see me.

RCT discusses the role of the *central relational paradox*, which people experience in their relationships (Jordan, 2001; Miller & Stiver, 1997). On one hand, we have a yearning for connection, and on the other, we leave important aspects of ourselves out of the relationship, precluding the opportunity for authentic relating. This paradox results in what relational-cultural theorists refer to as *condemned isolation* (Miller & Stiver, 1997, p. 72). Such experiences are not uncommon in relationships where there are ambivalent power differentials or where a lack of safety exists. In this case, it appeared that Amanda's need to hide her vulnerability, combined with her deep feelings of unworthiness, generated feelings of isolation and shame, contributing to her intermittent desire to die. Further, in experiencing betrayal, she became increasingly unwilling to risk exposing herself relationally. This was an important counseling consideration in my work with Amanda.

Beyond the relational issues, I listened for other important points and discovered that Amanda did not drink or use drugs; alcohol consumption had not been part of Amanda's family life, and she had never developed a taste for alcohol. Concomitantly, Amanda reported that no one in her family had ever committed suicide and that she had no firsthand experience with anyone who had. These were all good risk-assessment signs. However, her family had experienced a fair amount of grief following some family deaths, and she recalled feeling lonely and helpless during those times. It appeared that Amanda was used to feeling lonely; in fact, her state of loneliness had become internalized and chronic regardless of the good things that life brought her.

I also learned that Amanda was an overachiever and seemed to have little tolerance when she fell short of her anticipated goal. Amanda felt a deep allegiance to her family and felt responsible for being the best person she could be, given their trust and faith in her. Amanda grew up in the Catholic faith. In spite of the comfort she gained from her religion, she also learned to fear God and her own sinfulness. Amanda's impressions of what a "good person" looks like and her own self-perception as a "sinful" person seemed to exacerbate her pejorative feelings about herself.

I learned in this session of Amanda's idealized "death wish." When I asked her if she had ever fantasized about how she would die, she again replied that she would not actually hurt herself. However, she conceded that she did receive some relief from the idea that she would have the option to suicide if she chose to. Specifically, that option involved driving her car into a construction wall on an isolated highway. Amanda acknowledged that at times she would "cry so hard that the only thing I could think of is driving into that construction wall." Although she didn't have a "plan," she certainly had an "idea" about how she could suicide.

I asked Amanda to recall times when all she could think of was driving into the wall and then made the choice not to proceed. Her response was comforting. As much as the

"idea" of suicide seemed consoling, the idea of "executing" that suicide, of following through on her decision, brought her horror. "I couldn't do it," she whispered, adding, "I would hurt everyone. I would take away my last option to make whatever feels wrong with me feel better. And I would die and be remembered as someone who was reckless, someone who committed suicide. I couldn't live with that. It would all be too horrible." Amanda's faith and her fear that she would experience eternal damnation for committing suicide were also strong suicide deterrents.

At this point, I was comfortable proceeding with some more-formal suicide assessment questions. I asked Amanda: "On a scale of 1 to 5, with 5 being the highest number, how likely is it that you would suicide?" She replied, "2." Given that she had emphatically stated that she would never take her life, this gave me pause. Then I asked: "On a scale of 1 to 5, with 5 being the highest number, how likely would it be that you would have to live with these feelings the rest of your life?" Amanda replied, "2." Again, this was interesting because Amanda had previously indicated hopelessness about transcending these feelings.

Without a doubt, Amanda was clearly hard on herself. She had been a successful student as a child and grew into a successful adult. People with depression often describe symptoms that include problems with sleeping and eating, whereas Amanda did not. Her moods did not fluctuate often, and she did not necessarily feel pessimistic about her future. However, she clearly experienced feelings of worthlessness. And at times, she felt hopeless that things would change. During these times, Amanda would literally crawl into her closet, sit on the floor, and wish to die.

Amanda clearly suffered from suicidal ideations, but her suicide risk was not imminent. Although I continued to monitor her suicidal fantasies, my focus shifted to helping her address her self-loathing feelings through the therapeutic relationship; I also helped Amanda learn how to invest in mutually empathic relationships. My hope was to help her find more-constructive, self-supportive ways of managing her pain—while deepening her capacity for self-empathy.

TREATMENT

RCT does not speak in terms of "interventions" but rather describes relational conditions that must be present for genuine healing to manifest. For that reason, I chose to conceptualize the work Amanda and I did together in that context. According to RCT, all have yearned for connection. Yet, at times, all engage in disconnecting behaviors that keep us apart from the very connection we desire (Jordan, 2001). RCT describes the basic need for authentic relating and the consequences of hiding aspects of ourselves so we can make ourselves "acceptable" to others. In this case, Amanda was hiding important aspects of herself—important experiences—from her family—those she loved most. I had to wonder how isolating that hiding experience must be.

How was it that someone who described such a loving family could not allow herself to show her vulnerability? What were her fears? What did she see in herself that she felt compelled to hide? What experiences caused her to feel safer in silence? Finally, I asked myself what made her think the world would be better off without her.

From Amanda's account, thinking about suicide gave her "relief," yet the thought of executing a suicide plan appeared to both frighten and repulse her. Clearly, we had to work on alternate ways for Amanda to find relief. We had to identify and address the factors that caused her feelings of shame, guilt, and worthlessness.

Internalized Shame

Interestingly, one of Amanda's greatest sources of shame was the disparaging comments she heard about her ethnicity. Amanda carried memories of being "singled out" as different. Although some of Amanda's early childhood memories regarding her Hispanic ethnicity were uncomfortable, her more poignant and distressing memories revolved around being negatively labeled and tokenized at work. Amanda was very proud of her heritage. In fact, she cherished many ethnic-related values that had been passed down via her family and cultural community. However, she resented being the "resident Hispanic" in the larger community. She wanted to be seen as a competent and able professional who attained her advancement based on her merit and worth. She even wondered if Julie's interest in her stemmed more from a sense of curiosity about Amanda being Hispanic than from an interest in her as a person. Regardless of what Amanda believed Julie's intentions to be, Amanda felt small in relation to her friend. Julie's incessant discussions about *differences* added to Amanda's feelings. However, most distressing to Amanda were the societal stereotypes she encountered around the idea of *who Hispanics are*. In her words,

> Any time you hear about someone being Hispanic . . . they are poor; on drugs; in need of help. If you don't fit that mold, you're an exception. That doesn't feel good to me. Even well-meaning people can feel patronizing to me. It's easy to feel that, regardless of how much you do, you just aren't going to fit in.

Amanda had internalized shame surrounding the denigrating cultural images she had encountered, and she appeared conflicted about her "right" to her feelings or her experiences. Ruiz (2005, p. 33) described the importance of providing "culturally relevant [mental health] services" to the increasing U.S. Hispanic population. RCT offers this possibility by speaking to the experiences of people from diverse environments (Jordan, 1997; Jordan, Kaplan, Miller, Stiver, & Surrey, 1991). Thus, I used RCT in my work with Amanda.

Internalized Judgment

Amanda also had ambivalent feelings about some Catholic Church teachings. She described a deep love for God. At the same time, she felt completely inadequate to attain God's expectations. When asked to describe some things that could cause her worry, Amanda could not easily identify them. In learning Amanda's concerns, I wondered if her fears contributed to her feelings of confusion and shame. She described herself as being "the little girl proud to wear her beanie in chapel." She had tried to follow church rules and mandates. However, she never reached a place where she could feel good about herself and wondered whether she would ever reach that threshold, and if she did, whether she would, in fact, be sinfully "prideful."

Even Amanda's dreams haunted her. In one dream, Amanda was sitting on a bathroom toilet. The bathroom door swung open and a chorus of people, draped in black, taunted her: "Tell us, who is going to go to hell? WHO? WHO? WHO?" Then they cried out even louder: "YOU, YOU, YOU!" This dream, and others, haunted Amanda and reflected the very punishing internal messages she appeared to experience. Amanda had never committed any extraordinarily egregious behavior that would warrant such punishing unconscious afflictions. Still, she had a very strong superego, and in RCT terms, her relational images were such that she anticipated that others would not value her. Thus, clearly it was difficult for her

to value herself. More important, it became clear that there were times when Amanda felt deplorable.

In addition to these feelings of deplorability, stigmatization, and shame, Amanda described feeling that she lacked belonging. Specifically, she felt "too sensitive" and "helpless." Amanda was a "take-charge" person who "couldn't" tell others when she had reached her limit. In addition, she suffered from extreme perfectionism and was unduly self-critical. Many of these characteristics are commonly experienced by gifted individuals who have not yet learned that even they have limitations (Silverman & Conarton, 2005). And after getting to know Amanda, I found this to be true in her case. Keeping the challenges of the gifted in mind, in addition to the internal criticisms she reported and her relational disconnections and internalized cultural shame, we embarked on our work together.

We began with Amanda's belief that she would create problems if she told family members about her struggles. To assess her isolation level, I stated, "I understand how you wouldn't want to hurt your family." She nodded. And I continued, "Yet, I wonder what it would feel like to you if one of your family members was hurting and you didn't have the opportunity to help." She looked uncomfortable and replied that she wouldn't like it. After a moment, I said, "You seem to be in a difficult bind here. On one hand, you feel badly and want to protect your family. On the other, hiding how you feel has a cost for them and you, too." She nodded.

In treating women's pain, RCT addresses the impact that chronic disconnections can have on a person's psychological functioning (Jordan, 2001; Miller & Stiver, 1997). Apparently, Amanda's difficulty in authentically sharing herself with others created chronic disconnections. The societal messages she had internalized and her own critical self-talk made it very difficult for her to be genuine, vulnerable, and real in her relationships. Like all of us, her identity was formed through various contexts. RCT posits that each person carries multiple social and cultural identities, including race, class, gender, and spirituality (Walker, 1999). However, Amanda had not considered or put words to the diverse contexts that had influenced her worldview and shaped her identity. Thus, addressing these and finding meaning in them became an important therapeutic goal.

According to RCT, people in the American culture are seen hierarchically: dominant versus subordinate; better than versus less than (Walker, 1999). Amanda clearly identified with the subordinate, "less than" position. Given the messages she internalized, she also experienced shame. Differences among people are stratified, and it is these stratifications, not the differences, that limit our capacity for authenticity and weaken our inclination toward connection (Walker, 1999).

Furthermore, given that feelings of chronic disconnection has a deleterious impact on suicidal thought and the relationship of cultural contexts that engender those feelings of disconnection (Walker, 1999), I was interested to learn more about Amanda's cultural contexts. However, rather than asking her to describe herself culturally, I simply asked her to describe her life. I wanted to know the people in her life and the influences they had. It was in that context that I learned more about Amanda's pain and the shame she carried.

From Amanda, I learned how her family was close, Hispanic, and accomplished. She had an active social life but often felt like a fraud. She would often leave social situations relieved and ready to go home. Like her parents, she entered the business world and worked for a large corporation. However, she often retreated to her office and did not easily enjoy the camaraderie. Experiences such as those with Julie reinforced feelings of fear and isolation. Amanda preferred feelings of loneliness to those of vulnerability. Amanda conceded that her feelings of dread became particularly acute when she felt vulnerable.

In session, once Amanda began to speak, it was difficult for her stop. She told her stories and then monitored my responses to see whether it was safe to continue. I would respond by clarifying what I understood her experience to be and giving voice to her pain. When I was moved by her experience, I would say so. Then I would make reference to her resiliency and her courage to speak about these hurtful experiences.

Therapeutic Movement

As part of our therapy, we made distinctions between feeling responsible for actions that do not feel good and assuming responsibility for things we cannot control. We used the term *toxic guilt* to describe the bad feelings we assume—feelings that are incongruent with the facts. Some of our work involved helping Amanda distinguish the experiences of humility and accomplishment from the more self-serving expressions of pride and self-promotion. Working through these issues created a new healthy experience for Amanda. When Amanda eventually came to therapy without apologizing for what she had to say, I suspected she was incorporating these messages into our relationship. My hope was that her therapeutic and relational movement would be reinforced in other relationships.

Additionally, given the fact that the Hispanic culture and the Roman Catholic Church promote great respect for authority and given the way Amanda internalized and interpreted messages from both contexts, it was important that she understand how she "gifted" some authority figures with her trust. Conflict arose, as was the case with Julie and Amanda's supervisor; Amanda could not assume that *she* bore exclusive responsibility. In our work, we helped her find context for some of her feelings and expanded the possibilities for these new experiences.

Amanda began a journal, brought childhood pictures, and made a collage of her various life experiences. She wept at the denigrating ways she had viewed herself and felt compassion for the little girl that even *she* had only recently begun to support.

Amanda's suicidal ideations did not abruptly stop. From time to time, she would sheepishly apologize because she had had a "spell." However, she remained physically safe, her friendship base grew, and through her friendships, she began to experience mutually empowering relationships in which she could authentically represent herself. Although Amanda was slow to trust, we framed this reservation as a positive quality and discussed how in time relationships grow. Our hope was that she would provide enough relational space for a budding relationship, where trust could potentially unfold. Moreover, our hope was that she would no longer be haunted by her death wish. And in time, this happened.

CONCLUSION

I selected RCT for my work with Amanda because it is designed to avoid inadvertently misdiagnosing, stigmatizing, and mistreating clients. Some therapeutic perspectives would pathologize Amanda in ways that disconnect and feed shame. No doubt, Amanda would be first in line to read the *DSM–IV* and self-diagnose the most preposterous diagnoses. Further, as she was acutely "in tune" with how others perceived her, a therapist whose frame was pathology based could support the already hurtful self-images she carried.

However, by creating a space where Amanda could simply relax her critical voice, she was able to see how her loneliness and fears of being defective were instead the culprits. As she was able to see how "hiding" herself contributed to her hurt, she was able to increasingly take risks with people who appeared to be relationally compatible. Rather than continuing to seek rebellious and exciting friends, she became drawn to steady, fun-loving, and supportive

ones. And although she remained faithful to her church, she filtered messages through her healthier self-perception. She worked hard to believe that her God was as loving as He was just. And, most important, she began to learn about the meaning of grace.

Culturally, she examined how the value of *respeto* (Forst & Lehman, 1997; Garcia-Prieto, 1996; Ruiz, 2005), being respected by and respectful of others, had been confusing, particularly in relation to authority figures. This value, common in Hispanic culture, holds that people—and authority figures, in particular—have a person's best interest at heart. Regrettably, this is not always the case. Working through these experiences and coming to terms with them helped silence her critical inner voice. We examined her family—especially the hero position she often assumed. And although she continued to carry some societal pain over ethnic stigmatization, Amanda developed a strength base that helped her reframe the messages.

Amanda carried long-held suicidal ideation and shame. However, by looking at relational and cultural aspects and experiencing growth-fostering relationships that supported a more realistic self-appraisal, she was able to release the pain she had long carried. In this case, Amanda's relational disconnections, cultural stigmatization, religious interpretation, and apparent giftedness were all factors that we mutually explored. Amanda grew to recognize that she had a propensity to experience feelings of extreme dread. Now she also carries an appreciation for life and the people who genuinely love her. One of her favorite quotes is from Ernest Hemingway's *A Farewell to Arms* (1929): "The world breaks everyone, and afterward many are strong at the broken places." These words bring Amanda comfort—and more often than not, inner strength.

Case Reflection Questions

Suicide Issue Questions

1. Perfectionism can be a significant factor in suicidality. How does Amanda's need to appear perfect for her family and friends contribute to her feelings of loneliness and isolation?
2. What strengths of the client did the counselor use to help the client cope with her suicidal ideation? Would you have capitalized on these strengths in a different way?

Skill Builder Questions

1. How might you feel if you were counseling this suicidal client? What is your personal emotional reaction to this client's suicidal behavior?
2. What would you have done in order to ensure this suicidal client's safety? Utilizing the FED, described in Chapter 3, which indicates *frequency* of suicidal thoughts, *extent* of suicide plans, and *duration* of suicidal thoughts and impulses, indicate your assessment of this client's degree of danger to self. What would you have done to properly assess this client's immediate suicide risk?

3. What important suicide risk factors were present in the case? What unique individual factors or characteristics of this client would be important to your suicide risk assessment? As you read this case, which SAD PERSONS risk factors (sex, age, depression, previous attempt, ethanol abuse, rational thinking loss, social supports lacking, organized suicide plan, no spouse, and sickness) did you find most relevant to this case?
4. What would be your therapeutic approach to treating this suicidal client? What two pieces of information described within this case would be most helpful for your own work in intervening with potentially suicidal clients and their loved ones?
5. How would your approach be the same as or different from that of the clinician in the case? What interventions described in the case did you think were most helpful to the client?
6. How will you care for yourself when working with clients who are suicidal?
7. What strategies will you use to make sure you are competent and prepared to work with high-risk clients?

Dr. Thelma Duffey is a Profesor of Counselor Education at The University of Texas at San Antonio.

References

Forst, J. K., & Lehman, W. E. K. (1997). Ethnic differences in the workplace environment by employees in two municipal workforces. *Hispanic Journal of Behavioral Sciences, 19*, 84–96.

Garcia-Prieto, N. (1996). Latino families: An overview. In M. McGoldrick, J. Giordano, & J. K. Pearce (Eds.), *Ethnicity and family therapy* (pp. 141–154). New York: Guilford.

Hemingway, E. (1929). *A farewell to arms*. New York: Charles Scribner's Sons.

Jordan, J. V. (Ed.). (1997). *Women's growth in diversity: More writings from the Stone Center*. New York: Guilford.

Jordan, J. V. (2001). A relational-cultural model: Healing through mutual empathy. *Bulletin of the Menninger Clinic, 65*(1), 92–103.

Jordan, J. V., Kaplan, A. G., Miller, J. B., Stiver, I. P., & Surrey, J. L. (1991). *Women's growth in connection: Writings from the Stone Center*. New York: Guilford.

Miller, J. B., & Stiver, I. P. (1997). *The healing connection: How women form relationships in therapy and in life*. Boston: Beacon Press.

Ruiz, E. (2005). Hispanic culture and the Relational Cultural Theory. *Journal of Creativity in Mental Health, 1*(1), 33–55.

Silverman, L. K., & Conarton, S. A. (2005). Gifted development: It's not easy being green. In D. Comstock (Ed.), *Diversity and development* (pp. 233–251). Belmont, CA: Brooks/Cole.

Walker, M. (1999). *Race, self, and society: Relational challenges in a culture of disconnection* (Work in Progress No. 85). Wellesley, MA: Stone Center, Wellesley College.

Walker, M., & Miller, J. B. (2000). *Racial images and relational possibilities* (Talking Paper No. 2). Wellesley, MA: Stone Center, Wellesley College.

John

A Completed Suicide in an Outpatient Addiction Treatment Program

M. F. Sunich

EDITORS' COMMENTS

- This case illustrates the complexity of working with a dually diagnosed client.
- The counselor in this case must cope with his own feelings of loss and remorse concerning his client.

INTRODUCTION

It is Tuesday night. While retrieving my messages prior to leaving the office after a three-hour, intensive outpatient addictions group session, I hoped that I would hear only the usual excuses for canceling. Joe left a message stating that his car had broken down and that he would be in tomorrow. My wife called, reminding me to pick up whatever, whatever.... In the next message, John's wife, Jill, sounded very frantic and angry, urgently requesting that I keep John at the office after group and call her immediately. Considering that John had just pulled out of the parking lot following what seemed to be a rather shaky second session for him in group, I returned Jill's call.

As the phone rang, I reflected on John's behavior in group. He appeared superficially engaged, tentative, and preoccupied. He had been invited to share but declined, stating that he was still having some alcohol and cocaine withdrawal. He thanked the group members for their concern and support and assured us that he would open up when he felt a little more comfortable. My hunch was that his reported withdrawals were an excuse, but I chose not to confront him further, as this was only his second session and others had issues to process. Thus began a seemingly endless series of questions that I would ask myself regarding my professional judgment.

Jill answered the phone. Expecting to hear about how she had found his drug stash or other evidence that he was still using, I listened intently as she described an emerging crisis that would move me personally and professionally in an unanticipated and unwanted direction.

Jill informed me that her 16-year-old daughter, Sally, had disclosed to her that she had been having sexual intercourse with her father, John, for the past four months. She also indicated that sexual activity had been occurring between John and Sally's best friend. Jill could barely contain her rage. She stated that she had immediately called her minister and that her minister had already notified Child Protective Services, which would conduct an investigation of the allegations. According to Jill, John would be confronted as soon as he arrived home. I asked that she page me (this was in pre–cell phone days) after they confronted John and also gave her a time to come in the following morning to process her options.

BACKGROUND/REFERRAL

John was born and raised in a large, southeastern city. Both his parents were educated, upper-middle-class professionals. He was the first-born of three children and described his relationships with his siblings as highly competitive; he was always striving for the favored position based on academic achievement and social popularity. He described himself as an honor roll student throughout elementary school but said that he began struggling in high school. He was socially involved, played team sports, and had many girlfriends; he described his early high school years as relatively easy.

He began drinking alcohol on weekends with his friends at age 13 and also began using marijuana occasionally. He stated that his use remained recreational until about age 16, when he began smoking marijuana on weeknights and occasionally during the school-day. His drinking remained limited to weekends, at parties or at sporting events with his friends. At age 17, at the beginning of his senior year, he was arrested and charged with driving under the influence of alcohol. His parents intervened with the legal system, and the charges were reduced to reckless driving. He was not recommended for counseling. He stated that his parents began monitoring him more closely and began enforcing curfews and house rules.

John's drinking and marijuana use escalated to the point of frequent intoxications on the weekends, periods of blackouts, loss of control, and alcohol preoccupation and cravings. Toward the end of his senior year, he was no longer able to perform academically, and his grades plummeted. His use continued to increase, and he began having blackouts during the week, drinking alcohol in the morning, and remaining under the influence throughout the day. His parents intervened again, and he was referred to an outpatient counselor who diagnosed John as depressed. John began weekly therapy sessions to address his depression, but his drinking and marijuana use were left unaddressed.

Shortly after graduating from high school with a C-average, John was involved in a single-car accident when he lost control of his vehicle and went head-on into a tree. He was intoxicated and not wearing a seat belt. He was treated at a local emergency room and hospitalized with a closed-head injury, severe lacerations to his face, and a fractured collarbone. His blood alcohol level was .23. He was charged with driving under the influence, underage drinking, and reckless driving. His parents assisted him in having the charges reduced to reckless driving and underage drinking, and he was ordered by the court to complete an alcohol education program. He completed an eight-session program and continued to drink and use marijuana but stated that he was able to control the amount and frequency, using to excess only on weekends.

John began attending a local community college and eventually transferred to a large state university, where he completed a bachelor's degree in business. He was then hired into

a sales position with a large insurance provider. He quickly rose in the company's ranks and was managing a large sales district within three years. He stated that he continued to drink and use marijuana and saw this as essential to his business success. He also described himself as experiencing long periods of dysphoria, wondering why he wasn't happier with his accomplishments. He described his life as meaningless and empty. Although his parents were very pleased with his financial success and strong work ethic, John still felt as though he was an imposter. He continued to feel inferior to his younger brother, who was engaged, and his younger sister, who was excelling in her undergraduate premed studies.

After many brief romantic relationships, several of which terminated due to his drinking and drug use, John married Jill at age 27. He soon discovered that he was biologically incapable of having children. At age 29, John and Jill adopted a three-year-old daughter, Sally. John stated that his relationship with Jill changed immediately. He worked more hours, felt excluded from the mother-daughter relationship, and started feeling empty, bitter, and resentful. He would ruminate about ending his life and how this would affect his wife and child but stated that he never really considered suicide. John continued to drink and smoke marijuana on a daily basis but stated that he was in control during these years. He continued to function occupationally while his marriage slowly unraveled.

At age 40, John was introduced to cocaine while at a bar with his close friend and coworker. He immediately began using regularly, claiming that the "boost" helped him work more efficiently and productively. Jill began confronting John about his excessive use and continued impairment. The couple's sexual relationship came to halt shortly after John began using cocaine. Jill finally gave John an ultimatum—either get treatment or get divorced. John agreed to seek outpatient therapy. He was assessed for appropriateness for intensive outpatient therapy and enrolled in a structured program at our office. He was also seen by Dr. K., a psychiatrist, who prescribed antidepressant medication.

Key Suicide Risk Factors

During the initial assessment on Friday, John was provided time to discuss his current situation. He stated that he felt as though his wife was overacting to his drug use and that he was not as impaired as she claimed. He said that his marriage was "loveless," that their sexual relationship had ceased some time ago, and that he felt as though she was using him for a paycheck. He also indicated that he did not trust his close friend and business associate, Alan, stating that he was suspicious of Alan's feelings for his wife.

John went on to talk about his relationship with his daughter, indicating that he spent much of his time talking to her about his work and her friends. He said that he enjoyed the fact that she took interest in him and that they had become much closer over the past two years. When queried, John denied any inappropriate sexual behavior, stating that, given Jill's disinterest in him physically, he had resigned himself to the idea of not having sex.

John agreed that discontinuing his drug and alcohol use would be a good idea if that was what it would take to get his marriage back on track. He claimed to have stopped all drug use one week prior to the assessment and was able to commit to remaining abstinent from alcohol while in treatment.

An interview with Jill on the same day revealed that she had been confronting John for years about his substance abuse. She stated that, while John continued to claim that he worked more efficiently when using, he actually had begun missing appointments, getting up late, and staying out late on a regular basis. She stated that their communication had

deteriorated to the point of barely saying hello to each other and that she was concerned about whether she could remain married to John if he continued using. She voiced concern about his mood; he seemed down much of the time except when he was interacting with their daughter on the weekends. She had asked John to begin sleeping in the spare bedroom several months ago and was surprised when John agreed. Jill stated, "Something is wrong in our family, and I hope it gets right when he's sober."

Jill went on to say that John's coworker and best friend, Alan, had been very concerned about John and had been Jill's emotional support for some time. Jill claimed that she did not discuss John's condition with other family members or friends and that, with the exception of Alan, she felt alone in dealing with this situation.

Jill also mentioned that she had noticed that their daughter, Sally, had become more attached and attentive to John over the past month or so and that Sally spent a great deal of time defending John when they argued over his substance use. Jill claimed that her relationship with Sally was strained and becoming more distant. I explained how our Family Group worked on Sundays and asked that she commit to attending. Jill was eager to get involved and also agreed to attend weekly Al-Anon meetings.

ASSESSMENT

At the time of evaluation, John was a 42-year-old, married Caucasian male of average height and stature. His Mental Status indicated he was oriented to all spheres and did not present any disturbances of thought. His speech was of normal rate and rhythm, his sensorium was clear, and his thought process was logical and goal directed. His mood was rather dysphoric, and his affect was mood congruent and appropriate to his situation. His sleep was impaired with early insomnia, and his appetite was good. No changes in energy level were noted. He denied suicidal or homicidal ideation, hallucinations, or bizarre occurrences, and no delusional systems were noted. His immediate memory and his recent memory were intact, as he recited four of four objects and was able to recall four of four objects after a 10-minute delay. His concentration was disturbed as he struggled with serial threes, and he made one error in reciting the days of the week backward. He demonstrated poor insight into his situation and poor judgment with regard to initiating treatment. His motivation appeared dependent on his wife's prompting, and his prognosis remained highly guarded.

Diagnostically, John clearly met criteria for Alcohol Dependence, Marijuana Dependence, Cocaine Abuse, and Dysthymia secondary to polysubstance abuse. With many chemically dependent persons, depressive symptomatology often clears with abstinence and recovery. John agreed that he was chemically dependent and eventually stated that he had wanted to quit for some time but was not sure if he could. His greatest fear was that he would not be able to excel in his sales position without drugs.

As a routine part of the initial assessment, the SAD PERSONS Scale (Patterson, Dohn, Bird, & Patterson, 1983) was administered to assess suicide potential. SAD PERSONS is an acronym for the 10 literature-related suicide risk factors that the scale assesses (see Chapter 3). Each factor positively scored earns one point, and the scale provides score-dependent intervention guidelines. In John's case, he scored positively on sex, depression, previous attempt, and ethanol abuse. His single-car accident was considered a previous attempt. Although John did not acknowledge this as a suicide attempt, the fact that he had been drinking, was not wearing a seat belt, and had hit a tree head-on sounded like an impulsive suicidal gesture. While John denied any suicidal ideation or plan at that time, experience has shown that

alcoholics ruminate about ending their lives and that single-car crashes are often how they fantasize accomplishing this. With a score of four, John was not seen as an immediate threat for suicide.

Given that he denied an organized plan and demonstrated rational, logical thinking, he was encouraged to remain in the outpatient treatment sessions and continue seeing me individually on a weekly basis for the first eight weeks. John was in full agreement with this plan and agreed to begin attending the group the following Monday.

The Crisis

John arrived home after Tuesday's group and walked into a tsunami. As Jill described the situation to me at a later date, John appeared to know immediately what was taking place. Their minister was there, looking somber and concerned; Jill was outraged and barely able to contain her aggression; Sally was crying uncontrollably, saying that she was sorry that she caused so many problems; and Alan was stating that, whatever the problem, they could get through this. John was confronted with allegations that he had been having sex with Sally for the past two months and that, at times, he, Sally, and Sally's friend were getting high together and having sex. According to Jill, John broke down and admitted to the accusations, exhibiting great shame and remorse.

Jill paged me at that time, and I returned the call. After hearing a recount of the events prior to the call, I spoke with John. He was weeping, having difficulty talking, and yet expressing remorse and a great deal of fear for what was about to occur as a consequence of his actions. I tried to reassure him that the most important thing at this time was to get through this brief period, to keep his focus on the present. John was eventually able to contain himself and began speaking rationally of how he was going to deal with this situation.

Alan had agreed to stay with John through the night in an effort to support him and help him remain sober. Jill and Sally decided to stay with Jill's mother. Considering the issue at hand, Jill thought that it was about time to open up to her mother about John's substance abuse and their deteriorating marriage.

A brief mental status exam of John over the phone suggested that he was extremely distraught and fearful, yet rational in that he was planning how he was going to make it through the night without drinking and saying how he needed additional support from me, Alan, and his group. John agreed that he would see me the first thing the following morning, Wednesday, and that we would discuss how he was going to tell his group about his situation and ask the members for support.

After speaking with John, I spoke with Alan, who had agreed to spend the night with John. Alan stated that he was horrified and shocked that this had been occurring and at first wondered if Sally had been making up this story for attention. He stated that when John admitted to the accusations, he knew that John would need support and a good friend. Alan stated that he would remain with John that night and would accompany him to his session the following morning. Alan stated that as far as he knew, all of the alcohol had been removed from the house. I discussed with Alan the possibility that John might attempt to suicide, considering his current emotional state. Although John denied any current suicidal ideation or plan, the tendency to lose rational thinking when under the influence of alcohol increased the likelihood of an irrational, impulsive decision. Alan assured me that he would be in the same room with John throughout the night. Alan also agreed that if the situation got out of control, he would call the police for an involuntary commitment and page me immediately.

Jill and Sally had already left by this time. I spoke with the minister, who expressed great sorrow and sympathy. He indicated that he had already notified Child Protective Services of the situation and that they would begin an investigation; however, since Sally was in no immediate danger, they would not engage until tomorrow. The minister also had contacted Sally's friend's parents, who were furious and threatening criminal prosecution. I paged Dr. K. to apprise him of the situation and let him know that his assistance might be needed the next day. I knew, at this time, that I was in for one hell of a ride—that this was not just another substance abuse treatment case. I had no idea just how much worse this situation was going to get.

At 8:45 on Wednesday morning, I received a call from Jill. Expecting to hear that John had started drinking and would not be keeping his appointment, I sat in shock as Jill informed me that John had killed himself at around 6:30 A.M. Apparently, Alan had stayed with John through the night and at 5:00 A.M. had decided to leave John alone so that he could get ready for work. After Alan went home, John proceeded to drink a bottle of vodka he had apparently stashed in the garage. Most likely in an intoxicated state, he loaded a shotgun that he kept in the attic, returned to the garage, and shot himself through the mouth.

At about 7:00 A.M., Jill and Sally returned home to prepare for their day. Thinking that it was strange that Alan was not there, they both began looking for John. Sally went to the garage and found John's corpse. Jill called the police to report the incident, and John's death was listed as a suicide. I offered to meet with Jill and Sally that day. Jill declined but stated that they would both come in on Thursday.

It wasn't until I hung up the phone that I began feeling the impact of what had just happened. Fortunately, Dr. K. was up to date on the impending crisis and did not act surprised when I informed him that John suicided that morning. He reminded me that we deal with a severely impaired, impulsive, and self-destructive population and that suicide is not uncommon. While his words were temporarily reassuring, I struggled to get through my day. We decided to meet that evening to process what I was feeling and the numerous questions and doubts that I was having—questions like "What did I miss?" "Should John have been hospitalized?" "What am I going to do to help Jill and Sally?" "How do I inform the group?" "Am I really a competent therapist?" "Am I going to get sued for negligence?" "Why now?" "Why?"

Dr. K. and I spent several hours Wednesday evening piecing together a psychological autopsy with the information we had available. Dr. K. shared with me his concerns about John's suicide potential but indicated that John did not present an immediate threat under the circumstances that existed when he was admitted to the program—at least no more so than any other chemically dependent person. As we talked, I realized that I could deal with this intellectually, gathering factual data, analyzing the intervention process and the steps I had taken to ensure John's safety, and looking at other ways that I might have intervened.

We discussed John's background and history, his SAD PERSONS score, and my suspicions that there may have been some boundary violations with John and Sally as well as how common this is in alcoholic families. We reviewed my decisions concerning John's safety, once he had been confronted. Considering that John denied any suicidal intent or plan, he did not meet the criteria for hospitalization. The efforts that I made to provide John support through the night and to stabilize the situation at that moment were the best I could do under the circumstances. Dr. K. reminded me that it is just unrealistic to hospitalize every alcoholic who is in crisis over his consequences and that once an alcoholic in crisis starts drinking and impulsively decides to kill himself, there is very little we can do to prevent him from succeeding.

Intellectually, I took comfort in Dr. K.'s words of reassurance and was able to acknowledge that I had acted appropriately and competently. Emotionally, I was still pretty numb. Something about this case was not resolved, did not feel complete. I was still feeling a heavy, gnawing sense that I had yet to experience the full emotional impact of his suicide.

TREATMENT (FOR THE SURVIVORS)

Jill and Sally came in on Thursday. Sally sat, quietly crying, as Jill expressed her shock and disbelief that John had killed himself. I listened to Jill verbalize feelings of guilt, anger, shame, and fear and realized that I could easily overidentify with her. As I struggled to maintain some objectivity, Sally took the opportunity to express her feeling of responsibility for her father's death and her remorse over having told her mother about the incest. As Jill reassured Sally that she did the right thing and that she did not cause John's suicide, I became concerned that, while Jill talked about how she felt, she appeared detached and overcontrolled. As the first session concluded, we decided that I would meet with each of them individually on Friday and then decide if a referral was appropriate.

During my first individual meeting with Sally, she described how she, her father, and her friend would get high together and "play games." What started out as being subtly seductive and suggestive turned into the three of them having what Sally described as a "sex party." She went on to state that she did not feel taken advantage of by her father, that she had initiated the acts with her friend, and that they had both planned to seduce him.

Sally's only regret was that she had told her mother after being confronted. She stated that her mother knew something was going on, and when her mother confronted her, she told her mother the truth in an attempt to hurt her feelings. She stated that she had been angry at her mother for years and also believed that her mother was having an affair with Alan. Sally agreed that she would benefit from continuing to see a therapist and was open to a referral to a female child psychologist with experience in dealing with incest victims. She closed by telling me that she really loved her father and was afraid of what her mother might do to her.

My first individual session with Jill was stunning. Jill expressed anger at Sally for interfering in her marriage. She said that ever since they had adopted Sally, she had always been competing for John's attention and that John clearly wanted Sally more than her. She went on to say that John had taken out a $1 million life insurance policy and that he was at least considerate enough to have waited to kill himself for two years, so his policy would be effective in the event of his suicide. Interestingly, the two-year period expired three weeks before his death. She stated that she had wanted a divorce and was planning on leaving, once John was sober. Claiming that she had been ready to move on because her feelings for John had died long ago, she said that his suicide actually made it easier for her.

I listened, astounded and literally at a loss. I felt angry at Jill and also highly suspicious, wondering if, in some way, she had played a role in John's death. I knew that I would not be able to objectively continue with Jill and suggested that we find a therapist for her to see. She refused, stating that Alan had been a great source of support throughout the time John had been drinking and that she felt more comfortable with Alan than with some stranger. We closed with Jill agreeing to make an appointment for Sally to see her new therapist and to call me if she needed any further assistance.

Group convened at 6:00 P.M. I began with the usual structure of triaging to see if any members needed time that evening. I then informed the group that John had died on

Wednesday morning as the result of a self-inflicted gunshot wound. I did not reveal the precipitants or events leading up to his suicide. Although John had been with the group for only two sessions, several members expressed sadness and sorrow.

They all seemed to relate John's misfortune to the fatal consequences of alcoholism and addiction, recognizing that they no longer felt the hopeless desperation common among those so deeply enmeshed in their addiction. Several group members shared their experiences with suicide—their own ideations, their previous attempts, or those of others that they had known who had ended their own lives. As a group, they dealt with this event and moved on to other issues. It seemed so easy for them. I found myself wishing that I could do the same.

CONCLUSION

Through clinical supervision—or in this case, therapy for the therapist—I was able to put a better perspective on this case and emotionally let go of the personal responsibility I felt for John's suicide. I was sad for some time but not guilty. I also noticed a hypersensitivity to suicidal ideation presented by clients and began zealously intervening when a client hinted at suicide. Dealing with chemically dependent clients for eight years prior to this event, I had successfully intervened countless times in what appeared to be suicidal crises. John's story is like those of many others who are afflicted with addictions. The fact that he was the first client of mine to have completed a suicide made this particularly tricky in that, prior to this event, I had only heard of the emotional impact of suicide on the therapist. This was my first experience dealing with these feelings personally, while trying to attend to the needs of the family and others who were affected.

It has been nearly 20 years since John's death, and writing this article has brought back the emotional impact of suicide: the sudden shock, the questions, the self-doubt, the need to process and ventilate, and the need to remain objective and available to others while all hell is breaking loose inside. I have been fortunate in that, for the past 20 years, I have not experienced a client suicide. I do, however, still experience the uneasiness we all feel at times when we are not sure if we have done everything within our power to intervene and help keep a client safe. As a clinical supervisor and still a supervisee at times, I have found it essential to put words to my concerns and to remain open to feedback and suggestions. As a clinician for the past 27 years, I have learned a few important things:

> Some clients are going to suicide no matter what we do to prevent it;
>
> We never know for sure when we have prevented a suicide, only when we have not;
>
> We can only do our very best to ensure the client's safety;
>
> Some questions do not have answers;
>
> Clinical supervision helps;
>
> The choice to suicide seldom makes sense to us as clinicians, but at that moment, it makes perfect sense to the client who suicides;
>
> If you work with a seriously self-destructive population, you will most likely experience a suicide; and
>
> Some events in the life of a therapist are so painful that we never fully get over them; we just find ways to move ahead.

Rest in peace, John.

Case Reflection Questions

Suicide Issue Questions

1. Alcohol or other substances are frequently present in completed suicides. What role did alcohol and other drugs play in this suicide and the events leading up to it?
2. What kind of feelings would you have if you lost a client to suicide? To whom could you turn to help you process your own feelings?

Skill Builder Questions

1. How might you feel if you were counseling this suicidal client? What is your personal emotional reaction to this client's suicidal behavior?
2. What would you have done in order to ensure this suicidal client's safety? Utilizing the FED, described in Chapter 3, which indicates *frequency* of suicidal thoughts, *extent* of suicide plans, and *duration* of suicidal thoughts and impulses, indicate your assessment of this client's degree of danger to self. What would you have done to properly assess this client's immediate suicide risk?

3. What important suicide risk factors were present in the case? What unique individual factors or characteristics of this client would be important to your suicide risk assessment? As you read this case, which SAD PERSONS risk factors (sex, age, depression, previous attempt, ethanol abuse, rational thinking loss, social supports lacking, organized suicide plan, no spouse, and sickness) did you find most relevant to this case?
4. What would be your therapeutic approach to treating this suicidal client? What two pieces of information described within this case would be most helpful for your own work in intervening with potentially suicidal clients and their loved ones?
5. How would your approach be the same as or different from that of the clinician in the case? What interventions described in the case did you think were most helpful to the client?
6. How will you care for yourself when working with clients who are suicidal?
7. What strategies will you use to make sure you are competent and prepared to work with high-risk clients?

Dr. M. F. Sunich has a Doctorate in Counseling Psychology from Western Michigan University. He is Assistant Professor at Troy University and Licensed Psychologist in the state of Florida. Sunich has worked, trained and taught in the chemical dependency field since 1980.

Reference

Patterson, W. M., Dohn, H. H., Bird, J., & Patterson, G. A. (1983). Evaluation of suicidal patients: The SAD PERSONS Scale. *Psychosomatics, 24*(4), 343–349.

Frieda

A Woman with a Complex Diagnostic Profile

ROBIN GUILL LILES

EDITORS' COMMENTS

- This case illustrates the real-world frustrations that may result from having to work within the context of multiple systems of care.
- The counselor in this case must cope with a client who is ambivalent about her desire to live or die.

INTRODUCTION

When I met Frieda, I was working as an on-call assessment counselor for a local tertiary hospital that had contracted to provide mental health consult services to several area community hospitals. Frieda had been admitted to the intensive care unit (ICU) of one of those community hospitals, following an attempted suicide through overdosing on acetaminophen. In reading her chart, I discovered that Frieda had been admitted to the hospital the previous evening after being brought to the emergency room (ER) by her neighbor. Laboratory reports indicated that upon admission to the ER, Frieda was positive for diazepam and toxic levels of acetaminophen. Preliminary reports also suggested she had no physical (e.g., liver) impairment. She was negative for alcohol and other drugs. Frieda was subsequently transferred to the ICU for medical observation. Secondary to her medical status, the ICU, with its one-to-two nursing/patient ratio, was deemed the safest environment inasmuch as the hospital did not have a licensed psychiatric unit.

BACKGROUND/REFERRAL

When I spoke with Frieda's ICU nurse, I learned that Frieda was expected to be medically cleared that afternoon. Following hospital protocol, Frieda's attending physician had called for a mental health consult prior to her medical release. The nurse stated that since arriving in the ICU, Frieda had demonstrated acceptable mental acuity and was oriented to time and place and to the reason she was hospitalized. However, though polite and responsive to

staff interactions, Frieda had engaged in no substantive conversation with anyone since her transfer to the unit. The nurse went on to say that, whereas Frieda had been tearful and weepy during the early morning hours, she had appeared to have little anxiety and had demonstrated no angry, argumentative, or combative behavior.

The demographic information contained in Frieda's chart was sketchy, stating that she was a 43-year-old Caucasian woman with apparently no living relatives or other social support. Frieda was currently receiving disability payments and was a member of the state's medical assistance program. The name (Larry) and phone number of the neighbor who transported Frieda to the ER were provided; however, there was no chart documentation indicating that Frieda had given the hospital staff permission to release her medical information.

ASSESSMENT

As I entered Frieda's hospital room, I noted that she appeared to be sleeping, with her head turned away from the door. I called her name quietly, and at first, there was no response. I stepped to the edge of the hospital bed to determine if Frieda was asleep and saw that her eyes were open. Once more, I spoke: "Frieda, it's Dr. Liles, and I was wondering if we could talk awhile?" Frieda slowly turned her head, focusing on the ceiling, and then she nodded. It seemed that this small gesture took a great deal of effort.

I began the interview in the typical fashion, establishing the purpose of my visit. Once the demographic data were gathered, I posed questions about Frieda's psychosocial history. From this segment of the interview, I learned that Frieda had previously been a client with the local community mental health organization but had not seen a mental health professional in almost two years. Frieda explained that she did not have a driver's license or own a car, and given that she lived "out in the country," it was difficult for her to obtain transportation. Consequently, she had ceased to maintain her relationship with her counselor.

As a point of clarification, I asked Frieda if she had any access to transportation at all, and she related that a neighbor (i.e., Larry) who lived about a mile from her house would occasionally bring her into town for groceries. She also said that in the past three months Larry had transported her once to a medical appointment and twice to the pharmacy to fill prescriptions but that these trips were not "routine." I asked Frieda to give me the name of her physician, and she identified a local doctor who practiced family medicine. I inquired whether or not it would be possible for me to obtain a release of information such that I could talk with her family doctor, and Frieda said she would think about it.

At this point in the interview, I asked Frieda if she could talk a little about what had brought her to the ER on the previous day. Though she spoke haltingly, Frieda required little verbal prompting as she spent the next half hour telling me some of her life story. In brief, Frieda lived alone and had minimal contact with others; in fact, the primary theme of Frieda's narrative was one of loneliness and isolation.

Though it was not evident from chart notes, Frieda acknowledged that she had a daughter whom she loved very much and who lived in a neighboring state. Frieda further stated that although she and her daughter "got along" with one another, their contact was limited to the winter holiday season, when her daughter visited. Several times Frieda spoke of not wanting to "bother" her daughter, and on probe, Frieda refused to give her daughter's name or contact information, adamantly stating that she did not want her daughter to know about "this business." Further inquiry revealed that Frieda's parents were deceased and that

she had been their only child. She stated that her father died when she was an adolescent; however, her mother had passed away only five years earlier. Frieda stated that she had lived with her mother until she passed away. Following her mother's death, Frieda left "the home place," moving to a rental house in the same community.

Frieda went on to say that several years earlier she had been found eligible to receive disability payments and had not worked since that time. She continued to lace her comments with references to friends she "used to have," but now no one visited anymore, and she was terribly lonely. At this point, I asked her to tell me more about the nature of her relationship with the neighbor who had carried her grocery shopping and had brought her to the hospital the night before. Frieda was offhand, even dismissive, in her response, explaining that it was "a business deal," meaning that she reimbursed him for gas whenever he provided her with transportation. For clarification, I asked if she considered her neighbor to be a friend, and Frieda said no, she sometimes could not even remember his name.

I shared with Frieda that her chart indicated her neighbor's name was Larry and that I was confused and wondered how her neighbor knew to come to her house the previous evening. Once more, Frieda's response was offhand: "I don't know." (*Note:* The ER intake report suggested the neighbor brought Frieda to the hospital after looking in her window and seeing her passed out on the floor. No other details were provided.) I concluded by asking Frieda if she would allow me to give Larry a call to gather more information, and she said no.

Switching gears, I asked Frieda if she had intended to kill herself when she took the acetaminophen. With nonchalance, she replied, "I guess so." She further explained that she had been "stockpiling" acetaminophen for some time and that she had more of the medication at home. I then queried Frieda about the impetus for her suicide attempt. She denied that anything unduly distressing or upsetting had occurred recently; rather, she stated that lately she had found the loneliness and isolation just too overwhelming and her existence unbearable. I then returned to a discussion of Frieda's prior mental health treatments and hospitalizations. Frieda reiterated that she had established a relationship with a mental health counselor several years earlier but had not seen that counselor in two years. She denied any previous hospitalizations.

I asked Frieda if she believed having some time to rest in the hospital would be helpful to her now, and she said no. I asked her if she would be willing to contract for safety, allow me to contact a community mental health counselor, and follow up as an outpatient with the counselor the following day—all of which she replied to with an apathetic "I guess so." I concluded by asking if she would be willing to inform someone in her family (i.e., her daughter) or the community (i.e., Larry) of her situation and possibly ask that person to come stay with her or check up on her throughout the next few weeks. To this question, Frieda roused up from her bed and, with great emphasis, said no.

I excused myself from Frieda's room and returned to the nurses' station to page the attending physician. In relating the assessment information to the doctor, I explained that I felt Frieda was in a clearly confused and fragile state. Information gleaned from the interview suggested she was clinically depressed with suicidal features, was at best apathetic toward contracting for safety and seeking outpatient services, lacked (or was unwilling to accept) adequate social support, and had ready access to more acetaminophen. Thus, my safest recommendation would be that Frieda receive additional psychiatric care and observation as an inpatient at a behavioral health facility. (*Note:* The nearest behavioral health hospital was part of the health care system associated with my employing hospital.) I finished by saying

that it would be my preference for Frieda to admit herself voluntarily to the closest behavioral health facility; however, if Frieda refused to go into the hospital, then the physician would have to consider involuntary commitment to the state hospital, which was approximately $1\frac{1}{2}$ hours away.

The physician concurred and asked me to pursue hospitalization for Frieda. Given that Frieda had no private insurance and received state medical assistance, I made a preliminary call to the state psychiatric hospital designated for our community area to check bed availability. I found that the only available beds were "involuntary" ones. Subsequently, I contacted the closest private behavioral health center. In speaking with the on-call psychiatrist, I learned that, given low acuteness levels of cases currently on the adult unit, he could admit Frieda for inpatient care.

When I returned to Frieda's room, I explained to her that both her doctor and I were concerned about her welfare. I told Frieda that we did not have a clear picture of the ways she planned to manage her life henceforth and that this was worrisome in view of her recent suicide attempt. I told her that our concern related to her seemingly halfhearted willingness to contract for safety as well as her outright refusal to secure additional social support from family and friends. I described the difference between voluntary and involuntary commitment to the hospital and finished by saying that both her physician and I would like her to consider admitting herself to the hospital for some additional help. Frieda asked how she would pay for a private hospital, and I explained that private hospitals could accept patients receiving medical assistance. She also inquired about how long she would be in the hospital; I explained that the length of stay varied from patient to patient but that in most cases, three to five days was a reasonable hospital stay. This information seemed to make sense to Frieda, as she agreed to check herself into the hospital.

When filling out the paperwork, I asked Frieda once more if, in addition to the referral hospital, she would like to release information about her situation to any family or friends, and she said no. I explained that transportation could presently be provided between the community hospital and the behavioral health facility but that she may need to make arrangements for transportation home when she checked out of the facility at a later date. Frieda seemed unconcerned with this information, simply nodding her head.

The next time I saw Frieda was three weeks later. I was called to the same area hospital's ICU to assess a suicide attempt, and the client was Frieda. In reading her chart, I discovered that Frieda had been admitted to the ICU after being brought to the hospital by emergency personnel, presenting with cuts to her wrists and ankles. Some of the cuts were superficial, while others required minor surgery. None of the cuts was deemed serious or in need of more surgery. The cuts ran both vertically and horizontally to the anterior arms and legs.

The nurse reported that Frieda was receiving intravenous (IV) antibiotics as well as oral pain medication. The nurse continued, saying that although Frieda was cogent and oriented, she had been extremely angry and combative since her transfer to the ICU. The nurse defined "angry and combative" as cursing staff, throwing objects (e.g., drinking cups, pieces of ice, pillows), threatening to leave the ICU, and trying to remove her IV. The nurse indicated that Frieda's behavior was particularly violent whenever her "boyfriend" was in the room. From a medical point of view, the nurse said the physician thought Frieda would soon be suitable for a transfer to a medical unit with cases of lower acuteness. However, given her history of suicidal attempts, as well as her extreme irritability, the current plan included keeping Frieda in the ICU until she could be referred to a behavioral health center or psychiatric hospital.

Clearly harried, the nurse ended by saying that she felt Frieda needed to be transferred as soon as possible. I asked the nurse if Frieda's boyfriend was named Larry, and she said she thought so but was not sure. Looking around, I wondered aloud if Larry was still in the hospital. The nurse said he had gone home to freshen up but said he would return.

At this point, I phoned my employing hospital and spoke with the managing counselor on the assessment team. I asked if I could be briefed on Frieda's previous hospital stay, including her release disposition and follow-up plan. He said he would retrieve her medical records and get back to me. While waiting, I read the report filed by the emergency medical services team. In brief, around 4:00 A.M., their dispatch received a distress call from Larry, who said he had discovered Frieda walking up and down his driveway and crying. She had already cut herself and was bleeding from her arms and legs. Larry reported that the sight of Frieda standing in his driveway in this condition had frightened him badly. He was uncertain of the severity of her wounds and, for this reason, felt he should call 911.

My behavioral health colleague phoned back and stated that at discharge, Frieda's chart provided the following information:

- Axis I. Major depression with suicidal features, and rule out bipolar disorder;
- Axis II. Rule out borderline personality disorder;
- Axis III. Intermittent migraine headaches and stomach upset;
- Axis IV. Moderately severe psychosocial situation, including apparent lack of social support;
- Axis V. Continued stabilization through prescription antidepressant treatment, follow-up with mental health at discharge to establish a counseling relationship with a mental health professional, and psychiatric evaluation at the behavioral health facility within 30 days.

The chart further indicated that while receiving inpatient care, Frieda's behavior had been unpredictable—at times compliant and engaged in her treatment and at other times uncooperative and belligerent. Frieda continued to refuse to contact her daughter, although she was willing to call Larry to provide transportation at discharge. The psychiatric note suggested that Frieda may benefit from treatment of mania and that she should continue to be monitored for signs of Bipolar Disorder.

When I entered Frieda's room, she was sitting on the edge of the bed, inspecting her arm wounds. As I called her name, she glanced up and then back down, not responding. I told her my name and asked if she remembered me from her previous stay in the ICU. She did not respond immediately, continuing to look at her arms. I took a seat and, in a respectful tone, asked her, "What's going on?" At this, Frieda threw back her head, laughed loudly, and said, "You tell me!" For the next 20 minutes or so, I worked to engage Frieda in a cooperative dialogue, but Frieda was not interested in talking with me. She just kept telling me "to do what you gotta do." I found Frieda's change in affect, as well as her disinterest in treatment, confusing and worrisome.

After paging the doctor, I related Frieda's history, explaining that this was my second ICU consult with Frieda in less than a month. I also provided the behavioral health facility's discharge information. I concluded by saying that once Frieda had an opportunity to resettle herself, I would like to speak with her again. However, ultimately, I felt Frieda was not stable enough to be discharged to her own care and would need further psychiatric hospitalization.

The doctor agreed but stated that Frieda should remain on IV antibiotics for several more hours, so she would need to be transferred to a facility that could medically monitor

her as well. At this point, I called three private behavioral health facilities to determine bed availability, only to learn that due to high unit acuity, as well as the added complication of Frieda's medical situation, the hospitals could not admit Frieda that day. I then called the state mental health hospital and was told that no beds were currently open but that they were looking to free up space within the next 24 hours. I once more paged Frieda's attending physician and explained that psychiatric beds were tight and that immediate referral and transfer were not possible. I reiterated that I believed Frieda needed to be hospitalized. At this point, the physician decided to transfer Frieda to the community hospital's adult medical unit.

Once Frieda had been transferred downstairs to the medical unit, I met with her. I wanted to refine my thinking about what could be troubling her and to formulate a tentative treatment plan. As I considered practical avenues to help Frieda, it seemed that much of her unhappiness stemmed from her apparent lack of social support. It was not lost on me that Frieda was complicating the matter by refusing to contact her daughter and to acknowledge her relationship with Larry. It appeared to me that Frieda's life relationships were problematic issues.

On a different note, the connection between Bipolar and Borderline Personality Disorders and suicide and suicidal attempts is well established in the literature (Bowden & Maier, 2003; Bronisch, 1996; Krishnan, 2005; Pascolo-Fabrici, De Maria, & De Vanna, 1998. Inasmuch as the records from the behavioral health facility showed that these were potential concerns for Frieda and her suicide attempts were becoming more frequent and more lethal, I viewed Frieda's situation as grave and dangerous. Thus, my goal for our meeting that afternoon was to ascertain if Frieda could be suffering from the negative effects of mood and personality disorders or extremely distressful life circumstances or a combination of both.

TREATMENT

When I arrived at the hospital that afternoon, the medical nurse indicated that, whereas Frieda had complained about her "old room," she also had been fairly calm since transferring to the adult medical unit. Frieda was watching television when I came into her room. She glanced in my direction but did not speak or say hello. I asked her if it was a good time to talk, and she responded, "As good as any." I focused the first segment of the interview on reestablishing client/counselor rapport and again defining the nature of our relationship. Frieda seemed only mildly interested.

I then asked Frieda if she could help me understand her life circumstances since leaving the behavioral health center and what had happened the day before, leading up to cutting herself. Frieda only shrugged and said, "You don't understand. Nobody does." I explained that I wanted to help her, but in order to to accomplish that goal, I would need her cooperation, and she would have to talk with me. At this point, Frieda began to cry, telling me that she was a "hopeless case" and that I should not "waste time" on her. We continued in this vein for several minutes before Frieda relaxed.

Once calm, Frieda's demeanor appeared to take on a more hopeful tone, and she asked me if I could really help her. I indicated that in most cases those clients who sincerely desired to make improvements in their lives could receive the help they needed and that I saw no reason why she could not obtain a similar outcome. Frieda asked me if I could be her counselor; she stated that she felt unusually close to me and that she could "trust" me. I explained to Frieda that I would not be able to counsel her long-term but that we could

work together for awhile to develop a treatment plan to be implemented by Frieda and her next mental health counselor. Frieda seemed to accept this response and was willing to discuss possible treatment options.

Frieda admitted that one of the difficulties she had encountered since leaving the behavioral health facility related to remembering to take her antidepressant, and we agreed that it seemed reasonable to assume she had not fully benefited from the medication. I asked her about the structure of her days. For instance, did she tend to wake up, take her meals, and go to bed at the same time of day? I suggested to Frieda that if she could establish a rhythm to her day, then it would be easier to remember to take her medication. Frieda seemed agreeable to this notion but quickly said she was not sure she could follow through because she never really "made any plans" for her awake time.

At this point, I switched gears and asked about social support. Again, I pointed out that having a network of caring family and friends could help her maintain a balanced and healthful lifestyle. Frieda countered that she had no family and friends whom she felt she could "really count on." I explained that social support could also be found in other venues. For instance, she might find participating in groups or other outside organizations to be beneficial. Frieda argued that she had no transportation and that being "in crowds" made her feel anxious. I paused and then ventured that perhaps Frieda had thoughts about changes she could make to help her better organize her time, thus improving her chances that she would remember to take her antidepressants. Frieda shook her head.

In order to gain a better feel for Frieda's lifespan experiences, I asked her to tell me about her younger years, including memories of her marriage and times when friends used to visit. Frieda's face noticeably brightened up, and she began to talk about the time when her mother was alive. She said that, whereas she never had very many family members, there were always friends close by, dropping in and checking up on her and her mother. I asked what became of all the friends, and Frieda explained that once her mother died, everyone stopped coming. She did not know why.

When I asked her about her marriage and her daughter, Frieda began to cry. She said her daughter's father left her when her daughter was in elementary school. Frieda stated that she was still in love with her ex-husband but that she understood why he left her. When I asked her to tell me why she believed the marriage ended, she said, "Because I'm crazy, and I made him crazy, too." Frieda said she believed her daughter never recovered from her father's leaving, and that was the reason her daughter moved in with her father when she was 12 years old. I asked for her daughter's current age, and Frieda told me she was 21 years old. She further indicated that her daughter lived near her ex-husband and that she thought they shared "a real close relationship." Once more, I proposed to Frieda that she call her daughter, or let me call her, and again, Frieda refused.

A quick calculation indicated that Frieda's daughter had been approximately 16 years old when Frieda's mother passed away. I shared this with Frieda, asking if I had the math correct. Frieda nodded and began to cry even harder, saying that she still missed her mother and that she had never "gotten over her death." I pointed out to Frieda that I could understand how losing her mother just a few years after her daughter moved away must have been traumatic to her and how she would still be sad about these losses. Frieda countered by saying that pondering her mother's death made her days "impossible." I then turned the conversation back to circumstances surrounding the previous day and asked Frieda if that had been one of her "impossible days?" Frieda said yes. I asked Frieda if she had ever cut herself before, and she said "some" since she was a teenager. When her mother discovered

the cuts, it made Frieda cry. She admitted that she never completely stopped the cutting behavior but that she tried to "hide it" from her mother. I asked her how she hid it from her mother, and Frieda said she limited the cuts to her underarms, her inner thighs and groin, and the soles of her feet.

At this point, I asked Frieda to describe what had happened the "impossible" day before. Frieda said that there were gaps in her memories and that this was frightening to her. She said she remembered waking but having "no feeling" in her body. She said that she remembered standing in the kitchen and looking out the window at Larry's house and that his house looked as if it was underwater. She did not have any recollection of actually cutting her arms and legs or of walking to Larry's driveway. She said that she thought she remembered riding in the ambulance but that she could have "just dreamed that." As Frieda related this information to me, I noted that her voice became lower and lower.

As Frieda finished her narrative, she closed her eyes. I paused, allowing her a few minutes rest. Then I gently reviewed with Frieda that both her physician and I felt she would be best served by once more checking herself into the hospital. Frieda's facial expression hardened, and she said, "I'm not sure how much good that'll do." I went on to say that her life circumstances, and particularly those in the last 24 hours, were still unclear, and that any time situations were murky and dim, it was usually better to "play it safe." Frieda sneered, "Yeah, right!" She averted her eyes and stared at the television. I also shared with Frieda that I was impressed with her apparent willingness to talk with me about her life and some of its more painful aspects and that I thought this boded well for her future recovery. I concluded by saying that I would check in with her the following morning to discuss the next step in her care. I said good-by, but Frieda appeared not to hear me.

An hour after leaving Frieda, I was paged. The unit head nurse reported that Frieda had "become hysterical" and that I needed to return to the hospital as soon as possible. I asked if Frieda's physician had been informed, and she said yes; the doctor had also had the nurse notify hospital security.

I hurriedly returned to the hospital, where I discovered the chaotic scene. Frieda was rocking to and fro on her hospital bed. The floor of her room was littered with bedclothes, cups, pillows, and other objects. Frieda was crying loudly, while simultaneously screaming and yelling curse words and shaking her fists. Blood was starting to trickle from her left arm, possibly from the IV site or one of the arm wounds. Standing a safe distance from the bed, the nurse and hospital security officer were trying to talk with her, ostensibly to calm her down, but they appeared to be having little effect. Most of Frieda's anger seemed directed toward a man who was positioned at the corner of the bed. He was saying nothing, and I guessed this was Larry. A quick look at her chart indicated that the doctor had written an emergency commitment order, so I knew the police would soon be arriving. The doctor also had written an order for a tranquilizer through injection, but so far the nurse had not been able to administer the shot.

After speaking with Frieda's doctor, it was evident that she would need to be transferred to a psychiatric unit as soon as possible. I phoned the state hospital and explained the situation. As before, the expectation was for a bed to become available within the next 24 hours, but they hoped they would be able to admit Frieda by late evening. I asked them to call me back as soon as they could accept Frieda for transfer.

Over the next few hours, I had the opportunity to speak with Larry. Inasmuch as Frieda had signed no Release of Information, I could not share her medical or psychiatric history with him. However, I felt it was important to gather as much collateral information as

possible from Larry regarding Frieda's life circumstances. If her situation was as dire as I suspected, then it was important for the referral hospital to have this information when writing her discharge disposition.

Larry was a pleasant young man who told me he was "a lot younger" than Frieda. He said he first met Frieda five years earlier when she moved into the rental house next to his property. He said at first they were "just neighbors," but then after a couple of years, they had "gotten real close." I asked how he defined "real close," and he said, "You know, like husband and wife." He said that he had asked Frieda to marry him many times but that she had refused, saying that she was "no good" and that he "deserved better." It was clear in speaking with Larry that he cared deeply for Frieda but that he was essentially confused by her behavior and was uncertain about the true nature of their relationship.

Larry also related that Frieda's behavior had become increasingly bizarre over the past year and that every day for the last three months he had worried that something terrible was going to happen. I asked him about the first time she attempted suicide. He explained that they had argued and she had returned home, telling him never to speak to her again. He admitted he was angry and hurt, so he left her alone for the next two days. In an effort to make amends, he returned to her house to talk with her. When she did not answer the door, he looked into the kitchen window and saw her on the floor. Although groggy and disoriented, Frieda was not unconscious, and for this reason, he elected to bring her to the hospital himself.

The second suicide attempt was different, and Larry confessed he had never been as frightened as he was when he saw Frieda standing in his driveway, crying and bleeding from her arms and legs. I asked Larry if he had any knowledge about Frieda's other family or friends. He denied knowing she had family and friends other than him. On one hand, it seemed clear that Larry cared for Frieda. On the other, it was also apparent that maintaining a relationship with her had become increasingly difficult for him. I thanked him for sharing his story with me.

In the very early morning hours of the following day, Frieda was transferred to the state psychiatric hospital. My report included notes from my multiple sessions with Frieda, the previous psychiatric hospital's report, and Larry's narrative. I concluded by writing that I believed Frieda's deepening psychiatric disturbances were exacerbated by her difficult psychosocial situation and that I thought the converse was also true. In other words, a period of extended stabilization and care may be worth considering.

The last time I saw Frieda was approximately three months later. Once more, she was in the community hospital's ICU. Unbelievably, Frieda had yet again attempted suicide by cutting her jaw, neck, and upper chest with shards of glass. Interestingly, Frieda appeared to self-inflict the wounds just prior to the weekly visit from her local mental health adult-patient care team. Emergency medical services were called once again, and Frieda was brought to the community hospital. Surgery was required to close up her wounds. As I entered the ICU room, Frieda was resting. When I called her name, she opened her eyes, stared at me, and said, "How do you stand your job?" I asked her what she meant. She responded, "Mean Mama ain't never gonna let Baby live. You might as well give up. Mean Mama's gonna make Tommy Boy kill Baby."

For the next hour or so, Frieda told me about Mean Mama, Tommy Boy, and Baby. They were her other "Family." Frieda said that for as long as she could remember, the Family had been a part of her conscious life but that it was only with the death of her "real mother" that Mean Mama became dominant. Frieda had intermittent awareness of Mean

Mama's intentions, and during those times, she tried to control Mean Mama. But during Frieda's unaware periods, Mean Mama was "in charge," and Frieda could not control Mean Mama. Frieda said that she and Mean Mama "argued a lot" but that Mean Mama could also "slip away and hide" from Frieda.

Frieda said that when Mean Mama was hiding, Frieda was most frightened. Frieda knew that neither Tommy Boy nor Baby knew about her (Frieda); they related only to Mean Mama. Frieda said she wanted to protect Tommy Boy and Baby from Mean Mama, but she did not know how. I asked Frieda how she was cut, and she simply said, "Tommy Boy did it." Frieda went on to tell me that Mean Mama did not know about her daughter or Larry. She said she was afraid Mean Mama would find out about them and make Tommy Boy kill them. I asked if Mean Mama knew Frieda's real mother. Frieda smiled and said, "They were not real good friends, but they got along pretty well."

CONCLUSION

The case of Frieda poses multiple assessment and treatment questions and is a good example of the complex psychosocial issues that can and often do accompany clients presenting with Borderline Personality Disorder and suicidal ideation and behaviors. Such complex psychosocial issues challenge helping professionals to approach clients with a keen, yet caring eye and to probe more deeply for the true etiology of the psychological concern.

In assessing any client and developing a related treatment plan, concerns are necessarily ranked hierarchically, ranging from imminent danger, to urgent concern, to psychological maintenance. During Frieda's first hospitalization at the behavioral health facility, it was determined that Frieda could be suffering from Bipolar and Borderline Personality Disorders. These rule-out diagnoses were particularly powerful in view of Frieda's suicide attempt through overdose. Frieda appeared to fit the troubling bipolar/borderline profile, whereby she could be viewed as particularly vulnerable to poor impulse control, including suicidal behaviors. If this was the case, then every attempt should have been made to ensure that Frieda received the care she needed.

Though Frieda was given a follow-up psychiatric appointment and arrangements were made for her to seek additional help with the local mental health entity, the disposition failed to note the fragile nature of Frieda's social support network. Frieda's lack of a social support, combined with what was later determined to be a questionable assessment, placed Frieda at risk. Thus, attempts to continue psychological and behavioral stabilization through prescription medication and outpatient care failed.

Frieda's second hospitalization resulted in a more aggressive discharge disposition. Frieda was placed in the care of a visiting at-home adult services group intended to provide systematic support and observation, ensuring her medications were properly administered. The time line suggested that this method of outpatient care worked at least to the degree that Frieda could predict the team's arrival, thus allowing her to plan her own rescue just following the second cutting episode. Maltsberger, Ackerman, and Wheelis (2002) described a class of clients with Dissociative Disorder who split away or sequester their psychological and emotional pain and, during these detached periods, can engage in suicidal behaviors. It is hard to say what psychological mechanisms were at work when Frieda put the shards of glass to her face, neck, and upper chest. On the other hand, the nature of the attempt was

extreme and suggested that Frieda may well have been correct to be afraid of something or someone, be it Mean Mama, Tommy Boy, or herself.

With Frieda's third hospitalization, I wrote the recommendation that Frieda be considered for an extended period of stabilization and residential care. It seemed to me that Frieda's ongoing and profound lack of social support was the one area of her life that could be reasonably and effectively addressed through the mental health system. Clearly, her psychological concerns were treatable to some degree. Nonetheless, her long-term prognosis remained bleak without effective public health support. Designing the proper mental health maintenance plan was imperative.

In the many hours I spent with Frieda, it was never clear to me whether or not she was telling the truth about her relationship with her daughter. I always found it personally troubling that I could not help Frieda connect with the one family member whom she seemed to love so much. I never learned what became of her relationship with Larry. I do know that on discharge from the state hospital, she was placed in an adult residential facility and that her initial stay was to be for at least six months. I do not what know what became of her thereafter. I have pondered Frieda's case, and I remain skeptical that she was ever fully and correctly assessed. Treatment seemed to follow typical protocols, and this may be considered an acceptable practice as long as the assessment is correct.

Case Reflection Questions

Suicide Issue Questions

1. Many clinicians become frustrated with clients who have Borderline Personality Disorder or other chronic personality disorders. Yet these clients often have multiple and serious suicide attempts, which frequently lead to death either intentionally or accidentally. As a clinician working with AXIS II–diagnosed patients, what strategies would you employ to keep them safe?
2. What were the realities faced by this clinician in working with this patient within the mental health system? Were there unlimited resources? What resources did she capitalize on?

Skill Builder Questions

1. How might you feel if you were counseling this suicidal client? What is your personal emotional reaction to this client's suicidal behavior?
2. What would you have done in order to ensure this suicidal client's safety? Utilizing the FED, described in Chapter 3, which indicates *frequency* of suicidal thoughts, *extent* of suicide plans, and *duration* of suicidal thoughts and impulses, indicate your assessment of this client's degree of danger to self.

What would you have done to properly assess this client's immediate suicide risk?
3. What important suicide risk factors were present in the case? What unique individual factors or characteristics of this client would be important to your suicide risk assessment? As you read this case, which SAD PERSONS risk factors (sex, age, depression, previous attempt, ethanol abuse, rational thinking loss, social supports lacking, organized suicide plan, no spouse, and sickness) did you find most relevant to this case?
4. What would be your therapeutic approach to treating this suicidal client? What two pieces of information described within this case would be most helpful for your own work in intervening with potentially suicidal clients and their loved ones?
5. How would your approach be the same as or different from that of the clinician in the case? What interventions described in the case did you think were most helpful to the client?
6. How will you care for yourself when working with clients who are suicidal?
7. What strategies will you use to make sure you are competent and prepared to work with high-risk clients?

Robin Guill Liles is associate professor in the Department of Human Development and Services at North Carolina Agricultural and Technical State University. Liles is also a Licensed Professional Counselor and National Certified Counselor. Liles teaches applied research in counseling, testing and appraisal, and professional orientation and ethics. Her research interests include chronic disease among adolescents, ethical decision-making in counseling, and case writing and teaching efficacy. Prior to assuming her full-time teaching position, Liles worked for several years as a community agency mental health counselor providing both in- and out-patient services.

References

Bowden, C., & Maier, W. (2003). Bipolar disorder and personality disorder. *European Psychiatry, 18* (Suppl. 11), 9–12.

Bronisch, T. (1996). The typology of personality disorders: Diagnostic problems and their relevance for suicidal behavior. *Crisis, 17*, 55–58.

Krishnan, K. (2005). Psychiatric and medical comorbidities of bipolar disease. *Psychosomatic Medicine, 67*, 108.

Maltsberger, J. T., Ackerman, S., & Wheelis, J. (2002). Simon Muralis: Self-sequestration and psychotherapeutic failure. *Suicide & Life Threatening Behavior, 32*, 441–450.

Pascolo-Fabrici, E., De Maria, F., & De Vanna, M. (1998). Borderline disorders and the risk of suicide. *New Trends in Experimental & Clinical Psychiatry, 14*, 151–156.

Sergio
A Male Sexual Addict

W. Bryce Hagedorn

EDITORS' COMMENTS

- One important feature of this case is that it illustrates the limits of a counselor's ability to protect a client.
- The case also illustrates the relationship of severe depression and suicidality to a specific clinical population.

INTRODUCTION

In addition to my work as a counselor educator, I have maintained a small private practice for the last seven years. In that time, I have honed the skills I initially learned as a substance abuse counselor and have adapted them to working with those who struggle with sexual addiction. Even in such a large metropolitan area as the one where I work, there are few who specialize in such disorders. As a result, I am often called on by both clients and other support systems to render care.

BACKGROUND/REFERRAL

The initial contact regarding Sergio came from a local church's pastoral care department. It was Diana, the pastoral care specialist, who made the referral. Her call came one autumn afternoon. "Dr. Hagedorn, I have a parishioner named Sergio who is in crisis—it appears that his wife has separated from him as a result of her finding some pornography on his computer. He has expressed a lot of remorse to me and appears very depressed. I said that I knew someone who could help him with the pornography, and he seemed interested. Would you be able to see him?" I did not know if Sergio's use of pornography necessarily qualified him as a sexual addict, but given the crisis state in which he found himself, and hearing the concern in Diana's voice, I agreed to see him for an initial session.

ASSESSMENT

Sergio was a 47-year-old male of Brazilian descent. Although he spoke adequate English, his primary language was Portuguese. He presented as intelligent and articulate, tended to be cognitive and introspective, and initially was elusive as to the purpose of his visit.

The Initial Session

Our first session occurred late on a Friday afternoon. Sergio arrived 15 minutes late, a cultural norm to which I have become accustomed. After the initial pleasantries, a thorough discussion regarding my informed consent policies, and some answers to questions regarding his background, Sergio launched right into his reasons for seeking my assistance. "My wife asked me to move out after finding some pictures on my computer. I don't blame her. I feel bad about what I did and what I do—I don't like the fact that I keep looking at that stuff; it doesn't match my beliefs or my feelings about my family."

When asked for a more detailed account of what "stuff" he was looking at, Sergio shared that he struggled with Internet pornography, mostly centered on teenage girls. In exploring that further (in order to assess for the possibility of child pornography—a necessary caveat in my work with sexual addicts), he stated that the sites that he visited were all mainstream pornography and that the young women were highlighted as teens but all were over the age of 18.

"The thing that upset my wife the most was the fact that these girls are just three years older than my daughters—she was repulsed by the fact that I could be looking at young women in that way. She called me a 'pervert' and a 'sick man' and told me to get out of the house. That was two weeks ago, and now I'm living with one of the guys from work, sleeping on his couch. I hate the fact that I did that. I miss my family terribly." The level of disclosure surprised me but it also indicated to me how distraught he was. Sergio discussed his situation further, expanding on his current relationships with his wife, daughters, and other family members. He briefly explored his use of pornography and how much self-hatred he had for himself due to his inability to stop.

At this point, I was more interested in Sergio's apparent depression than his pornography use. Physically, Sergio looked underweight by about 15 pounds, he hadn't shaved in at least a week, and his affect was primarily blunted. "Sergio," I said, "you know that Diana from your church was the one that initially contacted me to see you. She mentioned that she was very concerned about you. Can you tell me what she would be concerned about?" He was silent for a long moment and then said, "Well, I had mentioned that I didn't see the point of living without my family, that perhaps I was better off dead. I mean, how can I even go back to that church, given what they know about me?" He further admitted that he felt "blue" most days, that he had lost pleasure in activities that he once enjoyed, and that his sleep had been impacted by his moods.

In exploring what he meant by "better off dead," I used the SLAP acronym as a way to assess his intent to self-harm. "Sergio, you mentioned that life doesn't seem worth living. Are you thinking about ending your life?" I asked. "I have considered it," he said quietly. "What have you thought about *Specifically*?" I asked. "Well, I thought that I could take some pills or something like that." Whereas overdosing is a fairly *Lethal* way to harm oneself, in checking on the *Availability* of these medications, he admitted that he had neither such pills nor any means to obtain them outside of buying over-the-counter medications. "On a scale of 1 to 10, with 1 representing no intention of buying these pills, or of seeking any other way to harm yourself, and 10 representing the clear intention of following through on a plan to hurt

yourself, what number would you rate yourself today?" "Oh, I guess about a 2 or 3—I've just been thinking about it—I mean, I would never actually do anything like that."

Finally, in assessing for the *Proximity* of supportive people in his life who knew what he was going through and the depth of his feelings, he mentioned that he had a couple of people at church who knew what was happening with him, that his coworker/roommate kept an eye on him, and that he would continue to check in with both Diana and myself.

As a result of this quick assessment, I determined that, whereas he was depressed, he was not an immediate threat to himself. We agreed to begin seeing each other on a weekly basis.

After the initial telephone contact with Sergio to set up our first appointment, I had emailed him a psychosocial form (which he received on his roommate's computer) that he was to complete and bring to our first session. From this form, as well as through the bio-psycho-social-spiritual interview that was part of our second meeting, I gleaned a wealth of background information.

Physically, Sergio rated himself as "average" in health, with a recent weight loss of an undetermined amount. He listed a back injury (as a result of a work-related incident three years prior) as his only physical ailment, no current medications, and no use of alcohol or other drugs. In terms of the *positive* elements of his physical health, he listed "exercise," noting that he walked on a regular basis at night.

Psychologically, he noted that he had been experiencing a severe emotional upset as a result of his separation, that he had no prior counseling experience, and that he had recently begun reading a book about pornography addiction. Further, he answered that he had "some" supportive people in his life (to include coworkers and people in his church) and that he had never taken medications or been hospitalized for any psychological reasons. Finally, he checked the following physical/psychological ailments as "currently experiencing": sleep difficulties, "blue" moods, difficulty concentrating, lack of energy, and addictive behaviors. In terms of the *positive* elements of his psychological health, he reiterated the book that he was reading and the fact that he was coming in for counseling.

Socially, Sergio noted that he had immigrated to the United States in the early 1980s with his wife, Isabelle, and had settled in the same city in which he currently lived. Both his and Isabelle's parents lived in Brazil, although his father had died when he was 13 and his mother had remarried when he was 17. He rated his marital relationship as "positive" prior to this current incident but as "very difficult" ever since. He stated that his wife would not want to join him in counseling as she had said this was his problem, not hers. Sergio had 15-year-old twin daughters, Catalina and Jesabel, both of whom were sophomores in high school. Sergio worked as a building contractor and had seen quite a bit of success as a result of the recent housing boom, ultimately allowing him to move into a home that a few years ago would have been beyond his means. In terms of the *positive* elements of his social health, Sergio stated that he had always been a very active parent, had made efforts to spend quality time with his wife (though he had felt emotionally distant from her for about two years), and prided himself on his ability to connect with others.

Spiritually, Sergio related how important his religious practice was to him. He shared that he had attended church on a regular basis for the last 14 years, had been an usher and small-group leader, and had been viewed as a "man of God" by others in the church. In terms of the *positive* elements of his spiritual health, he shared that he liked to devote some time each day to his spiritual practices, to include reading and praying. He admitted that unfortunately these two practices had decreased over the last year or so and that he currently felt unable to connect with God.

TREATMENT

By the third session, it was time to explore the behaviors that had been causing Sergio so much distress. I feel that it takes two or three sessions to establish the kind of trust that will allow someone to confidently dive into the murky waters of addictive disorders. After discussing how he typically dealt with his stress and other "negative" moods (as a way to determine if there was any other addictive use of a substance or behavior), I began probing for the presence of sexual addiction.

First, I had Sergio write on a dry-erase board the sexual activities that he used that were causing him (and his relationships) problems. He wrote (a) viewing Internet pornography, (b) visiting Internet chat rooms that were of a sexual nature, (c) viewing soft-core pornography in hotels when he traveled, and (d) sexualizing (in his mind) every encounter he had with women. I asked him to identify the behavior, of the four that he listed, that happened with the most frequency and that caused him the most distress, the one that he would most like to erase from the board (and his life). He chose Internet pornography. We would refer to his list later in our work. In essence, he would be "erasing" these areas of concern, once he eliminated them from his life.

Next, I utilized a diagnostic tool with the acronym *WASTE Time* (Hagedorn & Juhnke, 2005) as a means to further structure the assessment process. The letters of this acronym correspond to one or more of the known criteria for sexual addiction, and the tool itself was tailored so as to avoid any resistance or denial on Sergio's part. "Sergio, what happens when you are unable to log onto the Internet for long periods of time?" I asked (checking for any *Withdrawal* symptoms). "Well, I can usually go for about two or three weeks between episodes, and these episodes usually occur either when I'm overwhelmed with work or when my wife and I are in an argument of one sort or another. But, yeah, when I start feeling that 'itch' to log on and 'flirt' with sexual stuff, if there's something that gets in the way of my doing so, I usually get very irritable and moody."

Even though I thought I knew the answer to the next question, I asked it nonetheless. "How about any *Adverse consequences* as a result of your sexual behaviors? Have you lost anything dear to you?" As predicted, Sergio looked at me like I had lost my mind, but I find it important for clients to reiterate their consequences from time to time to address the minimizations and rationalizations that occur with addictive disorders. "Well, of course I have—I'm living on my friend's couch, and my wife hates me. I can't even spend time with my daughters!" Digging further, we determined that he had also (1) lost significant amounts of sleep due to his nighttime web-surfing, (2) not been as productive at work as he should have been due to being too tired (he even mentioned the possibility that his back injury may have been caused by his lack of attention at work), and (3) lost all belief in himself as a father, man of God, and husband. "In fact, I bet my whole depression is to be blamed on this stuff, too!" At this point, I assured him that sexual addiction impacts people of every gender, race, creed, and *religion*. "Many men, even those in the church, struggle with their sexual integrity, Sergio, and whereas this fact does not absolve you of your actions, it should help you to see that you are not alone."

"Sergio, have you attempted to cut back, control, or stop your sexual behaviors without success, even when you knew that continuing would cause you harm (*inability to Stop*)?" This is where Sergio teared up and became quiet for a while. "Doc, I've been trying to stop this stuff since I was in my twenties—that's more than 20 years of this roller coaster. I want to stop so much it actually hurts, and even after what happened with my wife, I still

find myself drawn to using my friend's computer when he goes to sleep! I hate this more than you know."

"I understand what a struggle it must be for you Sergio. . . . Over time have you found it necessary to increase the amount or intensity of your sexual behaviors to achieve the same effect (*Tolerance or intensity*)?" He asked me what I meant by that, so I explained that for an alcoholic, whereas one beer might have initially been enough to "catch a buzz," after a while it takes a minimum of a six-pack to get the same effect. "No, not really. I mean I have these, I guess you'd call them binge periods, every two or three weeks, and I haven't really done more than that. Then again, in the past I'd only spend 15 minutes or so searching for images, and now it's typical for me to spend at least an hour or more doing the same thing. In fact, I often intend to only spend 15 minutes online, but before I know it, something like a couple of hours have passed."

"Okay, Sergio, I think you already mentioned this. But can you tell me again about the events or moods that occur right before you choose to use the Internet as an *Escape*?" "Well, yeah, it's about my stress, my being overwhelmed by work or other things, fights with my wife—you know, typical stuff. And then for moods, I guess I use it to help me get out of feeling depressed or lonely. But isn't that the weirdest thing? I use it to stop feeling depressed and lonely, but here I am, more depressed and lonelier as a result. See how crazy I am?" I told him that I didn't think that he was crazy, but rather I shared that he was likely stuck in a destructive cycle from which there *was* a way out.

"Just one more question, Sergio, and then we're about done for today. You already mentioned the amount of time you spend on the Internet, how that has increased over time, and how you have wasted more time on the Internet than you had intended (*Time wasted*). But tell me about your pattern of using the Internet. What actually happens before, during, and after you log on?" With some additional probes, he noted that he would have to sometimes wait for hours until his wife fell asleep beside him; then he would sneak downstairs and use the Internet for several hours at a time—and suffer the entire next day as he struggled to get through work on three hours of sleep.

"Well, Sergio, I think that I have a pretty good picture of what has been going on with you. Given the answers you provided, I'd say that it's pretty certain that you struggle with sexual addiction. I think that you took a huge step toward seeking out some help for yourself, and I truly believe that there *is* a light at the end of the tunnel for your situation. In addition to our continued work together, next week we'll begin to identify some ways to set you up for success."

"To conclude for today, let me know where you are on that 10-point scale, especially in regard to your intent to harm yourself." He answered, "Well, we talked a lot about what I've lost and how crazy this has all been—to tell you the truth, I feel pretty crappy right now, not enough to hurt myself but not too great either. I'd say a 3 or 4, but again, I won't do anything silly." I reminded him that he had access to the 24-hour help line, knew my emergency number, and could go to the local emergency room if he should be in any danger. He acknowledged my suggestions and agreed to meet with me the next week.

The intent of our fourth session was to set some bio-psycho-social-spiritual goals to aid in his recovery and to address his depression. During the next hour, we identified several attainable goals for the upcoming weeks. Physically, he was encouraged to continue with his exercise (daily walks), as this would aid in both alleviating stress and increasing his self-efficacy. Psychologically, to supplement our work together, I provided him with a list of books that prior clients had found instrumental in their walk toward recovery. He reminded

me that he was already reading a book (nice one, Hagedorn!), and I admitted to being se-
nile (to bring a little levity).

In order to combat his shame and isolation, as well as to increase his social interactions,
I encouraged Sergio to attend a support group where the issue of sexual addiction was ad-
dressed. Whereas the mainstream 12-step groups that address sexual addiction [e.g.,
Sexaholics Anonymous (SA), Sex and Love Addicts Anonymous (SLAA), and Sex Addicts
Anonymous (SAA)] were available in our city, he mentioned a desire to have a more spiritual
approach to recovery. I knew of two such groups in the area: Faithful & True and Celebrate
Recovery. Both are Christian-based educational/support groups facilitated by trained leaders
(this lay-based training occurs through seminars held around the country). After providing
him with brochures about these groups, I suggested he attend a minimum of two to three
meetings per week, secure a temporary sponsor, and begin sharing his story with others in
the group. Given the nature of these groups, they could also meet his spiritual needs. In
terms of his current spiritual practices, I asked him to consider stepping out of the position he
held as a small-group leader and moving more into "receiving mode" by being a member
(versus a leader) of a group. He reluctantly agreed that this was probably necessary.

A Turn for the Worse

My work with Sergio continued for several months. Given that he was actively working on
the development of a strong support network, had been able to demonstrate several healthy
coping mechanisms, and had stated his readiness to use therapy explore the reasons why he
used sexual addiction as a way to cope with his life stressors, we began to do just that.
Progress was steady up until the fourth month, when Sergio experienced a significant crisis
that sent him into a depressive tailspin.

Sergio missed a session and did not call to cancel or reschedule. I was not concerned at
the time, given the positive steps he had been taking and his consistent low scores on the self-
harm scaling question. The following week Sergio arrived, and from the moment I saw him in
the waiting room, I knew that something terrible had happened—he looked physically worse
than he did during our first session. With two weeks' growth of beard, underweight to the
point of concern, and with dread in his eyes, Sergio related what had happened to him two
weeks ago: He had been arrested for voyeurism in the neighborhood where his friend lived.

Unbeknownst to me, during one of his evening walks about four weeks prior, Sergio
had witnessed a woman undressing through a downstairs window of a home along his normal route. Transfixed by the chance encounter, he had continued with his walks but had
spent more and more time in that same location, finding excuses to hang around that particular house. Then, two weeks ago, frustrated by the whole situation and yet unable to re-
strain himself, he had actually approached the house for the first time and peered in through
one of the windows. He was watching the woman undress yet again when he was tackled
from behind by the woman's husband, who had been taking the garbage out. The police
had been summoned, and Sergio was arrested and charged with voyeurism. A series of
events closely followed: His friend had had to bail him out of jail, his wife had found out
and had contacted the church, his name had appeared in the local newspaper, and he was
being touted as a sexual predator by the media. Sergio felt devastated and destroyed.

Without having to be asked, he shared that he currently rated himself as a 9 or 10 in
terms of how depressed he felt but wasn't sure about what he was thinking in terms of harm-
ing himself. "With you as depressed as you are, Sergio, I'm concerned about your health and
well-being. How will I know what kind of care to provide you if you don't let me know what

you're thinking?" "I'm not going to do anything to hurt myself," he replied sullenly. "In fact, I'm just going to go home and spend the weekend thinking about what I'm going to do about all of this. If I get close to wanting to do anything stupid, I'll be sure to call you."

Even with Sergio as depressed as he appeared, with no stated intent to self-harm, I did not have enough to move forward with any type of involuntary commitment at that time. I asked Sergio to call me at least twice before our next meeting to let me know how he was doing, shared that I was concerned about him, and reminded him about the resources available to him, should he find himself in a crisis between sessions. He again acknowledged having the necessary resources and restated that he would not harm himself. We agreed to meet again in three days to determine his current level of depression.

Key Suicide Risk Assessment Factors

Throughout my work with sexual addicts, perhaps the most significant and damaging impacts of this addiction on the addicts themselves include the shame, self-loathing, and despair that result from their behaviors. Whereas I have often heard from the "uninformed" that they wish they were "so lucky as to be addicted to *sex*," the reality is that people suffer greatly from their inability to stop their addictive cycles. This suffering comes from two primary sources. First, it results from an interaction of shame (which comes from within, as a result of one's inability to stop) and guilt (which comes from outside, as a result of being caught in compromising behaviors). Second, addicts' private lives (in which they have been able to secretly engage in their sexual behaviors, often hidden for years) suddenly collide with their public lives (the ones that others know and respect). Take, for example, the secret lives of politicians, athletes, clergy, and actors who have been recently exposed for the world to see and criticize. The shame, guilt, and exposure are so overwhelming that suicide often seems like the only solution. In fact, besides gambling, which has the greatest rate of suicide, such attempts and completions are very high among those who struggle with sexual addiction (Carnes, 1994; Hagedorn & Juhnke, 2005; Mahorney, 2002).

Sergio's risk of self-harm increased exponentially following his arrest. Several factors contributed to my concern about his well-being. First, given the collision of his private and public lives, as well as his deep despair (with an accompanying cycle of shame and guilt), his feelings of hopelessness and helplessness were acute. These feelings prevented him from continuing to seek assistance from his support group; he ceased attending. This lack of support was another significant risk factor. His wife filing for divorce was a third, and his pending court date was a fourth. Additional risk factors identified by the SAD PERSONS Scale (Patterson, Dohn, Bird, & Patterson, 1983; discussed in Chapter 3) included his being a male over 45 years old; yet he did not have any prior suicide attempts, was not abusing alcohol or other drugs, maintained the capacity for rational thought, did not have an organized suicide plan, and had not experienced any sickness or illness.

Three days later, at our next session, we decided to shift the primary focus of our therapy from his addiction to his depression, while at the same time noting how intertwined these two issues were. Given the aforementioned risk factors, the ones that we could feasibly address were reducing his hopelessness/helplessness, reengaging in his support group, and preparing for his two pending court dates (one the result of the arrest and the other the result of his pending divorce). Again, we acknowledged that all three of these goals were related to one another.

The remainder of that session was spent discussing Sergio's hopelessness and helplessness, as these were profound—he felt that he had no control over what was happening to him. He quietly admitted to his part in the current events. He noted that the choice had been

his (1) to return to the house on several occasions to try and catch another glimpse, (2) to not speak about his compulsions in either the therapy or the support group process, and (3) to approach the house that single time to look in the window. He did not see how the dire consequences of his choices fit the actual events, and I shared that I agreed with him as long as he was being completely honest about the events that he had shared. He maintained that the approach to the home had been his first, and I asked him how many more times he would have gone to that house, had he not been caught. "Oh, I don't know. I mean, I knew that what I was doing was wrong and that I probably needed to discuss what was happening with you and the group. But I mean, it was just that one time!" I reiterated the importance of accepting his piece of the events as a necessary step toward empowering himself to feel some sense of control—perhaps not control over what was to occur at his pending court date but control over his current feelings and behaviors. "I guess I accept that piece of it, but it still isn't fair. I'm not a sexual predator. I don't rape and kidnap people like those kinds of people do!"

"What would help you to get through the rest of this week, Sergio? What kind of support do you need?" He stated that he needed to have people spend time with him, that he needed to "get outta [his] head." He shared that the best support came from the men at the two groups he attended regularly and that he needed to return and bring them up to date on what was occurring in his life. "But I'm ashamed, doc. Up until this point, I was just another guy who struggled with pornography. Now they're gonna think I'm some kind of *real* pervert." To summarize the session, we explored the significance of that statement further, I reassessed his intent to self-harm, and we agreed to meet in four more days to continue our work.

Two days later I received a telephone call on my emergency number at 10 P.M. It was Sergio. He was at the emergency room (ER) at the local hospital and asked if I would be willing to come and support him. I agreed and left immediately. Upon arriving, I found that Sergio had come in around 9 P.M. and had admitted to the desire to end his life. The attending ER physician had put him in one of the curtained areas with a security guard to stand watch. In speaking with the physician, she stated that the hospital did not have psychiatric care available and that she was working on having Sergio transferred to a crisis stabilization unit (CSU) at another facility. I shared this information with Sergio, and he admitted that he probably needed that level of care. Asking what prompted his current level of despair, Sergio stated that that afternoon he had received notification of his court date related to the arrest. "I don't want to live with this hanging over my head—I can't go in there and face people who think that I'm some kind of demented pervert. I think that dying would just be easier and better for everyone."

Over the course of the next two hours, while we waited for the transport to arrive, we spent a lot of time being silent, and I allowed Sergio to share what was on his mind and in his heart. We also explored some of his specific reasons to keep living, and whereas he was able to note that he wouldn't want to hurt his daughters or wife, he couldn't think of any other good reasons to stick around. The transport finally arrived, we said good-by, and I asked that he list me as someone on his approved list of callers so that I could speak with him and help set up his aftercare.

Overall, I agreed with his need to be hospitalized until the current crisis could be stabilized. The problem was that the court date was not going to disappear. My primary concern was that I did not believe three to five days of inpatient care and a medical approach to his depression would sufficiently alleviate his desire to avoid the consequences of his actions. A step-down approach to treatment—from inpatient hospitalization, to intensive outpatient care, to individual counseling and support group attendance—would be my recommendation to the therapist in charge of his care at the CSU.

Unfortunately, I never got the opportunity to share my opinions with the CSU staff. Upon calling the next day, I was informed that they could neither confirm nor deny that Sergio had been admitted but that if I wanted to leave a message for someone, I could do so. I left a message both for Sergio and for the lead clinician, identifying myself as Sergio's therapist of record, reiterating that Sergio could add my name to his approved callers list, and stating that either of them should feel free to call me when they had an opportunity. I never received a return call, and after leaving a similar message the following day, I decided to leave the ball in Sergio's court.

A week and a half passed before I heard from Sergio. He had been discharged, was feeling a little better, and agreed to meet with me two days later. He didn't show for that session, and a telephone call to his cell phone netted no results. As he had listed his wife, Isabelle, on my consent form to contact in case of emergencies, I called her the following day. Isabelle stated that she hadn't heard from Sergio but that, interestingly, his bike had disappeared from the garage. A few more days passed and still no word from Sergio. Given my concern for his well-being, I contacted the coworker/friend that he had been living with, a man named Nathan. Nathan was notably confused and very alarmed, stating that he hadn't heard from Sergio since he was discharged from the hospital, which was more than two weeks ago. Further, Sergio had not shown up for work in that time. Finally, Nathan noted that nothing was missing from Sergio's room; in fact, his phone, wallet, and keys were where they usually were, near the front door. Nathan had gone so far as to file a missing person report on Sergio, but given that he hadn't known my name or contact information, he had not been able to bring me up to date. I thanked Nathan and left him my number, should he hear anything about Sergio.

I was notably worried about Sergio. I consulted with colleagues and determined that I had done all that I could until I heard from him again. The court date came and went, and again, I heard nothing from Sergio.

Finally, two weeks later, Isabelle called, very distraught. It turned out that the police had returned Sergio's bike (it had an identification tag), which had been found by a park ranger. This ranger worked in the alligator- and snake-infested swamps that border the southern metropolis where we lived and had found the bike alongside a dirt road, miles from any paved areas. Inscribed on the side of the bike in marker was one word: "Ciao."

CONCLUSION

Not every story has a happy ending, especially when working with clients who are suicidally depressed. As I never again heard from Sergio, Isabelle, or Nathan, though I did recommend that Isabelle seek counseling herself, I have to assume that Sergio took a long ride and then walked into the swamp: He had no intentions of returning. Too often we underestimate the power that shame and exposure can have on the lives of our clients. Whereas I recognized Sergio's despair, his loss still impacts me. In revisiting the main points of our therapy, I believe that I kept sufficient watch on his depressive symptoms and that he had been making some significant progress. But sometimes external events over which clients have no control can be so overwhelming that death seems like the only viable solution. It is still my job (and yours) to come alongside clients and assist them through their life trials and tribulations. Additionally, we help them recognize increased suicide risks. We also encourage them to make the appropriate choices that ensure their safety and care. My hope is that Sergio's story is one from which we can both learn and grow.

Case Reflection Questions

Suicide Issue Questions

1. Shame is a powerful emotion often linked to suicide. How would you have helped this client deal with his feelings of shame?
2. Control, communication, and avoidance are sometimes given as three underlying causes for suicides. How does avoidance figure as a possible cause in this case?

Skill Builder Questions

1. How might you feel if you were counseling this suicidal client? What is your personal emotional reaction to this client's suicidal behavior?
2. What would you have done in order to ensure this suicidal client's safety? Utilizing the FED, described in Chapter 3, which indicates *frequency* of suicidal thoughts, *extent* of suicide plans, and *duration* of suicidal thoughts and impulses, indicate your assessment of this client's degree of danger to self. What would you have done to properly assess this client's immediate suicide risk?

3. What important suicide risk factors were present in the case? What unique individual factors or characteristics of this client would be important to your suicide risk assessment? As you read this case, which SAD PERSONS risk factors (sex, age, depression, previous attempt, ethanol abuse, rational thinking loss, social supports lacking, organized suicide plan, no spouse, and sickness) did you find most relevant to this case?
4. What would be your therapeutic approach to treating this suicidal client? What two pieces of information described within this case would be most helpful for your own work in intervening with potentially suicidal clients and their loved ones?
5. How would your approach be the same as or different from that f the clinician in the case? What interventions described in the case did you think were most helpful to the client?
6. How will you care for yourself when working with clients who are suicidal?
7. What strategies will you use to make sure you are competent and prepared to work with high-risk clients?

W. Bryce Hagedorn holds a doctoral degree in Counseling and Counselor Education is a Licensed Mental Health Counselor, a Nationally Certified Counselor, and a Master Addiction Counselor and currently works as an assistant professor and clinical director of Counselor Education at the University of Central Florida in Orlando. A nationally and internationally recognized speaker and author, Dr. Hagedorn's research has significantly contributed to the development of assessment and treatment strategies for working with addicted clients and their families.

References

Carnes, P. (1994). *Contrary to love: Helping the sexual addict*. Center City, MN: Hazelden.

Hagedorn, W. B., & Juhnke, G. A. (2005). Treating the sexually addicted client: Establishing a need for increased counselor awareness. *Journal of Addictions & Offender Counseling, 25*(2), 66–86.

Mahorney, S. L. (2002). Point: Sexual addiction—A diagnosis whose time has come [Electronic version]. *Current Psychiatry Online, 1*(7). Retrieved July 19, 2003, from www.currentpsychiatry.com/2002_07/07_02_sexaddict.asp

Patterson, W. M., Dohn, H. H., Bird, J., & Patterson, G. A. (1983). Evaluation of suicidal patients: The SAD PERSONS Scale. *Psychosomatics, 24,* 343–349.

Mark

A Male with HIV and Depression

DANIEL R. CRUIKSHANKS

EDITORS' COMMENTS

- The counselor in this case clearly points out that suicidality is an expression by the client of his need for relief from pain and suffering.

INTRODUCTION

Unless you have lived with human immunodeficiency virus (HIV) or have entered the world of one living with it, it is almost impossible to imagine the difficulties those with HIV face on a daily basis. Although medical technology has advanced dramatically, allowing people with HIV to live much longer, the impact of the infection on people's lives is significant, and for some, the treatments can seem worse than the acquired immunodeficiency syndrome (AIDS) they are fighting. Imagine, for a moment, learning that you are HIV positive. How would you feel? Shocked, frightened, overwhelmed? As of this writing, HIV/AIDS continues to be a terminal disease, although many have come to see it as less of a "big deal," and as more of an illness to be managed like diabetes, than they might have 20 years ago. To date, however, there are no cures for the virus—only ways of keeping it virus at bay and delaying death.

HIV/AIDS is a terminal illness, and living with it is extremely stressful. The medications available to hold the virus at bay now can extend life almost to normalcy, but these treatments exact a heavy toll themselves. Many of those now living with HIV/AIDS experience significant medication side effects that can leave them feeling more ill than they did prior to treatment. These side effects can include chronic gastrointestinal problems like diarrhea and loss of appetite, neuropathy (numbness and tingling in the limbs), headaches, fatigue, and skin problems, to name a few. On top of these, many experience significant body changes as fat migrates, often out of the face and limbs and into the abdominal area; this frequently affects self-esteem. Depressive disorders secondary to HIV/AIDS are common. Unlike other types of depression, however, the suicidal ideation found here may be specific to the feelings of hopelessness associated with a life dependant on tens of pills a day that may cause misery while preserving life. Such was the case with Mark.

BACKGROUND/REFERRAL

At the age of 27, Mark had been HIV positive for nearly five years, and he had been living with AIDS for more than a year. Mark was referred to me for counseling by his Ryan White Program case manager. According to Mark's case manager, he had been struggling with depression for the past several months, following his transition to full-blown AIDS. With this change in the status of his illness, Mark had seen a dramatic increase in his medication regimen as his physician assumed a much more aggressive approach to his treatment. Mark had been suffering greatly from the side effects of his medications, and his quality of life had been suffering as well. Mark was no longer able to work, and he had been feeling increasingly useless. Although his partner had been supportive and understanding, Mark had fallen into a pit of despair and hopelessness. He had begun to express ideas of suicide both to his partner and to his case manager, and when he reported that he had acted on these ideas by stopping all of his medications, it was decided that he urgently needed counseling.

At that time, I was a Licensed Professional Counselor working in a small but busy psychiatric clinic in the large midwestern community where I lived. Moreover, I was one of a small handful of counselors in the community who was also a Provider through the Ryan White Fund. Because I was a specialist in counseling the terminally ill as well as those with mood disorders and suicidal ideation, Mark's case manager believed that I would have the best chance of helping this client. Given the circumstances, I arranged to see Mark right away for evaluation and counseling. Mark was brought to my clinic for his first session by his case manager.

ASSESSMENT

Upon meeting Mark, I was immediately struck by his appearance. He looked very obviously depressed. His affect was completely flat, his movement was slow and labored, his posture was slouched, and his grooming was poor. When I called him from the waiting area back to my office, his response was almost mechanical. He avoided eye contact and offered only the most minimal greeting. When I invited him to have a seat, it was as though he poured himself into the chair, looking like a sack of flour.

Mark presented as a homosexual Korean American and had been in a committed relationship for about three years. He and his partner both had knowingly been HIV positive when they met and got together. Mark reported that his relationship with his partner, Dale, was good. Dale had been supportive, but recently he had become more withdrawn and distant from Mark. Mark was the younger child of parents who had been born in Korea and immigrated to the United States long before Mark had been born. He had an older sister. Mark's family lived out of state. He had ended up in this community following a stint in the Navy, during which he had served as a cook on a ship. After he "came out," his parents had become more distant. They hadn't rejected him exactly, but they had difficulty understanding what they saw as his "choice of lifestyle." Mark acknowledged that he had been unable to bring himself to inform his parents of his HIV status.

Although Mark's health had declined in recent months, his partner's HIV continued to be managed effectively. Mark reported that initially HIV had not had a huge impact on his life. He knew that there were new treatments that could manage the virus, and he maintained a positive outlook. At the time of his positive test, Mark was working as a manager of a novelty shop, and he really loved his job. Despite the fact that he had completed only about two years of college, he was very successful. Under his management, the shop's revenue had increased, and

he had been promoted several times. Mark had big ideas for the business and had developed plans to venture out on his own. He had been working hard with long hours and a hectic schedule. The stress eventually took its toll, and Mark's T-cell count plummeted. Mark developed full-blown AIDS, becoming quite ill in a matter of weeks. With immediate aggressive treatment, Mark stabilized and even improved, but he never regained the strength to return to work.

Mark's life had become structured around a regimen of pills and dominated by nausea, vomiting, diarrhea, and exhaustion. His appetite lost, Mark's weight dropped more than 20 pounds in a matter of weeks. He began to despair of a life of illness and misery. Within a few short months, Mark's depression, secondary to his HIV/AIDS, had become severe. Mark lost his motivation, lost his sense of joy and humor, and became fixated on all that was negative in his life. He developed insomnia and became increasingly frustrated by the combination of his fatigue and his inability to rest. He became hopeless about his future. Ironically, the aggressive medical treatment of his AIDS was effective. Mark's T-cell count not only stabilized but also elevated. His AIDS-related illnesses remitted. Although he still had AIDS, Mark no longer had the physical symptoms of it. It was only the physical side effects of the medications that caused his suffering now. This only deepened his depression. He came to believe that, while he might be able to live a normal or near-normal lifespan, his life would have no meaning and no purpose and would be full of suffering.

About a week prior to his first appointment with me, Mark had become suicidal. He had quietly decided that he could not live his life like this. At 27, he might well live another 40 or more years, according to his physician, provided, of course, that he maintained his strict medication regimen. Mark decided to kill himself or, rather, to allow himself to die. In his mind, the easiest way to die was to stop his retroviral medications and allow the HIV to take over. It was only when his partner noticed that Mark was not taking his medications anymore that Mark admitted his intent. Despite the best efforts of his partner, his case manager, and even his physician, Mark stubbornly had refused to consider resumption of his treatment. Mark's T-cell count was falling already. He was now dying, and according to his physician, he might not live more than two or three months. AIDS is an autoimmune disease. HIV doesn't kill people; rather, it destroys the immune system, making us vulnerable to the myriad viruses and bacteria that all of us are exposed to all the time. Without the immune system, the body is attacked by opportunistic infections.

Initially, Mark stated simply that he had given up and was ready to die. He suggested that he was at peace with this decision and only wished that the people in his life could accept this. I wasn't convinced of this, however, and I pursued a line of questioning to assess further his decision. I had noticed that despite his profound depressive presentation, he had brightened and come to life as he talked about his work and the creative ways that he had made his store the most successful in the chain. It seemed obvious to me that this was a man who had loved life until relatively recently. Upon further assessment, it became increasingly clear that Mark's suicidal decision was more about his suffering and less about a genuine wish to die. He no longer wished to live if his life had no purpose or meaning, and he no longer wished to live if he would have to feel so miserable all of the time.

Mark had no prior history of depression or suicidal thinking. In the months since this depressive episode had manifested, Mark had not been in counseling, nor had there yet been an attempt to treat his depression with medications. Given this history, I believed it was highly likely that Mark would respond well to treatment; however, I also believed it would take some time before he would start feeling better. My immediate concern was that we did not have time under the current conditions. Since Mark had discontinued his retroviral

medications, he was now vulnerable to opportunistic infections. The course of his illness and the duration of his life would depend on which infection or infections attacked first. Moreover, as the treatment progressed, he would quickly start to feel sick again, which would only reinforce his depression and his decision to commit suicide.

I asked Mark a simple question: "If you were not suffering so much right now, would you still want to die?" Without too much hesitation, Mark confirmed my hypothesis. His wish to die was a wish to end his suffering rather than a wish to die. Mark wanted to live; he just couldn't continue to live like this. He was quick to point out, however, that it was not possible to alleviate his suffering, so the point was moot. "But if you were not suffering, you would want to live?" I reiterated. Mark agreed that this was true. At this point, I informed Mark that I believed that his suffering could be alleviated—if not completely, then at least substantially. I told him that his depression was a product of the stress and suffering that he had experienced after developing full-blown AIDS and starting the more aggressive treatment. Moreover, I suggested the possibility that the depression in part might have been a side effect of his medications. I noted that it appeared the suffering directly related to his medication regimen had started to get better and it was now the suffering associated with his depression that was predominant. Indeed, I observed that despite the fact Mark had discontinued all of his medications, he appeared to be feeling pretty miserable. He acknowledged that he was, in fact, still *very* miserable.

For the first time in this session, Mark looked directly at me. He asked if I *really* believed that he could be helped to feel better. I told him that I honestly did. I believe that it is important to be honest with clients, so I told Mark that I honestly I couldn't promise or guarantee anything but that in my experience, with the right treatment, he could expect to feel better and enjoy life again. I told Mark that, if he would be willing to work with me and give me some time, we might see progress within a few weeks.

Mark was skeptical and noncommittal. He wanted to know more specifically what I meant by "work with me," what I meant by "give me some time," and what I meant by "progress." Mark made it clear that he was not inclined to change his mind about his suicide. Since he had already enacted his plan, it was just a waiting game for him. Mostly, he was just going through the motions to appease his family. I told Mark that I would like to meet with him regularly to talk with him more about life with AIDS to see if we could discover some different ways of coping. Progress to me would mean that Mark was no longer seeing his death as the only viable solution to his problems, but I assured Mark that as far as I was concerned, suicide always is on the list of coping strategies and solutions. My immediate goal was to find a way to move it down the list, while finding less extreme coping strategies and options to implement first.

Over the years, I have worked frequently with suicidal clients. In my experience, most people who become suicidal do not really want to die. Rather, they want to end the emotional pain and suffering that results from their state. By the time they have begun to consider suicide as a solution to their pain, they have become pretty desperate and hopeless. In a strange way, the realization that they do have at least one controllable means to end their pain can give them a sense of hope and may actually allow them to face another day. They might think: "Here I am facing another miserable day, but if it gets too bad, I can always check out." Thus, when I work with suicidal clients, I feel that it is important *not* to attempt to take the suicide option off the list. Based on this assumption, I believe that when clients discover options that are more effective and less destructive than suicide, they will tend to choose them before the ultimate solution.

After talking with Mark about my belief that his suffering could be alleviated and his life could be better, I asked him if he would be willing to give me four weeks. I told him that, if, after working with me and following my lead for four weeks, he still felt that dying was his best option, then I would not stand in his way. In fact, I assured him that if in four weeks he still wanted to die, then I would work with him and his partner to help them resolve the conflict over his choice to die. Mark seemed to be stunned by this idea. For the first time since he had made his decision, someone had effectively affirmed his decision to die. All I was asking in return was for some time and cooperation. Mark agreed to accept my terms.

Once Mark had agreed to work with me in counseling, I began aggressively to establish a three-tiered treatment plan. First, I wanted Mark back on his retroviral medications right away. Second, I wanted Mark on antidepressant medication as soon as possible. Finally, I wanted to see Mark in counseling twice per week initially. In my assessment, Mark had made it clear that he could not face a life of physical suffering. While there was no doubt that Mark had suffered severely, it was my sense that as his physical symptoms had diminished, he was unable to focus on the positive because he had not found anything else on which to focus. Since losing his ability to work, he had not considered how to fill his time. Thus, he had way too much time on his hands. Counseling would focus on these issues.

In many ways, these are much the same issues as those faced by older adults who are adjusting to life after retirement and to the management of increasing health concerns. At the age of 27, Mark was facing a very long retirement, following a very short working life. Now what? Mark was having an existential crisis. In my mind, Mark's suffering was exacerbated by the fact that he had lost all sense of purpose and meaning in his life. Counseling would focus on helping Mark explore possibilities. Unless and until his health allowed him to return to the workforce, he would need to find a new way to structure his life and fill his time.

As a general rule, I assume a solution-focused, brief therapy approach to counseling, drawing on other models to help conceptualize the case. Especially given the nature of *this* crisis, I felt that it would be important to focus on short-term, immediate goals on which we could build as we progressed. The first and most immediate goal here was to convince Mark to resume his medications—the goals for a dying client would be different than the goals for a living but ill client. Next, I felt that it was important to help Mark find a reason to live. Based on my assessment, it seemed that the path to this goal would be found in vocational or avocational activities.

At this point, I did not feel that Mark was at risk of further or more aggressive suicidal behavior. There was no evidence that he had any plans for such, and he had no readily available means besides the discontinuation of his medication, which he had already done. Since he had agreed to give counseling a chance, I felt confident that he would honor his commitment and that any immediate risk of self-harm was minimal.

TREATMENT

Intervention began immediately. As it happened, Mark still had his medications. He hadn't thrown them away; he had simply stopped taking them. He agreed to start taking them again, as prescribed, right away and promised that he would make an appointment to follow up with his physician as well. In the meantime, I discussed antidepressant medications with him, and he released me to discuss options and recommendations with his physician. I was able to contact his physician later that afternoon, and she indicated serious concern for

Mark. She readily agreed to prescribe the antidepressant and also scheduled an appointment with him for the following day so she could assess his current health status and he could start the antidepressant immediately. Because of his particular symptoms, which in addition to the mood symptoms included pronounced weight loss, wasting, and insomnia, he was prescribed Remeron, an atypical antidepressant that is particularly effective when insomnia and appetite loss are of particular concern. Finally, I scheduled Mark to return for counseling in two days.

Mark returned to my clinic as scheduled, and already there appeared to be a marked improvement in his depression. When asked to talk with me about his thoughts and reactions to our first session, Mark reported that he had thought a lot about our discussion. Among the elements that he commented on was the fact that I was the first person he had encountered who did not try to talk him out of dying. I had not judged him for his suicidal act, and he appreciated this. I also had acknowledged his suffering, but rather than minimizing it, I had talked with him about the possibility that it might be alleviated. I had suggested, for example, that just because he couldn't work right now didn't mean that he would never work again or that he couldn't find other uses for his time. This had given him a sense of hope that previously he had lost, and he had started thinking already about new possibilities.

Mark reported that he had seen his physician the previous day. As promised, she had started him on Remeron, which he began taking that night. He reported that he had slept extremely well for the first time in recent memory. Although he was feeling very sleepy, he also was feeling more rested than he had in a long time, and he was pleased with this result. I assured him that the excessive sleepiness that he was experiencing would be short-lived but that the improvement in his sleep patterns should continue. In this session, Mark also reported that he had been thinking about what to do with himself and his time, but he was reluctant to explore this much in this session. When asked how he was feeling, Mark reported that his depression wasn't much different than what he had reported at our first session. That said, he admitted that simply getting a good night of sleep had made a significant difference in his state of being. He suggested that he was feeling more hopeful. Although he was nowhere near ready to relinquish his plan to die, he remained committed to the counseling process. We agreed to meet again in one week.

Mark returned a week later, as scheduled, but for the first time, he drove himself to the appointment. He was feeling better. Mark reported that he was sleeping well and that the excessive daytime sleepiness had mostly subsided. He reported that he was enjoying more energy than he had felt in a long time and that he had found himself motivated to do some things around the house. Mark's mood clearly was lifting. His affect was less depressed, he was more animated and talkative, and for the first time, I was getting a sense of Mark's personality. He was quite an engaging person, and I was beginning to understand why he had been so successful in his work.

In this session, Mark reported that he and his partner were looking fort a house to buy (this was the first I had heard of this). They had started looking at homes over the weekend, and he was excited about the possibilities. Mark had wanted to get a dog for some time. A house with a backyard would allow this. Mark wanted a border collie. "Really?" I asked. "I hear that they are a lot of work; that's quite a commitment." "I like training dogs," he explained.

I asked Mark how he was feeling. As expected, he was having some problems with side effects since resuming his medications. But for some reason, he was not as bothered by them as he had been previously. He remembered that to a degree the worst of these had

passed eventually. Also, his physician had discussed these with him on their last visit. It turned out that Mark had not talked much about them with her before, so she had been unable to address them. Mark explained that he had been raised with the attitude that he shouldn't bother people with his problems. Now that his physician was more aware of the medication side effects he was experiencing, she would be able to address them, at least some of them, through a variety of strategies. This had given Mark a sense of hope. In only a week, it seemed that the suicidal crisis largely had resolved. Nevertheless, I was very much aware that I was working under a deadline.

Mark returned a week later, as planned. For this session, he was accompanied by his partner, Dale. He asked if Dale could join us in session, and I agreed. We were now in week three of our four-week agreement, and I was curious to see how Mark would present. Since Mark had brought his partner, I asked them to talk about their relationship and how Dale understood the problem that Mark was having. As they discussed their relationship, interacting with each other and with me, I had the sense that Dale cared deeply about Mark.

Dale seemed to be a warm, quiet, and patient man about two years older than Mark. Dale worked as a computer systems support person for his company. While Mark previously had indicated feelings of guilt about not being able to help financially in their relationship, Dale insisted that he made plenty of money for both of them. So far, despite his own HIV positive status, his health was good, with no indication that it would not remain so for the foreseeable future. Dale reported that he understood that Mark could not do as much, but he didn't mind. He just wanted Mark to take care of himself. He wanted them to have as much time as they could. They had continued to look at houses and had found one that they liked and could afford in the area where they wanted to live. Mark was particularly enthusiastic about the house and talked about the possibilities. It seemed that he was making plans already. He even talked again about getting a dog.

Mark reported that his symptoms of depression were getting better. He was less obsessed with his physical symptoms. He was feeling much more positive about his situation and more *future* focused. This was clearly evident in Mark's newfound enthusiasm for the possibility of a new home and a new dog. To me, this future-oriented thinking was particularly important and hopeful. As Mark focused on what might be, he became more goal oriented. Working on the house and training the high-maintenance dog were projects that would give him a sense of purpose. Indeed, even though the house and the dog were merely possibilities at this point, they already seemed to be giving Mark a sense of purpose. He was still feeling crappy, but he didn't care as much—his suffering had decreased. As Frankl (1997) tells us, suffering is a state of mind that has little to do with a person's actual physical state.

I began our fifth session by informing Mark that we had reached the end of our agreed-on time frame. During the preceding weeks, I had not made the time frame an issue, but I wanted to bring it back now as a way of reevaluating Mark and evaluating the counseling process. So I said to Mark, "We've reached the end of the four weeks that I asked you to give me to work on this problem with you. Where are you now with regard to your wish to die?" Mark reported that he didn't want to die. He reiterated that he had not wanted to live if it meant feeling the way that he had when he had first seen me four weeks earlier. But he was not feeling that badly now. He admitted that he was not thrilled with the regimen of medications that he again was managing every day. Indeed, thanks to me, it was even worse now, as he had the added antidepressant to take at bedtime. Moreover, he continued to experience a number of physical problems that were bothersome to him.

That said, his appetite was back, and he had gained back some of his lost weight. He was sleeping well, feeling more rested, and enjoying a lot more energy, which he was using to get back into life. Mark indicated that he had shifted his thinking about work. Four weeks earlier he had resigned himself to a life of suffering and uselessness—sitting around with nothing better to do than feel sorry for himself. But now Mark was feeling more positive. I hadn't told him that he would be able to return to work, but I had suggested that he might eventually find some way of working. Moreover, I had worked with him to find alternative avocational activities. Although in my mind these might include things like volunteering, I had simply facilitated a discussion of what kinds of things would be enjoyable to him. Mark had come up with the realization that now that he was unable to work, he had time to do things that he had never had time for before, such as training a border collie and working on a house. As he had considered these and other ideas, Mark had become more hopeful. As he and Dale had looked at houses, Mark's creative juices began to flow, and his brain started working with all of the possibilities. He had found enjoyment with Dale as they worked on this new project—finding a fixer-upper.

Mark reported that he was not willing to take the option of suicide off the table, but at present, he wanted to live. He was satisfied. He was enjoying life again and looking forward to a new home, a new dog, and whatever else might come along. Mark asked me if, now that we had come to the end of the four-week time, we would be ending counseling. I told Mark that it was up to him and asked him what he would like to do with this counseling process now if we were to continue. Mark indicated that he didn't feel that he was "out of the woods" and wanted to continue with counseling if I thought it was OK. I agreed that it would be good to continue.

At this stage, new goals were in order. While the immediate suicide crisis was over, Mark still faced many challenges. He was still a sick man. He was vulnerable to stress, and his depression was still an issue. Now counseling would focus on the longer-term goals of helping Mark manage his illness and cope with the inevitable emotional ups and downs that come with any serious illness. Mark needed to learn how to be a productive person living with AIDS rather than a person dying of AIDS. He had taken some significant steps in that direction, but after only four weeks, this may well have been a rebound effect. Mark would need to be followed for some time. I was pleased that he had suggested this.

CONCLUSION

I worked with Mark, and at times with Dale, for another 12 sessions. As Mark became more stable, we decreased the frequency of sessions to once monthly before finally terminating. Mark and Dale purchased the home that they had found, and Mark took charge of designing and planning the renovation project. On weekends, they worked together on projects. Mark did get his dog, which seemed to bring him great joy. As expected, there were ups and downs as Mark's body changed and he required changes in medications and dosages. But Mark's health improved. Over time, his viral load dropped to almost undetectable levels, and his T-cell counts were near normal. Eventually, Mark was doing so well that we agreed to terminate with the promise that, if he found himself struggling again, he would call me to resume counseling. I never heard from Mark again.

I have worked with many suicidal clients over the years. As of this writing, I have been fortunate that I have not lost a client to suicide, although I assume that it will inevitably happen. I don't look forward to this inevitability. Mark's case is unusual in my experience because

he had actually followed through on his suicidal plan before he had entered counseling with me. Most times the problem is to respond to existing clients who become suicidal. We assess risk, determine appropriate interventions, and act accordingly—hopefully interrupting a successful suicide. But in this case, Mark had pulled the trigger already. The bullet was on its way. We could see it coming, and there was nothing we could do about it. Only Mark could stop the bullet.

Others had tried to talk Mark into changing his mind about dying, to no avail. I believe one mistake that others made was to try to take suicide off the table as a viable option. As mentioned previously, I have adopted the attitude that suicide always is an option. As long as we are trying to wrestle it away from clients, we get stuck in a tug-of-war that may well miss the point. In my experience, the salient point is that most people who become suicidal don't really want to die; they just don't want to suffer any more. If we can focus with suicidal clients on what it is that defines their suffering and on how their life needs to be different in order for them to experience less suffering and then empower them to take action, clients are more likely to discover that life is bearable.

When Mark's case manager referred him to me, initially I felt a little panicked; somehow I had to get him to change his mind before it was too late. But by the time I met with him the next day, I had shifted my thinking. I remembered my hospice background and reminded myself that Mark was suffering from a terminal illness and that ultimately, if he chose to discontinue treatment and die, this was his choice. Who was I to judge that decision? How do I know that I wouldn't have made the same one if I had been in his shoes? Indeed, as I reflected on this case, it occurred to me that, if I were in his shoes and I made a similar choice, I would probably be offended by those who judged the decision a bad one and tried to talk me out of it.

It's been more than 10 years since I worked with Mark. I have yet to be faced with a similar case, but whenever I encounter suicidal clients, I make a point of letting them know that I respect their position and that I will not try to talk them out of it. But I also ask this: If given a choice between living and dying, if you could live without suffering, which would you choose? So far all my suicidal clients have agreed that they would choose life, and so far we have always found a way to alleviate their suffering—if not completely, at least enough that they are willing to continue to live and work on making their lives better.

Case Reflection Questions

Suicide Issue Questions

1. Edwin Schniederman, called the grandfather of suicidology, coined the term *psychache* to describe the intense psychological suffering that suicidal people experience. How does this case embody the idea that suicidal people do not really want to die but rather just want their suffering to end?

2. HIV is actually one of the few diseases that has been shown to increase suicide risk even after factoring out depression. How will you modify your approach to working with a suicidal client if he or she also has a serious chronic disease?

Skill Builder Questions

1. How might you feel if you were counseling this suicidal client? What is your personal emotional reaction to this client's suicidal behavior?

2. What would you have done in order to ensure this suicidal client's safety? Utilizing the FED, described in Chapter 3, which indicates *frequency* of suicidal thoughts, *extent* of suicide plans, and

duration of suicidal thoughts and impulses, indicate your assessment of this client's degree of danger to self. What would you have done to properly assess this client's immediate suicide risk?

3. What important suicide risk factors were present in the case? What unique individual factors or characteristics of this client would be important to your suicide risk assessment? As you read this case, which SAD PERSONS risk factors (sex, age, depression, previous attempt, ethanol abuse, rational thinking loss, social supports lacking, organized suicide plan, no spouse, and sickness) did you find most relevant to this case?

4. What would be your therapeutic approach to treating this suicidal client? What two pieces of information described within this case would be most helpful for your own work in intervening with potentially suicidal clients and their loved ones?

5. How would your approach be the same as or different from that of the clinician in the case? What interventions described in the case did you think were most helpful to the client?

6. How will you care for yourself when working with clients who are suicidal?

7. What strategies will you use to make sure you are competent and prepared to work with high-risk clients?

Daniel R. Cruikshanks is an Associate Professor in Counselor Education and Clinical Director of the Graduate Studies in Counseling Program at Heidelberg College in Tiffin, Ohio. He has a Ph.D. in Counseling and Family Therapy from Saint Louis University, a master's in counseling from the University of Missouri, St. Louis, and a BA in Psychology from the California State University, Sacramento. He is a Supervising Professional Clinical Counselor (PCC-S) in Ohio as well as a National Certified Counselor (NCC). In addition to his work at Heidelberg, he maintains a small private practice in Tiffin, and he serves as the Clinical Supervisor for Christian Counseling Center of Tiffin, Ohio. Dr. Cruikshanks routinely consults with the Department of Job & Family Services providing psychological and forensic evaluations and serving as an expert witness in cases of child abuse, neglect, and parental competence. Prior to joining the faculty at Heidelberg College, he spent over four years working in hospice, counseling the terminally ill and bereaved. During this time, he developed a program called The Life Review Project with which he creates video autobiographies of terminally ill folks by which they can create a legacy for future generations of their families. He continues to work with hospice creating video Life Reviews for people of Northwest Ohio. In his clinical work, Dr. Cruikshanks specializes in working with people with mood, psychotic, and personality disorders. Dr. Cruikshanks' other scholarly interests include ethical issues in clinical supervision and counselor identity. He has published research on suicide, sexual boundaries in clinical supervision, and the role of counselor supervisors in the formation of counselor identity. A leader in the counseling field, Dr. Cruikshanks served as President of the Ohio Counseling Association in 2007–2008.

Reference

Frankl, V. E. (1997). *Man's search for meaning* (Rev. & updated ed.). New York: Pocket Books.

Terri

A Completed Suicide with Bipolar Disorder; Obsessive Compulsive Disorder; and Borderline Personality

PETER ZAFIRIDES

EDITORS' COMMENTS

- Suicide has multiple causes—it may result from biologically based disorders, social factors, and stressors as well as individual psychological traits. This case illustrates a strong biological basis for suicide.

INTRODUCTION

It is well known within psychiatry that Bipolar Disorder has the potential to be very lethal. Extra caution is warranted when a patient presents with a "mixed" subtype of Bipolar Disorder, which carries a significant risk of mortality. This can be understood if one considers that the patient is simultaneously expressing extreme symptoms of depression as well as mania (hence the "mixed" designation). Manic symptoms such as irritability, anger, and impulsivity combined with severe depression can be a very deadly mix. A comorbid psychiatric conditions (BiPolar and OCD) as well as an existing severe characterological disorder (Borderline Personality Disorder) further heightens the risk of suicide.

This is the story of Terri. She came under my care almost at the start of my career as an attending physician and remained my patient for almost five years. Chillingly, Terri and I had a running dialogue about her eventual suicide from nearly the beginning of our treatment relationship. I can clearly remember her saying throughout the course of our sessions, "Dr. Z, you know I am eventually going to take my life. You know I cannot live like this. I really hate the fact that I will do this on 'your watch,' but I know you will be my last doctor. I know I cannot live the rest of my life like this. I won't." Terri would make these points even when she was feeling better and was not actively suicidal. This was an ominous backdrop to our five-year treatment history.

Terri struggled tremendously with the combination of her Bipolar Disorder, Obsessive-Compulsive Disorder, and Borderline Personality Disorder. She is perhaps the most challenging patient I have treated to this point in my career. She is—without a doubt—one of the *strongest* patients I have ever treated. I know that may seem like a paradox to you. How can a patient who is struggling with so many illnesses and who ultimately ends her life be considered "strong?" Perhaps it is because I have rarely seen someone in such a perpetual state of chronic impairment and pain secondary to emotional illness. Terri's periods of happiness were but fleeting moments against the backdrop of severe depression and mania. The fact that Terri lived as long as she did was a testament to her strength and perseverance in the midst of this pain. I remember discussing this with Terri's family at her funeral. We marveled at Terri's ability to make it through the darkest days despite her illness. We could barely imagine the stress she endured in dealing with this illness. We spoke of the humility and helplessness we felt in not being able to "do more" to keep her alive. This is a story of a very troubled but very remarkable young woman.

BACKGROUND/REFERRAL

Terri was a 38-year-old, single female when I first met with her in 1997. She was a transfer case from one of my resident colleagues, Dr. John Blanchard. We were just completing our residencies, and John's fellowship was taking him to New York. He had been treating Terri for nearly two years at our residents' clinic. As I was planning to remain in practice locally after residency, he asked me if I would be interested in assuming Terri's care. He said, "She is a very interesting patient." Now it must be noted that when a physician tells you that a patient is *interesting*, it usually means that this patient's case is very *challenging*, if not downright *difficult*. He briefly presented Terri's case to me over a cup of coffee in the hospital cafeteria. I remember thinking her case truly was a challenge. Challenging cases were nothing new to fourth-year residents at a large university psychiatric clinic, but the more John described Terri's case, the more intrigued I became. She had made some progress in their treatment, but John acknowledged the difficulties and frustrations caused by the chronic nature of her illness.

After thoughtful consideration, I agreed to accept Terri's case. We arranged an appointment for the three of us later the following week. I remember that first visit quite vividly. Terri was very upset and crying nearly inconsolably. Although she and John had discussed his move to New York in prior sessions, our meeting marked the finality of their treatment together. It was at that point I realized how strong her transference to John was. I remember her looking at me and—at first—refusing to agree to the transfer of care. She was feeling extremely abandoned and vulnerable at that moment. So strong was her transference to John that several times throughout our treatment relationship, Terri attempted to contact him by telephone in New York. It would take the better part of two years of treatment together before she truly accepted the fact that I alone was her treating psychiatrist. It was quite a challenge during those years to provide the needed level of psychotherapy and medical treatment, knowing this tranferential barrier was in place.

ASSESSMENT

Terri had an uncomplicated birth. Her mother carried her to a full-term pregnancy. Terri reached her developmental milestones appropriately. She described her childhood as "fairly pleasant." She denied abuse of any kind in her childhood years. She remembered many

warm and loving times with her family. She described her parents as caring people. She got along well with both of her siblings. Terri's grades early in school were good. She enjoyed learning and had a good network of friends. She often reminisced about her childhood, finding it the most pleasant time in her life.

As Terri approached adolescence, however, she began to notice subtle changes in her mood. At first, her depressive symptoms were mild and transient. She described them as periods of melancholy and lethargy. These symptoms were fleeting. She never really thought much about them, as they were mild and seemed to resolve rather quickly. She figured it was just "teenage angst." At age 14, however, Terri had her first episode of severe depression. She remembered being overpowered by profound feelings of sadness, tearfulness, anxiety, and lethargy. For the first time in her life, she encountered feelings of desperation, hopelessness, and helplessness. "I had no idea what was happening. This had never happened to me before," she would say. I still can remember how upset Terri became as she spoke of this first episode of depression. She sadly reflected on it, stating that "I still can't believe [the first depressive episode] really was the end of happiness as I knew it."

As she entered into her late teens and twenties, Terri's depression became more severe. Terri would become very withdrawn with very little interest, energy, or drive. Her feelings of isolation and hopelessness were profound. During these episodes, Terri would reflect existentially on the meaning of her life and its purpose. She wondered if everyone contemplated his or her life in this constant fashion. She began to consider—and worry about—the possibility these depressive symptoms might never remit.

Terri remembered symptoms of mania beginning in her early twenties. Her mania had an evolution of its own over the years. Initially, Terri had very distinct periods of mania with pressured speech, decreased need for sleep, impulsivity, and grandiosity. These episodes had a very euphoric nature to them and at times would occur outside of the depression. This was clearly a classic bipolar-manic presentation. However, as Terri entered into her late twenties and early thirties, the disorder evolved into a bipolar-mixed picture. During these times, Terri would have simultaneous symptoms of depression (profound sadness, tearfulness, hopelessness, and isolation) and mania (agitation, irritability, impulsivity, and anger). This is the basis behind the *mixed* presentation of Bipolar Disorder.

During her midtwenties, Terri began to have suicidal thoughts. At first, these thoughts were quite fleeting. As her emotional illness worsened—and with it, her hopelessness about getting better deepened—her suicidal thoughts intensified. It was during these mixed episodes that Terri had her worst suicidal thoughts. It was during these episodes that she attempted suicide several times. Terri had many hospitalizations during her life, beginning at age 25. Invariably, the vast majority of these hospitalizations occurred during an exacerbation of a mixed episode of her Bipolar Disorder.

Terri's Obsessive-Compulsive Disorder (OCD) began at a very early age as well. Her obsessions focused around neatness and order. She required all of her possessions to be arranged in a very specific manner. She would become extremely agitated and anxious if this order was disrupted. Terri would compulsively write as well. She would take copious notes, documenting and charting her mood. She would present those notes to the treatment team and me—in highlighted, outline form—during our visits. She often would break down in tears as she discussed the level of impairment the OCD caused. I remember her saying that "I am a total slave to my rituals."

Terri was a hoarder as well. It was very difficult for her to dispose of trivial possessions (newspapers, circulars, magazines, articles, etc.). She had a great love for *The New Yorker*

magazine. At one point, however, she felt paralyzed by what had become a stack of several years' worth of unread *New Yorkers*. It was impossible for her to dispose of them unread because she might "miss" something of profound importance. I recall many treatment team meetings discussing how Terri's apartment had become one large pile of magazines and papers. I remember case managers reporting the difficulty in physically navigating through Terri's apartment due to the sheer volume of her "collections." At times, case managers would help Terri clear a path simply so she could move about the apartment. Despite feeling totally overwhelmed and exhausted by the thoughts and actions caused by her OCD, she felt powerless to change her behaviors. This only added to her desperation and hopelessness.

In addition to the above disorders, Terri met the criteria for Borderline Personality Disorder (BPD). Much of our early work involved educating her on this diagnosis and establishing a psychotherapeutic framework to address her BPD. Terri greatly resisted the diagnosis of BPD, insisting she had only Bipolar Disorder. There are many similarities in the clinical presentations of Bipolar Disorder and BPD, but clearly both disorders can—and often do—exist together. Therapy involved educating Terri on this disorder and trying to bring her to an understanding of the reasons for her behavior. She met many of the diagnostic criteria of BPD, including a pattern of chaotic relationships, impulsive acts, marked mood instability, an extremely negative self-image, chronic feelings of emptiness and worthlessness, feelings of abandonment, and recurrent suicidal behavior. Although she could appreciate the diagnosis on an intellectual level, she was furious about the possibility of being labeled a "Borderline." She felt physicians and therapists would never take her emotional symptoms seriously if she had a personality disorder. Some of our most difficult sessions revolved around the BPD diagnosis.

TREATMENT

Terri initially sought treatment in her late teens. At that point, she had been through a couple of exacerbations of her depression. The symptoms at that time included profound sadness, lethargy, decreased concentration, decreased appetite, and insomnia. She had some suicidal thoughts but without intent or plan. Early in her life, Terri had had a strong support network. Both family and concerned friends made sure she was engaged in treatment. Now she began to slowly withdraw from family and friends.

Terri's primary care physician initially treated her with Anafranil, a tricyclic antidepressant (TCA). Although Anafranil did seem to alleviate some of the mood symptoms, Terri's experience was quite negative secondary to the side effect profile of the medication. She felt extremely sedated. It was very difficult for her to think clearly while taking the medication. While she acknowledged some benefit, her side effects were clearly limiting. Her care was quickly transferred to a psychiatrist, and in the ensuing months, she tried several different TCAs. Unfortunately, she never completely tolerated any of the medications in this class (this is very common). She acknowledged this as a very trying process. Not only was she struggling emotionally, but also the side effects of these medications added to her frustration, anxiety, and hopelessness.

It must be understood that at that time (the early 1980s), treatment options for depression were significantly more limited than they are today. The selective serotonin reuptake inhibitor (SSRI) antidepressants were not yet available (Prozac, the first SSRI, was approved for depression in 1987). Monoamine oxidase inhibitors (MAOIs) were available at that time, but patients were required to follow very rigid dietary restrictions with this class of antidepressants

secondary to the risk of stroke and sudden death. Other pharmacological options at that time included lithium, typical antipsychotics (e.g., Haldol, Thorazine, Mellaril), psychostimulants (e.g., Dexedrine, Ritalin), and thyroid supplementation.

Terri had a tendency to become agitated on the antidepressants as well. In fact, later in the treatment course, she became floridly manic while solely on Imipramine. Treating Terri (or any patient with Bipolar Disorder) solely with an antidepressant creates the potential to exacerbate a manic episode. Unintentionally in Terri's case, the treatment with Imipramine became a diagnostic trial. It was clear from that point on that she had Bipolar Disorder. (The diagnosis of Bipolar Disorder greatly changes a physician's pharmacological treatment approach. Treatment *must* include a mood stabilizer [lithium, Tegretol, Depakote, atypical antipsychotics, etc.]. Antidepressants may be used in treatment but only *after* a mood stabilizer has been initiated. This is due to the risk of exacerbating a manic episode if a patient is on only an antidepressant.) Terri's psychiatrist began lithium in combination with the antidepressant treatment. Terri remained on this combination of medications for several years. While she did notice some stability on the medication, she was greatly impacted by the side effects. Lithium treatment also involves regular blood monitoring. Terri found this very inconvenient. This led to long periods of noncompliance in her treatment.

By the late 1980s, Terri had been hospitalized several times due to her emotional illness. All of these hospitalizations were secondary to worsening symptoms and expressions of suicidality. Although Terri had not made an actual suicide attempt to this point, on several occasions she had threatened to overdose on her medications. Lithium and the TCAs in overdose are quite lethal. This posed a great treatment challenge. Fortunately, Prozac and the other SSRIs—with their low risk of lethality in overdose—were approved in the late 1980s. Over the next several years, Terri would be tried on various SSRIs, including Prozac, Zoloft, and Paxil. She continued on lithium for her Bipolar Disorder. She clearly did better on the SSRIs. She acknowledged that the SSRIs were the only class of medications she felt made a difference, albeit slight, in her depression and OCD.

Even though Terri acknowledged feeling better on these medications, her condition was clearly deteriorating. By the mid 1990s, she was no longer working. Her mood fluctuations, along with the aggressive nature of her OCD, left her unable to work. During very difficult exacerbations of her condition, Terri was barely able to perform even basic activities of daily living (ADLs). By now, she had transferred her care to Ohio State and had begun her treatment with Dr. John Blanchard. The availability of a new class of antipsychotics opened up new treatment opportunities and hope for Terri. This new class—the atypical antipsychotics—was found to be very effective for mood states such as Bipolar Disorder in addition to treating Schizophrenia. Also, compliance was enhanced with the more tolerable side-effect profile that this class of medications provided.

In the next two years of treatment, Terri was relatively stable with a combination of an atypical antipsychotic, an antidepressant, and an anxiolytic medication. A key to her ongoing health at this time was her dedication to regular psychotherapy. This was the first time she had maintained in psychotherapy for an extended period of time. It made a significant difference in Terri's health. The psychotherapeutic stance was a combination of cognitive-behavioral therapy and psychodynamic therapy, but a highly structured form secondary to her BPD.

By this time in her life, Terri had alienated or abandoned most of her family and friends. She spent most of her time in solitude. Her therapist was a weekly focal point and a critical source of support. In 1997, Terri was to lose both her psychiatrist and her therapist, as they

were completing their residencies and moving out of state. This had a devastating impact on Terri. Unfortunately, it was one from which she would never completely recover. The loss of these critical sources of support ignited her ultimate fears of abandonment and isolation.

Over the next five years, Terri remained in regular treatment with me. We made some adjustments in her medications, but the basic combination—antidepressant, mood stabilizer, and anxiolytic—always remained in place. It took her about two years to develop a transferential relationship in which she truly trusted me. Eventually, she began to discuss with me her frustration at not being able to be in a relationship. She told me of various failed relationships as well as impulsive encounters with men that put her at great risk. She also told me of occasional episodes of binge drinking. She continued to have exacerbations of her Bipolar Disorder. She also continued to comment on the frustration of having to be on medications. She would then become noncompliant with her meds in response to this frustration and anger.

Terri transitioned with me from the university to a local community mental health center in 1999. This change—while difficult at first for Terri—allowed for a level of care (in the form of case management and a treatment team) that had never been in place for her before. Both my treatment team and I were shocked to see Terri's state of affairs when home visits were initiated. Clearly, she had underreported the level of her impairment from her emotional conditions. Her apartment was nearly filled with a mass of papers, magazines, and circulars. Her OCD was significantly worse than she had reported.

Over the course of the next three years, a consistent combination of case management, psychotherapy (individual and group), and medication management maintained Terri at a baseline that allowed her to attend to her basic ADLs. She was not able to work due her emotional condition. This greatly affected her self-esteem. Her unemployment and lack of a boyfriend continued to be a source of anger, frustration, and hopelessness. Perhaps in response to this anger and frustration, Terri's course was also marked by periods of medication noncompliance. She would continue to stop her medications, as she wanted to be "normal." She often saw her medications as a "crutch" or a sign of weakness. Also, they were a daily reminder of her illness. Invariably, discontinuing her medication led to an exacerbation of her condition.

In 2002, Terri began to miss more appointments at our clinic. These included visits with me as well as with other members of the treatment team. She had stopped her group therapy as well and was coming only occasionally to her individual therapy. In our discussions, Terri stated that she was "tired" of all of the sessions. She wanted to spend more time on her own and actively try to find a relationship. The entire team tried to impress on her the importance of regular follow-up and her tendency to decompensate when she fell away from treatment for any extended period of time. She did agree to meet regularly for our medication management sessions and have home visits by case managers. During this time, she presented somewhat depressed, but over the weeks, she seemed to do better. She enjoyed having fewer commitments at the clinic. In my monthly follow-up sessions, I was pleased to see how well she was doing. She had entered into a relationship that—by her accounts—was a supportive one. Everyone on the team was cautiously optimistic.

In late 2002, Terri began to regularly miss our appointments. We spoke by telephone, and she assured me she was doing fairly well, but her relationship had ended rather abruptly. She felt she was doing the best she could under the circumstances. I told her I was concerned with the decreasing frequency of our visits, but she would not commit to a more regular schedule. She continued with her meds, but it was clear from pharmacy

records that she was not being totally compliant. When I confronted her during one of her follow-up appointments, she admitted to her noncompliance. Although she was depressed, there was no indication that her mood was any worse than it had been in the several months prior. She agreed to redouble her efforts to stay on the medication regimen. She also agreed to a follow-up visit in two weeks.

I never met with Terri again. About 10 days after that last visit, I received a phone call from the case manager on my team. She informed me that Terri had taken her life in her apartment. Apparently, none of the other residents at her apartment building had seen Terri for over a week. She always took her dog out daily, irrespective of her mood. Neighbors had heard the dog barking for a couple of days and became concerned when Terri was nowhere to be found. Her landlord—fearing the worst—called the police to investigate the residence. The police found Terri's body in the bathroom. She died of a self-inflicted gunshot wound to the abdomen. According to her suicide note, she chose to take her life in the shower with the water running so as to not cause a mess for those that would find her body. She was the first patient I had ever lost to suicide.

CONCLUSION

According to Kessler (as cited in National Institute of Mental Health, 2005), 5.7 million American adults or about 2.6 percent of the population age 18 and older in any given year, have bipolar disorder. As Terri's case above illustrates, Bipolar Disorder is associated with significant morbidity and mortality. Symptoms of Bipolar Disorder can have a devastating impact on patients and their families, while placing a heavy burden on society (Calabrese et al., 2003). Psychosocial functioning is greatly impaired in these individuals.

Bipolar Disorder has been shown to be associated with higher rates of unemployment, work loss, relationship difficulties, and divorce rates than found among nonbipolar patients. The unemployment rate in those individuals with Bipolar Disorder is six times the U.S. average (Kogan et al., 2004). Significantly greater amounts of work loss and short-term disability are seen in bipolar patients (Matza, 2004). The diagnosis of Bipolar Disorder can have devastating consequences on interpersonal relationships as well. According to recent studies, only 38% of patients with Bipolar Disorder reported being married, with almost an equal number of patients (34%) either separated or divorced. A large majority of patients report significant difficulty in maintaining long-term intimate relationships due to their illness (Hirschfeld, Lewis, & Vornik, 2003). Clearly, one can see how the potential for isolation, helplessness, and hopelessness exists in the bipolar patient.

Bipolar Disorder is very lethal. It has been estimated that 25% to 50% of patients with Bipolar Disorder will attempt suicide (Chen & Dilsaver, 1996; Goodwin & Jamison, 1990, pp. 227–244). The mortality rates due to suicide in those who have Bipolar Disorder and Major Depression have been reported to be as high as 15 to 20 times the mortality rates due to suicide in the general population (Harris & Barraclough, 1997). Goodwin and Jamison (1990, pp. 227–244) estimated that a mean of 19% of the deaths of patients with Bipolar Disorder were due to suicide. It has also been estimated that the suicide rate among those with Bipolar Disorder is more than 20 times higher than that among the general population (Tondo, Isacsson, & Baldessarini, 2003). The World Health Organization ranks Bipolar Disorder sixth among all medical disorders in terms of years of life lost to death or disability.

As a practitioner, one must be keenly aware of multiple risk factors for suicide during the assessment and ongoing treatment of the bipolar patient. Prior attempts are one of the

strongest warning signals for eventual completed suicide (Lopez et al., 2001). Other risk factors for suicide include a history of drug abuse and severe depressive episodes as well as a family history of affective disorders and early traumatic stressors (Lopez et al., 2001). The presence of other psychiatric disorders is another critical risk factor for suicide (Leverich et al., 2003).

Terri possessed many of these risk factors. Clearly, her ongoing suicidal ideation was a signal. As she transitioned from John's care to mine, Terri had been hospitalized after overdosing on her psychiatric medications. Although Terri did not use illegal drugs, she would drink alcohol. On occasion—particularly during periods of mania—her consumption would be to excess. This is quite common among patients with bipolar illness. Terri's bipolar illness was marked by severe periods of depression. In fact, the majority of her life was spent in depression, with few classically manic episodes. The presence of Terri's severe OCD also put her at risk for suicide. Although Terri denied early traumatic stressors, her family history was notable for depression and alcohol dependence. This suggested a genetic predisposition to her illness.

Terri's diagnosis of Bipolar Disorder, mixed type was also a very significant risk factor for suicide. There are significant differences in the rates of suicidality associated with the various subtypes of Bipolar Disorder. Although suicidality occurs in the bipolar-manic patient, the risk is significantly greater for those with bipolar-mixed. In fact, the risk of suicidal ideation or attempts increases nearly 50-fold in the bipolar-mixed patient compared to the bipolar-manic patient (Goldberg, Garno, Leon, Kocsis, & Portera, 1998).

In the evaluation and treatment of the bipolar patient, one must aggressively search for symptoms that suggest a diagnosis of the mixed subtype. In Terri's case, this diagnosis was very clear from the beginning. Terri struggled primarily with depression. Rarely did her manic symptoms occur in isolation. When she had an exacerbation of her bipolar symptoms, they were often a simultaneous mixture of depression (sadness, lethargy, tearfulness, anhedonia, and suicidality) and mania (irritability, racing thoughts, pressured speech, insomnia, and anger). When Terri felt suicidal, she often discussed high levels of anger. She felt very angry about being diagnosed with Bipolar Disorder. Much of her anger was due to the global impairment Terri experienced across all domains of her life—psychosocial, occupational, and interpersonal. She often discussed the self-hatred that grew out of her anger. I have no doubt it was this anger and self-hatred that led Terri to take her life.

Case Reflection Questions

Suicide Issue Questions

1. Bipolar Disorder is a high-risk diagnosis for suicide, as is Major Depression. How do you think an understanding of the etiology and typical clinical course of these mood disorders would help you to effectively treat clients with these diagnoses?

2. Aside from crisis management, do you actually "treat" suicide, or do you treat the underlying disorders that lead clients to feel suicidal?

Skill Builder Questions

1. How might you feel if you were counseling this suicidal client? What is your personal emotional reaction to this client's suicidal behavior?

2. What would you have done in order to ensure this suicidal client's safety? Utilizing the FED, described in Chapter 3, which indicates *frequency* of suicidal thoughts, *extent* of suicide plans, and *duration* of suicidal thoughts and impulses, indicate your

assessment of this client's degree of danger to self. What would you have done to properly assess this client's immediate suicide risk?

3. What important suicide risk factors were present in the case? What unique individual factors or characteristics of this client would be important to your suicide risk assessment? As you read this case, which SAD PERSONS risk factors (sex, age, depression, previous attempt, ethanol abuse, rational thinking loss, social supports lacking, organized suicide plan, no spouse, and sickness) did you find most relevant to this case?

4. What would be your therapeutic approach to treating this suicidal client? What two pieces of information described within this case would be most helpful for your own work in intervening with potentially suicidal clients and their loved ones?

5. How would your approach be the same as or different from that of the clinician in the case? What interventions described in the case did you think were most helpful to the client?

6. How will you care for yourself when working with clients who are suicidal?

7. What strategies will you use to make sure you are competent and prepared to work with high-risk clients?

Dr. Peter Zafirides is currently President of Central Ohio Behavioral Medicine, Inc. in Columbus, Ohio. Since 1997, this multispecialty practice—employing 15 psychiatrists and behavioral health therapists of differing disciplines—has been committed to meeting the behavioral health care needs of the Columbus community. Dr. Zafirides maintains his clinical appointment with Ohio State University where regularly teaches medical students and residents. Dr. Zafirides' practice is quite varied. His specific area of interest in Psychiatry involves the psychiatric treatment of those patients suffering with chronic physical pain. He has been published in this specialty of psychiatry. He has also spoken internationally on the psychiatric aspect of chronic pain. Dr. Zafirides is also staff psychiatrist at Southeast Mental Health Center in downtown Columbus. Since 1997, he has been the medical director of the Homeless Team Clinic at Southeast. As a certified acupuncturist, Dr. Zafirides regularly administers acupuncture at Southeast to patients as part of their recovery treatment from substance abuse. He has been involved in community mental health since his residency and is actively involved in the treatment of schizophrenia, schizoaffective disorders and other chronic psychotic disorders. Dr. Zafirides is originally from Youngstown, Ohio. He completed his undergraduate work at Youngstown State University. He attended Ohio State University College of Medicine. He completed his residency in Psychiatry at Ohio State University. He has lived in Columbus for over 20 years.

References

Calabrese, J. R., Hirschfeld, R. M., Reed, M., Davies, M. A., Frye, M. A., Keck, P. E., Jr., et al. (2003). Impact of bipolar disorder on a U.S. community sample. *Journal of Clinical Psychiatry, 64*(4), 425–432.

Chen, Y. W., & Dilsaver, S. C. (1996). Lifetime rates of suicide attempts among subjects with bipolar and unipolar disorders relative to subjects with other Axis I disorders. *Biological Psychiatry, 39*(10), 896–899.

Goldberg, J. F., Garno, J. L., Leon, A. C., Kocsis, J. H., & Portera, L. (1998). Association of recurrent suicidal ideation with nonremission from acute mixed mania. *American Journal of Psychiatry, 155*(12), 1753–1755.

Goodwin, F. K., & Jamison, K. R. (1990). *Manic depressive illness.* New York: Oxford University Press.

Harris, E. C., & Barraclough, B. (1997). Suicide as an outcome for mental disorders: A meta-analysis. *British Journal of Psychiatry, 170,* 205–208.

Hirschfeld, R. M. A., Lewis, J., & Vornik, L. A. (2003). Perceptions and impact of bipolar disorder: How far have we really come? Results of the National Depressive and Manic-Depressive Association 2000

survey of individuals with bipolar disorder. *Journal of Clinical Psychiatry, 64*(2), 161–174.

Kogan, J. N., Otto, M. W., Bauer, M. S., Dennehy, E. B., Miklowitz, D. J., Zhang, H-W., et al. (2004). Demographic and diagnostic characteristics of the first 1000 patients enrolled in the Systematic Treatment Enhancement Program for Bipolar Disorder (STEP–BD). *Bipolar Disorders, 6*(6), 460–469.

Leverich, G. S., Altshuler, L. L., Frye, M. A., Sappes, T., Keck, P. E., Jr., McElroy, S. L., et al. (2003). Factors associated with suicide attempts in 648 patients with bipolar disorder in the Stanley Foundation Bipolar Network. *Journal of Clinical Psychiatry, 64*(5), 506–515.

Lopez, P., Mosquera, F., de Leon, J., Gutierrez, M., Ezcurra, J., Ramurez, F., et al. (2001). Suicide attempts in bipolar patients. *Journal of Clinical Psychiatry, 62*(12), 963–966.

Matza, Louis S., Rentz, Anne M., Secnik, Kristina, Swensen, Andrine R., Revicki, Dennis A., Michelson, David, Spencer, Thomas, Newcorn, Jeffrey H., Kratochvil, Christopher J. (2004). The link between health-related quality of life and clinical symptoms among children with attention-deficit hyperactivity disorder. *Journal of Developmental & Behavioral Pediatrics. 25*(3), 166–174.

National Institute of Mental Health (2005). *The Numbers That Count: Mental Disorders in America*. Retrieved June 2006, from http://www.nimh.nih.gov/health/publications/the-numbers-count-mental-disorders-in-america.shtml.

Tondo, Leonardo, Isacsson, Goran, Baldessarini, Ross J. (2003). Suicidal behaviour in bipolar disorder: Risk and prevention. *CNS Drugs*, 17, 491–511.

John and Marlene

A Couple with Depression, Marital Problems, and Religious Issues

JAMES O. FULLER

EDITORS' COMMENTS

- This case demonstrates how suicidality can be related to long-term relationship stress.
- It also shows how a counselor can work in a respectful way with a client who has strong religious beliefs.

INTRODUCTION

John and Marlene were both "born again" Christians who attended a nondenominational fundamentalist church. The church was conservative in its theology and firmly believed in the authority of the elders of the congregation over the laity. John and Marlene were stepping outside the zone of the church's authority by seeking help from a counselor who was not a member of the church's ecclesiastical hierarchy.

BACKGROUND/REFERRAL

John and Marlene were referred by friends to the counseling center where I was a doctoral intern. John was 44 years old, 6'2" tall, and around 185 pounds. He was moderately built and seemed to be in good physical condition. Marlene was 41 years old, about 5'3" tall, and around 200 pounds. John presented with a sober countenance and was relatively quiet throughout our first few sessions. Marlene was gregarious and would often answer for John, especially if he was hesitant in responding. Based on my informal assessment of John's and Marlene's responses during the interview, it was obvious that he was highly intelligent, though extremely shy and dependent on Marlene. Marlene was of moderate intelligence but determined and confident in her social interactions.

Their presenting problem was that there was little or no physical intimacy in their marriage. They had been married for almost 23 years and had no children. Marlene stated that she desperately wanted to be a mother and three times had gotten pregnant, only to miscarry each time. John reported that those three miscarriages were extremely hard on him emotionally and that he

felt personally responsible for their occurrences. John and Marlene had been to "counseling" at their local church but had discontinued when they realized that their issues were far beyond the training of their pastor and church elders.

Based on this initial session, I would diagnose John, the identified client, as having dysthymia with intermittent major depressive episodes and tendencies toward avoidant personality disorder. Although John had a history of depression, there was no history of suicidal ideation or para-suicides.

ASSESSMENT

John came from a very dysfunctional home. His father had died when he was a toddler, and he had no memory of him. John's mother was domineering and demanding, even to this time in his adult life. According to reports of both John and Marlene, she was manipulative and expected John to be ready and willing to take care of her needs at the "drop of a hat." They reported that she did not like Marlene, as Marlene would stand up to her and occasionally would encourage John to not respond to her demands. John had one brother, Phillip, who was nine years older than he. Phillip was a practicing homosexual. John and Marlene, from their conservative church background, considered Phillip to be living a sinful lifestyle. Although John's relationship with his brother was peaceful, he did not describe them as being close. John often sought ways to avoid being around his brother.

As John became more comfortable with the counseling process, he revealed that he had been sexually molested when he was four years old by his brother. He reported that, at this point in his life, he had no feelings. He loved Marlene but had no desire for sexual relations with her. Marlene, on the other hand, desperately wanted to have children and also wanted a "normal marital sexual relationship."

During the early sessions, John and Marlene spoke freely about his regular bouts with depression. He reported that some of these episodes had lasted for months. In addition, he battled low self-esteem and often believed that whatever he might do would be wrong. He found it overwhelming to deal with his interpretations of what people thought of him. It was much easier for him to think lowly of himself than to build himself up.

An additional issue that emerged during the counseling process involved John's unreconciled feelings for another woman in their church. This other woman was divorced and was, at one time, a close friend of both John and Marlene. During that time, John had expended much time and energy helping her with odd jobs and chores at her house. At this point in the counseling process, there was little relationship between the woman and John and Marlene. Marlene had discovered that John was secretly writing and sending letters to the woman. Although the letters were not sexual in nature, the woman was disturbed that he was writing to her, and she revealed the letters to Marlene. In turn, Marlene demanded that John not go to her house or be alone with her.

Marlene came from a larger family, which she described as "dysfunctional." Her father was an alcoholic, and her mother was "emotionally disturbed." Even though her father was an alcoholic, she was close to him, and she avowed that he was never abusive. Her mother had moved away when Marlene was eight, and even up to the time of our counseling, they had not restored a healthy relationship. Marlene reported that, though she loved her mother, she did not want to see her or have any involvement with her. On the other hand, Marlene dearly loved her stepmother. Marlene's father had died of a heart attack 10 years earlier. Even at this point, Marlene continued to feel intense grief at this loss. In addition,

John had developed a close relationship with Marlene's father and viewed him as the only positive male role model he had known in his life. John had experienced severe grief and depression when Marlene's father died.

One of Marlene's fears was that she would turn out like her mother. This fear was so vivid with her that each time she mentioned it, she began crying. John was in agreement with Marlene's assessment of her mother. He said he never liked her, but he got along well with Marlene's stepmother. He consistently reassured Marlene that she was nothing like her mother and never would be.

A major part of John and Marlene's psychosocial history was their involvement with their church and their commitment to their religion. As previously mentioned, the church was conservative, evangelical, and nondenominational. It was a charismatic community that believed in and practiced the expression of "spiritual gifts," including prophetic utterances, healing, and speaking in tongues (i.e., unknown languages). They also strongly believed in the hierarchy of the elders.

John and Marlene were highly involved in the church's programs. Marlene was active in Sunday school, the women's ministry, and outreach ministries, and she also sang in the choir. She was extroverted by nature and gregarious and had no problem with physical demonstrations of her faith, such as lifting her hand during the worship and prayer times or speaking in tongues if the Spirit of God would so direct her.

John was much too shy to be involved in any such demonstrative form of worship. He had agreed to be an usher, and at the time of our counseling, he had just become comfortable enough to actually sing during the worship service. He was dreadfully fearful that someone would hear him sing or, even worse, would look at him and notice that he was participating. He sought desperately to not be noticed in any way. In fact, Marlene would often run interference for John at church so that no person could actually get to him for any reason without going through her. They gave examples of people who wanted to simply chat with him or who were interested in arranging a time to have dinner with them. Marlene would see them moving in John's direction and cut them off to find out why they were approaching him. If she deemed it to be "safe," then she might allow them the opportunity to talk directly to John, but often she would tell them that she would get back with them after she had talked to John.

John's introversion (or avoidance of people) spilled over to other areas of his life. He explained that, though he was "better" now, there had been a time when they would even leave restaurants without being seated if the waiter attempted to seat them at a table in the open. He required a booth or table in a corner so as to not be noticed by anyone.

TREATMENT

As counseling progressed, one significant difficulty revolved around their church and their beliefs. By this time, they had changed churches. Although the name of the new church was different, the style and organization of the church were very similar to those of the first: charismatic, nondenominational, evangelical, and conservative. John was not comfortable in this new church situation, but he faithfully attended with Marlene.

During one counseling session, he related an experience he had at one of the church's special meetings. At the end of the service, the pastor had called for people to come to the altar for special prayer. John did not want to go, but Marlene was insistent that he do so. Eventually, he succumbed to her pressuring and went forward to the altar, where he was

anointed with oil and a public prayer was offered for his "healing." John said the prayer itself had little impact on him, but after he returned to his seat, he felt an unusual "presence of the Holy Spirit," and for at least a half hour after that, he was almost frozen in place as he communed with God.

Marlene had wanted John to receive the "healing prayer," a special type of prayer touted by this church, whereby God does a special work in a person's heart that is outside the realm of what can happen during regular prayer times. Although she was pleased that John was reporting a significant experience with God, she was not at all happy that he had not been willing to seek this "healing prayer." John said he didn't feel any need for it and thought he was doing well in his spiritual life.

During this time in their relationship, Marlene also had some significant "discussions" with God and came to some conclusions: First, if John wasn't going to do things her way and seek the kind of prayer that would "set him free from his bondage to his past," then she would take things in her own hands to set herself free from her past. She decided that she would get a job working outside the home. This was the first time during their married life that she had suggested this, and John was extremely distressed at this idea. His distress was not related to any concern with her working and having an income, as that would be a welcome assistance to him. Rather, it was related to the fact that she no longer wanted to rely on him as the family "breadwinner." At the news of this decision, John sank into an even deeper depression.

A second conclusion that Marlene reached was that John had to begin to take their relationship seriously, especially in the area of seeking "healing prayer" to "fix" his problem, or else she would consider leaving him. This was an especially noteworthy revelation of Marlene's independent thinking and demandingness, as they were in a church that taught that divorce is a sin. Although John was occasionally critical of Marlene (e.g., he disliked her demandingness, and he wanted her to lose weight because her size was a definite turnoff to him), he was highly dependent on her for many things and could not bear the thought that she would not be part of his life. His depression intensified. At this point, I was concerned about his fragility and suspected that he would be a candidate for self-harm, although he denied it when I probed in this area. So counseling continued to focus on marital issues and John's self-esteem issues.

John and Marlene continued counseling, on an as-needed basis, over a period of about three years. During the first year, they experienced significant progress in their relationship, so they discontinued counseling. Although their issues were not "resolved," they both decided to cope with the situation as it was and to be happy to be in a loving relationship. During that time, I received notice that they were planning a wedding vow renewal ceremony for themselves on the occasion of their 25th wedding anniversary. Later reports indicated that it was held at their church, that about 100 people were in attendance, and that there had been a reception and program after the ceremony. Although John was willing to participate in this ceremony for Marlene's sake, he felt "exposed" and self-conscious. He did not relish being "in front of all those people" and took every opportunity to migrate to the outskirts of the room to escape the scrutiny of the attendees. Marlene reported that she enjoyed herself immensely and had great hopes for the future of their marriage after their public recommitment to each other.

In the area of self-esteem, John made some significant positive strides. He took the initiative to ask his boss for a raise (he was a professional welder) and received a positive response. He was increasingly using his talent as an artist to assist people in his church in

decorating their homes. He was excellent at oil painting and also excelled at painting murals. He even started a small part-time children's mural company, had business cards printed, and marketed himself in his local community. He was still shy and hesitant about his progress, and although he recognized his improvement, he was unsure of how he might continue and what his next steps might be. He described himself in one session with a metaphor. He said he was like a hermit crab that had outgrown its shell and was out seeking a new, better fitting shell. He saw himself as growing but vulnerable and fearful of the future.

They soon returned to counseling. The "issues" of the past had resurfaced. At one session, Marlene was exceedingly upset. She and John had argued intensely over whether or not they would or should have children. Marlene claimed John had said that he did not want children. She "felt" as though God had confirmed in her mind that they would have their own kids, biologically, and John's lack of desire was another instance of his thwarting of God's will. She threatened John with becoming his "roommate" rather than his wife.

John was flustered with this turn of events. He claimed that her weight deterred him from feeling sexual attraction to her and that at that point in their relationship, there was no desire at all. Although he would occasionally get erections, he could not sustain them. He firmly stated that he wanted kids but was afraid of failure, both in the possibility of miscarriage, which he assumed as his personal responsibility, and in not being able to perform sexually. He also worried about his ability to be successful as a father, especially since his own father had died when he was so young and since he had been sexually molested by the only other male in his family. I wondered about John's testosterone level and inquired about it. He readily agreed to have it tested. Subsequent tests revealed that his testosterone level was normal.

At the next session, John and Marlene were much better. Marlene seemed to be trying to reconcile her personal desires with living her life without physical affection (sex) from John. They had gone dancing the Friday before the session and enjoyed themselves immensely. Marlene said that John was going out of his way to be nice to her but that this was not what she really wanted. John said he remembered normal sexual arousal as a teenager but had very little or no desire at that point in his life.

During the next session, we discussed Marlene's disappointment at not having children, while having to associate with children at a friend's house. I inquired as to whether they had considered artificial insemination with John's sperm and whether they would consider adoption. I also wondered if Marlene needed to take a "solo retreat" to help her deal with her negative and intense feelings.

In continuing with the discussion of John's self-esteem, he and I discussed his image of himself. As noted before, he was relatively tall, moderately built, and muscular. Even so, he thought of himself as ugly and unattractive. I encouraged him to restructure his thinking by imagining himself as manly and attractive to women in a sexual way and by telling himself the truth about his muscular and trim physique. Marlene saw him as attractive. John was embarrassed to even think of himself in those terms and images.

With Marlene, I discussed the possibility that she think about what she would be willing to do to make the relationship to work. She feared "falling out of love with John." I suggested that she go on a weight-loss program for her own benefit, and not just to please John. From a systems perspective, I suggested that she reframe the situation in such a way that her weight loss would be an indication that she no longer needed to "protect" John from having to perform sexually. Her commitment to lose weight for herself and concomitantly to stop enabling

John's lack of desire could reap sexual benefits for her. At this point, if the resolution to their sexual problems was to be effected, it seemed important that they both have positive attitudes toward John.

In the next session, John said there was no change in their relationship. He desperately wanted to feel and do better but was not able to make any lasting changes. At times, he reported waking up in the early hours of the morning and watching television to get sleepy. He sometimes found his mind racing, his thoughts moving in a sequence from one idea to another. At times, he reenacted in his mind "insignificant" events of the recent past. At times, he would dwell on his shortcomings. We talked about his going to church alone. He did not like doing that. He felt secure with Marlene and very insecure without her. Although he was avoidant of people, at the same time he felt ignored and rejected if people did not approach him when he was alone. Based on his report, it seemed as though he was sending out signals that he did not want interaction with people, although he very much desired interaction. We discussed methods of maintaining eye contact with people. We also discussed thought control—that he could, in fact, control his thinking and not be controlled by it, that he was not a victim of his own mind. I encouraged him to practice using open-ended questions in social situations. I also encouraged him to continue to use his diary to have a more concrete view of the impact of events and his feelings on his self-concept.

During one session when John came alone, as Marlene was visiting her stepmother, who was ill, John confessed that he was still having difficulty with Marlene's weight. He was trying to encourage her to lose, but she was now refusing. This was becoming an increasingly intense problem for him, and Marlene was taking the stance that he should love her for who she was and not for someone who she was not. Her opinion was that he would be sexually attracted to her, even though she was overweight, if he really loved her.

John also confessed that he continued to be concerned about not being able to talk or relate to the woman who was formerly a good friend of his and Marlene's. Marlene did not want him even talking to her in public places (e.g., church). Marlene believed those kinds of casual conversations would again develop into a problem in their marriage if allowed.

Key Suicide Risk Assessment Factors

At this point in the counseling, I administered the Taylor-Johnson Temperament Analysis (TJTA). Since the key treatment issues revolved around John's inability to perform sexually with Marlene, John's long-standing depression, and John and Marlene's overall marital health, the TJTA seemed to be a potentially helpful assessment tool. It gives a profile of each person in the marriage relationship, and in addition, its "crisscross" portion requires that each member of the couple respond to the items on behalf of the other member. The subsequent profile indicates how each person in the relationship views himself/herself at the time he/she responds to the items as well as how he/she presents himself/herself to the other. It is based on nine bipolar traits: Nervous versus Composed, Depressive versus Lighthearted, Active-Social versus Quiet, Expressive-Responsive versus Inhibited, Sympathetic versus Indifferent, Subjective versus Objective, Dominant versus Submissive, Hostile versus Tolerant, Self-Disciplined versus Impulsive.

As was expected, John's profile indicated high scores on many of the negative traits, not the least of which was Depressive, as viewed by John himself and as viewed by Marlene. His profile indicated high scores on Nervous, Depressive, Quiet, Inhibited, Sympathetic, Subjective, Submissive, Hostile, and Impulsive. An additional bit of vital and

pertinent information arose when patterns of traits were noted. The Nervous, Depressive, Subjective pattern is indicative of anxiety; the Quiet, Inhibited, Subjective pattern is characteristic of social withdrawal and deep feelings of inadequacy; the Depressive, Impulsive pattern is a red flag for self-destructive tendencies. John's profile indicated all of the above patterns. Although suicide and other forms of self-harm had been discussed throughout the counseling process, John had always denied that he was prone to suicidal ideation. Once again, the teaching of John and Marlene's church was that suicide is a sin, from which one could never repent. John's TJTA result was the first concrete indicator that his situation was more dangerous than he had been willing to admit in the past.

Marlene's scores were more positive. She scored high on Composed, Lighthearted, Active-Social, Expressive-Responsive, Sympathetic, Objective, Dominant, Tolerant, and Impulsive. This profile confirmed her sense of competence in social situations and her strong, domineering personality.

A subsequent test of depression, the Beck Depression Inventory, also indicated that John was severely depressed. This fact did not stop Marlene from pursuing her goal of finding a job outside the home. She soon was hired as a secretary for a contractor and began her role as a working woman and wage earner. As her sense of accomplishment and self-worth grew in this newfound position, she and John grew more and more distant from each other. Marlene became more determined to have things the way she wanted them in her life, including her job, her church, and her marriage, and John was more and more frustrated with the fact that he was helpless and impotent. John's depression spiraled downward.

Marlene's attendance at counseling sessions was sporadic. She was still convinced that John needed "healing prayer," and he was still hesitant to seek such prayer. After about three years of intermittent counseling with this couple, Marlene finally said she had "had enough; John will never change." She moved out of their house and rented an apartment for herself.

John called me the morning she left. He told me the progression of events that had led up to this latest decision. She had threatened to leave before, but he had never taken her seriously. John had hit an all-time low in his life and was completely overwhelmed with feelings of helplessness, hopelessness, and despair. He spoke freely of not wanting "to go on," of having "no reason to continue." I talked to John for over 45 minutes on the phone that morning, and I was able to get him to agree to enter into a verbal no-harm contract and to come in for another session of counseling.

At this point, several factors seemed to be having significant impact on John's depression. These included John's (1) sense of low self-worth; (2) dependency on Marlene for protection from an encroaching and threatening world; (3) overall passive response to his external world (i.e., his victim mentality); (4) view of religious authority; (5) childhood sexual abuse; (6) feelings of impotence, which were highlighted in his inability to perform sexually but were pervasive in his view of himself; and (7) sense of personal helplessness and hopelessness.

Although Marlene would not come with him, John was true to his commitment to participate in additional counseling. At our next session together, I asked him to sign a no-harm contract, and he complied. He specifically agreed to not inflict physical harm on himself or anyone else and, if he did have thoughts of self harm, to call one of the three people listed on his contract. I was his first resource for help, followed by the pastor of his church and the associate pastor. Both of these gentlemen had been involved with John in church-related programs and had learned something of John's struggle with depression. If none of us could be reached, John agreed to call the local crisis/suicide hotline.

I began to process with him how he would respond to these recent devastating events in his life. John persisted in his thought that there was no reason for him to go on living. All the difficult parts of his life had "come crashing down on him." And in the midst of this despair, he saw no relationship between his lack of desire to continue living and his church's belief regarding suicide. He asked, "What kind of God would want me to live this way?" I asked John if he had made any plans for ways that he would end his life. He said that he had not thought of any specific ways. All he knew was that he was hurting, and he said, "I don't want to hurt any more." When I pressed him on the precise meaning of this statement, he admitted that he would not choose any means that involved pain or that would leave him in a still living and painful state. Even more specifically, he would not choose to kill himself with a gun or in a self-caused automobile accident. If he was to kill himself, it would be with pills or carbon monoxide. But he continued to explain that the real meaning of his statement that he "didn't want to go on living" was that he just simply wished that he would die—that God would take him. He adamantly stated that he never intended to kill himself.

Although John's statement was encouraging, I recognized that he might act impulsively when in the throes of depression. In the light of his despondency, I asked John to consider antidepressant medication. Although he was amenable to this idea, he did not want to see a medical doctor for a prescription. In addition, I was concerned about John's not being able to withstand such a deep level of depression during the four to six weeks it often takes for antidepressants to start working. However, he reluctantly agreed to make an appointment with his family physician for an assessment. I agreed, with John's permission and a signed release form, to speak to the doctor about John's depression. As a result of that appointment, John was started on a high dose of Prozac.

John's initial depression related to Marlene's leaving was so intense that I considered the possibility that he might need to be hospitalized. I suggested this to John. Although he was not adverse to hospitalization, he thought he would be better off if he continued with his regular schedule of work and church. He stated that when he was at work or church and his mind was busy, his sense of hopelessness was less. With the no-harm contract in place, I agreed to John's plan, but only if we would monitor his moods closely and he would agree to be hospitalized if the suicidal ideation increased.

Another treatment issue that concerned me was John's unreconciled sexual abuse by his brother. It seemed that John's passive victim mentality regarding this issue was a factor in his lack of ability to be proactive in relationships and work. I indicated to John that I thought he would benefit from continued regular counseling sessions and that he should move in the direction of confronting his brother and mother (who knew about the abuse and did nothing to prevent it). John agreed to continue with me in the counseling process to work on his past abuse issues.

A third treatment issue was his overwhelming loneliness and sense of inadequacy, which had been present since Marlene's departure. I processed with John the possibility of finding a support group for divorcees or widows and widowers. He was predictably reticent to join a group of "people I don't know," but he also understood his need to be with others—especially while adjusting to life without his spouse. As we explored the possibility, I located a support group administered by a local church. It was called "Single Again," was intended for divorcees and those who had lost spouses to death, and was based on biblical principles. John was happy to know about such a group, and he and I arranged with the leader of the group for him to attend the group's next regular meeting.

A fourth concern that was of supreme importance to John was the possibility that Marlene might, at some point, want to return to him. Although Marlene's resolve to "be on my own" and to be "free from the bondage of the demons of my past" was strong, John's desire to have her back was also strong. Therefore, I assisted John in developing a contingency plan. When Marlene first left, John wanted her back at all costs. After a time of adjustment, he realized that some things would have to change before a peaceful reconciliation could be effected. Marlene would have to reenter counseling with John to resume processing the unresolved issues in their marriage. Marlene's strong and domineering personality had overwhelmed John for their entire married life, and he realized that marital happiness depended partly on his ability to be assertive in the marriage as well as in life in general.

During the weeks following Marlene's departure, John was faithful in carrying out our plans for his treatment. He attended the support group meetings and found others who were dealing with loss, grief, and loneliness. They were eager to help him overcome the initial intense feelings of separation, and he was especially comforted by the integration of Christian doctrine, scripture, and prayer into their meetings.

He was also faithful in coming to weekly counseling sessions. He was open and willing to process his sexual abuse and made plans to write letters to his mother and brother, including details of how the abuse and the lack of protection had adversely affected his life. Part of his plan for confronting his brother and mother included forgiving them, as would be consistent with his faith commitment. As I have also been trained in the integration of faith and counseling, I was able to incorporate John's belief system into our counseling. That was reassuring to John and coincided with the work he was doing in his support group.

I received two calls from John as a result of being on his no-harm contract. At those times, alone at home and reminiscing about his former life with Marlene, he had once again begun the descent into despair and despondency and had had increasing thoughts of not wanting to continue living. His phone calls to me and our resulting reaffirmation of reasons for living seemed to break the thought processes, allowing him to take control of his thinking. In time, he also incorporated into our sessions a desire to forgive Marlene, although he could not bring himself to that point for several months.

CONCLUSION

John and I continued our counseling sessions until John felt comfortable and secure in not meeting. At that point, Marlene had still shown no interest in returning, but John had formed some strong relationships with men and women in his support group. In addition to their weekly meetings, they had formed a social club, which organized monthly activities such as dancing, bowling, cards, and more. John also learned the practical and sustaining side of his faith. Rather than his faith being something he followed because Marlene insisted that he do so, he came to "own" his faith as his. He continued to present with a somber attitude, but he was more secure in his ability to depend on himself in social and work situations. John continued to work as a welder but also continued to market and use his artistic talents, which gave him great fulfillment. John was able to send letters to his brother and mother and has forgiven them for his abuse. Although he feels a sense of release in that forgiveness, he still chooses not to associate with his family.

Case Reflection Questions

Suicide Issue Questions

1. Could you work with a couple if one of the partners expressed suicidal ideation? Are there any advantages to working with both partners in a relationship? What are the disadvantages?

2. Spiritual beliefs are a significant factor in suicide cases. Clients' beliefs may either exacerbate shame and guilt or encourage resiliency by providing a sense of meaning and purpose. How does spirituality or religiosity play a role in this case? How can you as a counselor have respect for clients' spiritual beliefs yet also prescribe therapeutic approaches that may challenge those beliefs?

Skill Builder Questions

1. How might you feel if you were counseling this suicidal client? What is your personal emotional reaction to this client's suicidal behavior?

2. What would you have done in order to ensure this suicidal client's safety? Utilizing the FED, described in Chapter 3, which indicates *frequency* of suicidal thoughts, *extent* of suicide plans, and *duration* of suicidal thoughts and impulses, indicate your assessment of this client's degree of danger to self.

What would you have done to properly assess this client's immediate suicide risk?

3. What important suicide risk factors were present in the case? What unique individual factors or characteristics of this client would be important to your suicide risk assessment? As you read this case, which SAD PERSONS risk factors (sex, age, depression, previous attempt, ethanol abuse, rational thinking loss, social supports lacking, organized suicide plan, no spouse, and sickness) did you find most relevant to this case?

4. What would be your therapeutic approach to treating this suicidal client? What two pieces of information described within this case would be most helpful for your own work in intervening with potentially suicidal clients and their loved ones?

5. How would your approach be the same as or different from that of the clinician in the case? What interventions described in the case did you think were most helpful to the client?

6. How will you care for yourself when working with clients who are suicidal?

7. What strategies will you use to make sure you are competent and prepared to work with high-risk clients?

James O. Fuller is a Ph.D. in Counselor Education and a Licensed Mental Health Counselor (LMHC), NCC, NCSC. He is currently Dean, College of Graduate Studies, Indiana Wesleyan University. Previously, he worked as Professor of Counseling. He maintains a small private practice in Marion, IN, even while doing administrative work.

Earl

An Older Adult Male

DARCY HAAG GRANELLO

EDITORS' COMMENTS

- This case illustrates working with a population at high risk for suicide: depressed elderly white males.
- A key component of this case is how the counselor shares her reaction to the loss of a client to suicide.

INTRODUCTION

When I first met Earl, he was a 74-year-old businessman who had lived his entire life in a small community in the Midwest. Earl was the son of immigrants who came to the United States from Germany after World War I. Growing up, Earl's family was poor but hardworking and extremely committed to making a life for themselves and their children. Earl married a local girl, began a small business, and had several children. By the time I met Earl, he had a very large and very successful business, a wife of over 40 years, grown children, and grandchildren. Earl had spent his entire life as a businessman, working long hours to build up his company and finding meaning in his standing in the town. He was an outspoken member of the local business community, and he was active in the local Rotary Club. Whenever an important issue came before the group, Earl's opinions were sought and respected by others. Although he never held public office, many in the town considered Earl the unofficial representative of the town, seeking his advice and input on everything from traffic planning to construction of the new library. He was generous with his money and funded many charitable activities.

Within the past couple of years, Earl's older son had taken over the family business, and Earl was retired. Anyone looking at Earl's life would say that he had truly experienced the American dream. Now all that was left was for Earl to relax, enjoy the fruits of his years of hard work, spend time with his family, and take pleasure in his retirement.

Of course, anyone who works in the field of mental health knows that things are not always what they seem. Earl's "perfect life" wasn't quite so perfect after all. First, Earl was extremely reluctant to retire. His older son, who was in his midforties at the time, started pushing his father to step aside and leave the day-to-day decision making to him. Although Earl had

officially retired five years earlier, he still went into the office every day and made most of the decisions regarding the business. His son expressed frustration that everyone in the community still saw Earl as the business owner and saw him, although he was 45 years old, as still just "the son." For his part, Earl said he trusted his son and thought the business was in good hands with him. He just couldn't give up the daily interactions that the business provided.

Meanwhile, at home, Earl's wife had gotten used to filling her time with family and community commitments. For more than 40 years, Earl was busy attending to work, and she was left to raise the family and participate in charity work within the community. When Earl started spending less time at work and more time at home, she found that he was often underfoot and started questioning her daily activities. For example, he decided that glasses that were used only once for meals should be washed by hand, thereby saving the number of times the dishwasher needed to be run during the week. After doing some comparison shopping, he decided his wife should start shopping at a different grocery store, which offered double coupons and could save them as much as $20 per trip to the store, assuming that she clipped the coupons and brought them with her (although she hadn't used coupons in years). Next, Earl decided that his wife stockpiled too many groceries in the house, which was a waste, and that she should engage in a more efficient system to keep track of what food they actually needed. He developed a complex tracking system for her to use to help in this endeavor. The last straw came when Earl stepped in, uninvited, to help her organize a fund-raiser for the church. She yelled at Earl, telling him that she was sorry he had retired. She said she liked him better when he was working.

BACKGROUND/REFERRAL

I met Earl when I was a counselor at a partial hospitalization program. Like many older adults, Earl did not come directly into the mental health system for treatment. Instead, he spent several years traversing through the medical system, looking for physical explanations for what turned out to be a very serious case of clinical depression.

Earl had always had high blood pressure, which he attributed to the high-stakes world of business. Like his father before him, who died of a heart attack at age 60, Earl had heart problems and high cholesterol. Earl had been on blood pressure medication, cholesterol medication, and blood thinners for at least 10 years. At age 64, Earl suffered a heart attack and underwent a triple bypass surgery. In spite of these health problems, Earl declared himself in fine physical shape and was reluctant to visit the doctor's office or complain of any health problems. He believed that admitting to any deteriorating health was a sign of weakness and old age.

It should be noted that the link between cardiovascular disease and depression has been well documented in the research, and about one in three people who survive a heart attack has diagnosable clinical depression (National Institute of Mental Health, 2002). Depression is caused not just by the transitory feelings of having a chronic and/or life-threatening illness but also by the changes in serotonin levels that accompany heart disease (although the direct mechanism or cause and effect remain uncharted). Thus, Earl's cardiovascular problems and depression were inextricably linked.

Although Earl was clearly exhibiting signs of a significant major depressive episode when he had routine visits to both his primary care physician and his cardiologist, neither doctor asked about or diagnosed the depression. Unfortunately, this is typical. Study after study has found that in spite of the clear links between depression and heart disease, it remains extremely uncommon for medical personnel to initiate conversations with heart patients about

depression, to diagnose depression, or to make a behavioral health referral for depression to a counselor or psychiatrist. In this area, Earl's experiences were hardly unique.

When asked directly, Earl told his physician that he was having trouble sleeping, that he was feeling tired much of the time, and that he was having trouble concentrating. He answered direct questions about his difficulty withdrawing from the world of business and his inability to find meaning in his new retirement. His primary care physician suggested that he consider some volunteer work or other community service to keep himself busy and recommended that he and his wife travel and see the world, now that they had time on their hands.

It was about five years after Earl's "official" retirement that he first entered the behavioral health-care system. Earl's wife was vacuuming her husband's home office one day when, on a whim, she sat down at his desk and started looking in his desk drawers. When the treatment team and I talked with her later about what caused her to investigate, she said it was simply "a sign from God." She said he had been getting quieter and quieter and had started spending more and more time away from home. She had had a nagging feeling that perhaps he was having an affair, although she admitted that this was quite out of character for him and that realistically she didn't think this was a possibility. Nonetheless, one day she found herself carefully picking through the files and notes in his desk drawers, something she had never done in the past.

Deep within Earl's desk drawer was a "to do" list of everything he needed to get in order before he could commit suicide. The list contained items from his business life, his personal life, and his life in the community. Attached to the list was an instruction sheet for his son on how to handle news of his death in the business community and ideas and suggestions to further expand the business. Also attached was a letter to his wife that he was in the process of drafting.

Earl's wife immediately called her daughter, who came over and read the information. Soon Earl's two sons also were called to their home, and the entire family was waiting for Earl when he arrived home later that afternoon. Earl was confronted with the information but denied that he had any serious intention of killing himself. He was angry that his privacy had been violated and shouted to the family that they were blowing things out of proportion. Earl insisted that it was just some idle rambling one afternoon but nothing that they should be alarmed about. To the family's credit, they refused to accept Earl's answers and insisted that he be assessed by a psychiatrist. Earl protested that he didn't need psychiatric care, that he wasn't crazy, and that they were making too much of the list. Finally, when all else failed, he protested that his standing in the community would be greatly diminished if other people knew he had seen a psychiatrist.

Earl's daughter tearfully insisted that they take him to the hospital emergency room that same night regardless of the repercussions. Earl insisted that he was fine, but it was clear that his family would not take "no" for an answer. In the end, he agreed to see a psychiatrist if the family agreed not to take him to the hospital that evening. Because of the family's financial resources, they were able to get Earl in to see a psychiatrist within the next few days. In the meantime, the family kept constant vigil with Earl, never allowing him out of their sight. By the time Earl met with a psychiatrist a few days later, he was feeling extremely angry with his family, agitated over his life situation, and clinically depressed.

ASSESSMENT

In spite of his initial resistance to the idea of talking with a psychiatrist, Earl completed a comprehensive suicide assessment. Corroborative interviews with Earl's family helped the psychiatrist piece together the history of clinical depression and the suicide risk.

With the recognition that Earl's suicide risk was high, the psychiatrist made arrangements for Earl to enter a partial hospitalization unit located about an hour from Earl's hometown. Earl found this arrangement more acceptable than seeking treatment locally, and the promise of anonymity that came with the plan allowed Earl to voluntarily enter treatment rather than being admitted against his will. Whenever possible, voluntary admission to psychiatric care is preferred, and finding a way to help Earl accept this level of intervention was an important component of his treatment.

Earl's Suicide Risk Assessment

At the partial hospitalization unit, Earl went through a full bio-psycho-social assessment. He had many risk factors for suicide. As an older, white male, he already was in the highest risk category. Added to that, Earl had a very clear (although undiagnosed) case of clinical depression. More than 90% of older persons who commit suicide have clinical depression at the time of death (Kennedy & Tanenbaum, 2000). Earl's cognitive rigidity and poor problem-solving also were significant risk factors for suicide. He had developed a solution to the problems that he saw facing him, and once he had hit on suicide as the only logical answer, he had appeared to lose the ability—or desire—to look for other solutions. Finally, and perhaps most significantly, the cumulative losses that Earl was facing (retirement, loss of prestige in the business world, loss of control over his life, loss of power, loss of identity) were simply too much for Earl to bear.

TREATMENT

Earl was diagnosed with clinical depression and started on a selective serotonin reuptake inhibitor (SSRI). He was admitted to a five-day-a-week, full-day regimen of group counseling, expressive therapy, medical rounds, relaxation therapy, and individual counseling. At night, he was to stay in a respite house located on the premises rather than driving an hour back to his home.

Earl had difficulty in his initial adjustment to the program. He frequently told the staff that he felt uncomfortable being around people who were clearly so low functioning. In group, he would often tell other clients to "just get over it" and "buck up—nobody likes a whiner." Within a few days, however, he started to open up. As I saw him more often in group counseling, he started to talk about his feelings of being worthless, of being "used up," of being unable to find any meaning in his life, and of fearing that things would get worse and worse until he died. In Earl's mind, suicide was the only logical solution. He argued that it was not an emotional response, based on feelings of hopelessness or helplessness (a statement about suicide that he heard often from the staff and other clients), but a rational choice that was born out of logic and reason. He argued that he had completed his work, left his family in good financial standing, and was now ready to die. He said that although he felt good physically, he knew it was just a matter of time before all the health problems caught up with him, and he didn't want to end up old and infirm.

In individual sessions, he said he had an image of himself as an old man, sitting in a wheelchair with a lap blanket over his knees, wearing an adult diaper, and being condescended to by his well-meaning family. In Earl's mind, that image summed up everything he needed to know to make a decision about his life. For a man who had worked his entire life

to have control and power and to be respected by others, this was intolerable. Yet Earl saw no other way out.

In our work together, Earl continued to be very emotionally reserved, which according to his family was the way Earl had been his entire life. Cognitive-behavioral interventions designed to challenge his defeatist vision of the future had little effect. Earl could follow all of the rational discussions and challenge his own thinking, but in the end, he always ended up at the same conclusion. I had the opportunity to work with Earl in expressive therapy, and he engaged in the drawing and writing activities, but he never seemed to connect with them at any meaningful level. At the end of the day every day, as the group prepared for the evening, Earl's comments were always pretty much the same. Yes, he would be safe for the evening; no, his decision about suicide had fundamentally not changed.

About a week after his initial admission, Earl's wife, who had visited frequently, moved into a local hotel room so that she could be with Earl more often and more available to assist with his treatment. The treatment team arranged for Earl and his wife to engage in couples counseling, and she participated eagerly, hoping to help her husband in any way she could. The couples counselor discussed Earl's recent behavior at home that had so irritated his wife as evidence of his desire to find ways to control his life and to assume power in the relationship (to replace the power he used to have at work). She also questioned whether Earl may have been using these behaviors as a way to distance himself from his wife, to make her angry with him, or to give her an excuse to allow him to spend more time alone, thereby giving him time to make his final plans.

Over the next week, Earl spiraled into more and more severe depression. He now was more adamant that he would kill himself, as soon as the time was right, and that there was nothing anyone could do to change his mind. All of the members of the staff—the psychiatrist, the psychiatric nurses, his group counselors, his individual counselor, his marriage counselor, and I—all worked tirelessly to help him turn around. I saw Earl in group counseling for at least two hours every day, and I found him to be a likable and intelligent man who was easy to talk with, sharp-witted, and engaging. However, whether I tried a head-on approach to attack the suicidal ideation or a roundabout method to challenge the assumptions that allowed the ideation to continue, I could not make progress. Nor, for that matter, could anyone else.

By the end of the second week, there was a general feeling among the treatment team that in spite of what Earl was saying in group at the end of each day, we no longer believed he would necessarily be safe at the respite house. Because we knew Earl would kill himself when "the time was right" and we had no way of assessing when that right time would be, we all understood ourselves to be on borrowed time. On that Friday afternoon, Earl was admitted to an inpatient psychiatric unit.

By this time, Earl's wife and family were beside themselves with anxiety and fear. Things appeared to be spiraling downward faster than anyone's ability to control them. Whereas just over two weeks ago Earl's family thought that their husband and father was learning to adjust to retirement, having a few health issues, and getting a bit quiet, they now faced the very real possibility that they could lose him. They were frustrated and angry with the treatment team and our inability to help Earl turn around. They were frustrated and angry with themselves because they hadn't done something earlier. In the middle of it all, Earl was calmly and rationally determined to die.

In the inpatient unit, Earl's medications were adjusted, and he was put on round-the-clock watch. Nevertheless, the depression worsened. A few days later the psychiatrist met with Earl's family and said that he wanted to try electroconvulsive therapy (ECT). Although

many practitioners consider ECT a treatment of last resort for depression and suicide, the National Institute of Mental Health's multisite research consortium findings suggest that it is a highly efficacious treatment. In fact, more than 80% of persons with severe clinical depression and suicidal ideation who engage in ECT have significant decreases in suicidal intent with only one to three treatments (Kellner et al., 2005). The rapid resolution of suicidal intent and the reports of low side effects made ECT a logical choice for Earl, whose other treatment options appeared to be quickly fading.

Although Earl and his family were initially quite resistant to the option of ECT, it became clear in conversations with them that they had a very distorted view (gleaned from one horrible scene in *One Flew over the Cuckoo's Nest*) about what ECT entailed. Once they had a more accurate understanding of the procedure, the family became more open to it. For his part, Earl was simply resigned to their decision. In many ways, he had simply given up. He no longer cared. He no longer demonstrated the will to fight for independence or dignity, or anything else. For me, this was perhaps the most frightening development of all. Earl, who had come into treatment with such resolve, such strength, and such determination had now become, for all intents and purposes, the "frail old man" that he had so feared.

I walked away from a visit with him with a sense of impending dread. When I went back to the treatment team the next morning to report on my visit with Earl, I remember thinking "We are going to lose him." The psychiatrist talked to the treatment team about Earl's impending ECT and changes in medication. The team talked about ECT and its likely positive effects, and there was some widespread optimism about Earl's recovery. But most of the people on the team hadn't seen Earl since he went into the hospital. If they had, I wonder if they would have been nearly so optimistic. I wonder now if we were all just trying to protect ourselves by saying that we thought he would get better. What else could we do?

Over the next several weeks, Earl transitioned between inpatient and partial hospitalization care. He went through a series of about 10 ECT treatments, and at times, there appeared to be a spark of hope. There were times over those weeks when he would laugh and talk and appear more animated. He could be a model client, telling other group members to hang on, to keep working and things would improve. At other times, however, he was withdrawn and quiet and nonresponsive in group counseling. Regardless of his affect, he still could not find a reason to stay alive.

In individual and group sessions, he told us that as much as he appreciated all of the hard work that everyone was doing to keep him alive, he wanted us to stop. He was tired—tired of taking all the invasive medications and undergoing ECT, tired of spending his life talking to strangers in groups, tired of drawing or writing about his emotions, tired of rehashing it all. He was angry for what we were putting his wife and family through. He told us that, if he had simply killed himself several months ago, as he had originally intended, his family would have "moved on" by now. Instead, he was in limbo, and they were forced to come along for the ride. I can remember him saying one day in group, "We've all given it the old college try. Can't we just admit that it isn't working?"

As we neared Thanksgiving, Earl seemed to rally a bit. His affect was brighter, and he was more talkative and animated. One day, during medical rounds, he told the psychiatrist that maybe he might be turning the corner. His wife asked if there was any way we could allow him to come home for Thanksgiving dinner. The grandchildren were asking about him, and the family thought a day of normalcy might do Earl a world of good. They agreed that he would spend just one night at home, and then he would come back to respite care.

Earl seemed eager to "take the day off" from his illness. He said he wanted to see the grand-children, and he assured us that he would be safe.

After much discussion with Earl and his family and many conversations within the treat-ment team, it was decided to allow Earl to go home for Thanksgiving. At one point, Earl told us that he felt pretty sure that he could be safe through the holidays—that he had always said that he would kill himself when "the time was right"—and Thanksgiving certainly wasn't the right time to do it. We thought we had bought a little more time.

On Thanksgiving Day, after what was reported later by his family to be a very nice din-ner with his children and grandchildren, Earl excused himself to go to the bathroom. Instead, he stepped into the garage, opened the trunk of his car, took apart the wheel well, found the gun that he had stashed there months before, and shot himself.

CONCLUSION

In many ways, Earl represents the case we all fear. In spite of everyone's best efforts, we couldn't save him. Looking back, I'm not sure what we could have done differently. We had medical interventions, counseling interventions, and help from his family. Unlike so many situations where we have limited resources, or family members who don't care or are so wrapped up in their own mental health problems that they can't assist, or a client with psy-chosis or substance abuse problems that make it difficult to intervene, everything about Earl's case was stacked in his favor. I don't know where we went wrong, or even if we did go wrong. If it was a different situation, if it involved something we could pinpoint, a place where we made a mistake in our treatment, we could say, "As painful as that was, I learned from it, and in the future, I will (or will not). . . ." Unfortunately, what I learned from it was that we can't save everyone. In retrospect, of course, we could have refused his trip home for Thanksgiving. But I'm not sure that would have saved him. We did everything we could, and we tried one more thing—allowing him back into his old life, just for a day, to see if it would help. Did it save him? Of course not. But did it kill him? I'm not sure.

In a culture where productivity and financial success are valued and where men are at-tributed value based on what they do, how much they make, and how much power they have, it perhaps isn't surprising that the highest suicide rate in the country is that of older white males. White males over age 65 commit suicide at a rate of 40 per 100,000, nearly 4 times the rate of the U.S. population at large. After age 85, the rate is even higher—a stun-ning 70 per 100,000—making this, by far, the demographic group most likely to commit sui-cide (Murphy, 2000). More than 70% of elderly Americans who commit suicide have visited their family physician in the month prior to their death, 40% within the last week, and 20% on the day they die (National Alliance for the Mentally Ill, 2003).

And when individuals in this demographic group decide to kill themselves, like Earl, they find highly lethal means. It is the age group with the fewest number of attempts for every completion, possibly as low as 4 to 1 (compared with as many as 59 attempts for every completion in other age groups). In other words, when older white men decide to take their lives, they are more likely than individuals in any other age group to make active and lethal plans and to carry them out.

I provide this context as much for myself as for the reader. I think we sometimes believe that as counselors, we should be able to save everybody. We think that we should somehow be able to make everyone safe and that, if we work hard enough, we can make a difference. And I believe that, if we follow the right protocols, engage in the right interventions, and have

the right relationships with our clients, most of the time we can save lives. But sometimes we can't. One in four counselors has had a client commit suicide, and most who have experienced a client death call it the most profoundly disturbing event of their professional lives (McAdams & Foster, 2000). Some people leave the profession. Others find ways to learn from the experience and move on. But no one is ever the same.

In a book about suicide prevention and intervention, it would be wonderful if all the cases had happy endings—positive outcomes where, as a result of outstanding clinical care, all of the clients improved. But in the real world in which we live and practice, that's not always the case. So I tell you my story, my clinical failure, my inability to save a life. I hope the case helps provide some insights, helps improve our clinical care, and helps offer a starting point for discussion. I also hope that it helps provide a mechanism for us to have a conversation about client suicide.

Clinicians who lose a client to suicide often feel a deep and profound sense of guilt, a loss of self-efficacy, and extraordinarily high levels of stress. They may feel isolated from the professional community and afraid to process their therapeutic failures with those who are in the best position to help them. They may fear impending litigation, worry about their ability to help others, or fear professional embarrassment or the financial implications of reductions in referrals if the word gets out. We know so little about how clinicians react to client suicide. What we *do* know is that they don't tend to talk about it. I'd like to break that cycle. I don't think it's healthy to keep this a secret. We need to process it and learn from it and share our grief and our insights with others.

I learned so much from my work with Earl. He was a strong, intelligent man with a good heart, and I am glad I got to know him. I am grateful that Earl shared a part of himself with me, that he trusted me enough to let me into his world. I hope I am a better counselor because of what he taught me. In the end, maybe that is part of the legacy that Earl has left us. I wish I could have helped him. As I reflect on the experience, I recognize how much he helped me.

Case Reflection Questions

Suicide Issue Questions

1. Oregon is the only state in the United States that has a procedure for legal physician-assisted suicide. Should clients that are elderly or suffering from an illness have a right to commit suicide?
2. What would you have done differently in this case? Are there limits to what treatment teams can do to help keep a client alive? How can a clinician learn to accept the loss of a client from suicide?

Skill Builder Questions

1. How might you feel if you were counseling this suicidal client? What is your personal emotional reaction to this client's suicidal behavior?
2. What would you have done in order to ensure this suicidal client's safety? Utilizing the FED, described in Chapter 3, which indicates *frequency* of suicidal thoughts, *extent* of suicide plans, and *duration* of suicidal thoughts and impulses, indicate your assessment of this client's degree of danger to self. What would you have done to properly assess this client's immediate suicide risk?

3. What important suicide risk factors were present in the case? What unique individual factors or characteristics of this client would be important to your suicide risk assessment? As you read this case, which SAD PERSONS risk factors (sex, age, depression, previous attempt, ethanol abuse, rational thinking loss, social supports lacking, organized suicide plan, no spouse, and sickness) did you find most relevant to this case?

4. What would be your therapeutic approach to treating this suicidal client? What two pieces of information

described within case Chapter would be most helpful for your own work in intervening with potentially suicidal clients and their loved ones?

5. How would your approach be the same as or different from that of the clinician in the case? What interventions described in the case did you think were most helpful to the client?

6. How will you care for yourself when working with clients who are suicidal?

7. What strategies will you use to make sure you are competent and prepared to work with high-risk clients?

Dr. Darcy Haag Granello is an Associate Professor at The Ohio State University in Counselor Education. She has conducted research, presented nationally and internationally, and written extensively on the topic of suicide.

References

Kellner, C. H., Fink, M., Knapp, R., Petrieds, G., Husain, M., Rummans, T., et al. (2005). Relief of expressed suicidal intent by ECT: A consortium for research in ECT study. *American Journal of Psychiatry, 162*, 977–982.

Kennedy, G. J., & Tanenbaum, S. (2000). Suicide and aging: International perspectives. *Psychiatric Quarterly, 71*, 345–362.

McAdams, C. R., III, & Foster, V. A. (2000). Client suicide: Its frequency and impact on counselors. *Journal of Mental Health Counseling, 22*, 107–121.

Murphy, S. L. (2000). Deaths: Final data for 1998. *National Vital Statistics Report* (DHHS Publication No. (PHS) 2000-1120, Vol. 48, No. 11). Hyattsville, MD: National Center for Health Statistics.

National Alliance for the Mentally Ill. (2003). *Depression in older persons*. Retrieved December 27, 2005, from http://www.nami.org/Template.cfm?Section=By_Illness&template=/ContentManagement/ContentDisplay.cfm&ContentID=7515

National Institute of Mental Health. (2002). *Depression and heart disease*. Retrieved January 30, 2007, from http://www.nimh.nih.gov/publicat/depheart.cfm

CONCLUDING THOUGHTS

We hope you have learned something about working with suicidal clients by reading the cases contained in this book. These clients' cases were varied in terms of treatment setting, developmental stage, age, gender, and cultural background. Even so, you will in your work settings encounter individuals who may not fit any of the specific demographic profiles highlighted here, so it is important to treat each client as unique. Remember that each individual is worthy of our respect and should be taken seriously, especially with regard to suicidal ideation, plans, or attempts. In a profession such as counseling, there are few "hard and fast" rules, and counselors must learn to think with complexity. However, one rule concerning suicide is that it is always better to err on the side of caution with suicidal clients. The result of not taking a client seriously is too final and unfixable for us not to be very cautious.

INDEX